Introduction to Human Resource Management

A guide to personnel in practice

Donald Currie worked as a personnel officer for over 15 years before joining the Southampton Institute as a lecturer in personnel management. In 1990 he was appointed to be a fellow in human resource management, and for over 10 years led the CIPD Professional Education Scheme. Since retiring in 1995, Donald has worked as a consultant to the Southampton Business School, and has been running the CIPD-CPP course.

The CIPD would like to thank the following members of the CIPD Publishing Editorial Board for their help and advice:

Pauline Dibben, University of Sheffield

Edwina Hollings, Staffordshire University Business School

Caroline Hook, Huddersfield University Business School

Vincenza Priola, Keele University

John Sinclair, Napier University Business School

Introduction to Human Resource Management

A guide to personnel in practice

Donald Currie

Chartered Institute of Personnel and Development

Published by the Chartered Institute of Personnel and Development, CIPD House,
151 The Broadway, London SW19 1JQ

First published 2006

Typeset by Curran Publishing Services, Norwich, Norfolk
Printed in Great Britain by Cromwell Press, Trowbridge, Wiltshire

British Library Cataloguing in Publication Data
A catalogue of this manual is available from the British Library

ISBN 1 84398 139 4
ISBN-13 978 1 84398 139 8

Chartered Institute of Personnel and Development,
151 The Broadway, London SW19 1JQ
Tel: 020 8612 6200
Email: cipd@cipd.co.uk   Website: www.cipd.co.uk
Incorporated by Royal Charter   Registered Charity No. 1079797

To my daughter Susan

Contents

Part 1: The role of HR in the organisation

Part 3: Contemporary issues in HR

Figures

Tables

Preface

The first edition of this book was entitled *Personnel in practice* and was published in 1997. It was aimed exclusively at Certificate in Personnel Practice (CPP) students, but experience shows that it also proved useful to those undertaking the early stages of the CIPD Professional Development Scheme (PDS) and to undergraduates in their studies of the human resources (HR) content of business degrees.

Change of title

You may need an explanation why I have changed the title of this book from *Personnel in practice* to *Introduction to HRM*. Since 1997, the adoption of human resource management (HRM) has become widespread, it has had a significant influence over how HR activities are carried out, and has changed organisations' perceptions of the importance of people. Undeniably the term 'HR' has become synonymous with 'personnel', since the large majority of people who work in what were 'personnel departments' now say they are in 'HR'. While the use of the term HR is now more widespread than personnel, there are significant differences between the traditional personnel management approach and the more recent HRM approach to managing people and employee relations.

HR as a career

If I had to nominate just one thing that I think attracts and sustains people's interest, I would say that it is other people. The fact that we are all different from each other is a source of fascination to most, and like millions of others, I find contact with people interesting and exciting. To me, therefore, HR is the most interesting and exciting function in any organisation because it is all about the organisation's people. If you are serious about entering the profession, then I hope you enjoy it as much as I do.

For whom the book is intended

My main purpose with this book is to introduce to those who are new to HR the theoretical concepts and ideas they need to understand, and the practical skills they need to develop at a level that is appropriate to their studies. Those to whom this book would be of interest are either employed and have embarked upon their chosen courses as part-time students, or undertaking the CIPD-PDS on a full-time basis. Alternatively, they could be doing a full-time degree which includes an HR module and are considering HR as a career after graduation. I hope that if you are in any of these categories, you will be able to carry your new knowledge and skills with you into the organisation. The book, therefore, is for those undertaking:

- the early stages of the Chartered Institute of Personnel and Development (CIPD) Certificate in Personnel Practice (CPP course)
- the first year of the professional development scheme (CIPD-PDS)
- a different professional course, such as marketing or finance, which contains HR elements
- an HRM degree.

It is also for those who work in HR and are serious about furthering their career in the profession.

It is worth bearing in mind that membership of the CIPD, gained by examination, is regarded as the standard career qualification, and it is the one that employers ask for. To qualify for such membership you need to be able to demonstrate appropriate levels of knowledge and understanding and that you have developed within yourself the core competences that will enable you to achieve good practice. The content of this book has been specially designed to provide you with the required knowledge and understanding, and to offer guidance on how the competences may be developed.

A new phase in HR

Many changes have taken place in organisations since this book was first published, and undoubtedly further changes lie ahead. This second edition of the book takes account of the changes that have affected the strategic and operational activities of HR professionals, and considers some of the changes that the future might bring.

First, important changes to the structure and content of the CIPD professional courses took place in 2002 when new provisions for the education and development of student members were introduced. The educational institutions that are approved by the CIPD to prepare people for the various levels of membership examinations redesigned their courses to take account of these changes.

Second, largely as a result of European directives, new UK legislation has had an important impact on HR, especially in the areas of data protection, working time, disability, equality, family friendliness and other employee rights.

Third, the more widespread adoption of the principles and practices of HRM has resulted in a redefinition of the employee relationship and a greater emphasis on the importance of employee development, performance management, organisational structure and culture. HRM has also influenced the role of HR in that in an increasing number of organisations, it has become integrated with top-level strategic decision-making groups.

The aims of the book

Clearly, the changes mentioned above have implications for the content of a book such as this. The main aim is still to provide the knowledge requirement, and explain how you can develop the core competences that will enable you to meet the new requirements and to do a good professional job in the organisation.

A further aim is to encourage the building of self-confidence and the improvement of performance as an HR worker. People who develop a skill in a classroom are sometimes reluctant to try it out in the workplace, often because they lack the confidence. Confidence is the most essential ingredient of success in the application of newly acquired knowledge and skills to a practical situation. I have, therefore, modified the style of the book so that now, hopefully, it will assist your understanding and build your confidence to a greater degree. There is a greater number of worked examples, activities and case studies. At the end of each chapter there is a set of test questions, and you will also find examples of essay and assignment topics.

You are encouraged to carry out the activities and pay particular attention to the examples and case studies, since they are designed to deal directly with the core skills and key concepts that you will need to develop; not only to pass examinations and succeed with your assignment and project work, but to enhance your understanding and achieve good practice in the workplace.

Obviously you cannot fully develop practical, in-job skills by reading a book, but it is hoped that from this text you will gather the knowledge and understanding that will enable you to see the organisational relevance of applying the skills you acquire on your course; which means knowing why you are doing what you are doing. This brings us back to the question of confidence again, since in addition to self-confidence, you also need to feel confident that the skills you develop will actually be effective in the real situation. The only way to test that is to dip your toe in and try it. It is when you discover that they really are effective that you begin to build confidence.

When you have finished your course, you may decide to stop studying, but it is impossible to stop learning, so you might as well carry on studying in a structured way order to ensure that you do not develop any bad learning habits such as picking up poor practice or failing to keep abreast of developments. The CIPD calls it continuing personal development, which can mature into lifelong learning. I wish you good luck with your studies and hope that your career in HR will be a fulfilling and rewarding experience.

Good luck.

Donald Currie

Overview of the book

Part 1 The role of HR in the organisation

Chapter 1 Organisations

To be effective in the HR role, you first need to develop a sound understanding of organisations: how they are classified and designed, and how corporate strategy, policy and objectives are formulated as the means through which they achieve their goals. It is also essential to understand how the organisation interacts with its business environment; for example, how the internal and external pressures of an ever-changing society influence decision-making in terms of strategy and policy. You also need to understand the factors that trigger change, and the impact that change has upon managers and employees.

Chapter 2 Human resource management

This is an explanation and discussion of human resource management (HRM). The main discussion sees HRM as a set of principles and practices that influence how the whole organisation is managed and in particular its influence on the activities of the HR department. The chapter discusses the differences between the personnel management approach and that of HRM, and compares the principles of HRM with those of traditional management.

Chapter 3 The role of the HR practitioner

Clearly, if you intend to make a career in HR you need to understand how the HR practitioner role operates within the organisational context; how the HR department functions and inter-relates with the rest of the organisation's departments in terms of its role in offering expert advice and assistance to managers and employees. The view taken here is that the line managers are responsible for the human resource, while the HR department uses its expertise to advise and assist them. The interdependent nature of the relationship between corporate and HR strategy is explained. The chapter also explains and discusses the administrative roles of HR specialists and advisers, including the establishment and maintenance of records and a discussion of the law on data protection.

Chapter 4 Human resource planning (HRP)

This chapter begins with a brief historical account of HRP and then shows how the elements of manpower planning have been adapted for modern strategic purposes. Comparisons are made between different definitions of HRP, which leads to an explanation and discussion of the systems and techniques that occupy the HR planner. The chapter takes account of the fact that many organisations have not fully adopted HRM, and distinctions are drawn between *traditional* and *modern* systems. This section of the chapter concludes with an examination of the planning process, after which we demonstrate the techniques used for forecasting HR demands, calculating staff turnover and workforce stability; forecasting HR supply and explaining the internal and external labour markets. Throughout the chapter, HRP is integrated with business strategy.

Chapter 5 Recruitment

This chapter is about recruiting and selecting employees, and takes you through the 'recruitment cycle', which is a set of guidelines that begins when a vacancy has been identified and ends when you start to examine the responses to the recruitment advertising. This includes working with line managers, developing the documentation such as the job description/role definition, the person specification and recruitment advertising.

Chapter 6 Selection

The selection process that follows recruitment involves screening applications and compiling a shortlist of appropriate candidates. Also included are organising and administering the interview and applying selection techniques, such as psychological and occupational testing, assessment centres and job simulation/work sampling, questioning and listening, employment decision-making and making an offer of employment. The legal aspects are explained in broad terms, including the law on discrimination and contract.

Chapter 7 Induction and retention

The purpose of this chapter is to explain and discuss the various approaches to induction, including corporate and departmental induction. The *induction crisis* is explained, its typical causes are discussed and there are recommendations for action designed to avoid, or at least reduce its frequency. The importance of retention has increased in recent years, and the steps that may be taken to ensure that the organisation holds on to its key staff are discussed.

Part 2 People and performance

Chapter 8 Learning

The aim of this chapter is to provide a basis for Chapters 9 and 10, since learning is the foundation stone of training, development and performance. The chapter outlines the strategic importance of learning as a critical factor in achieving a competitive advantage and then goes on to discuss the prime beneficiaries of learning: the individual, the organisation and the state. After a brief discussion of human capital and knowledge management, the chapter moves on to explain and discuss the principles of learning. From there, learning theories are examined, followed by a section on learning styles, with an exercise demonstrating how you can identify your own learning style.

Chapter 9 Human resource development (HRD)

Here we define, explain and discuss HRD. The chapter starts by examining the relationship between learning, training and development. We then explain how people learn and the various learning theories that have emerged; learning cycles and learning styles are also considered. The chapter then moves on to training, which includes systematic training, training needs analysis (TNA), planning and delivering training, applying training techniques such as using examples, case studies, exercises, group work, and coaching and counselling. This part of the chapter concludes with an explanation of the various approaches to the evaluation of the effectiveness of training. After an explanation of government initiatives for a national framework (VET), the chapter concludes with a section on management development.

Chapter 10 Performance management

The chapter opens with a definition of performance management and then goes on to explain its objectives, the traditional and modern systems, and techniques. This includes continuous assessment, the appraisal interview and feedback, performance agreements and the factors that influence performance, such as managerial and employee attitudes, motivation, competence, the work environment and job security.

Chapter 11 The employment relationship

This chapter includes explanations and discussions about employee relations perspectives and policies, and managerial and employee attitudes. The various types of employment contract are explained and discussed, as are the psychological contract; the internal justice system and the modern role of the trade unions. This is where we examine the most recent legislation on working time, data protection and family-friendly policies such as maternity and paternity rights. There is an introduction to organisational culture, types of culture and culture as an important determinant of behaviour. The section concludes with a discussion about the building of a culture that is conducive to the purposes of the organisation, and how such a culture may be managed.

Chapter 12 Employee reward

This chapter explains the concept of reward, including payment and non-cash rewards. An explanation and discussion of the systems of reward distinguishes between different types of payment system, and the variety of approaches to job evaluation, performance-related pay (P-rP) and profit-related pay (PRP). The chapter presents discussions on traditional and HRM approaches to reward.

Chapter 13 Health, safety and well-being

The chapter covers health, safety and well-being including the legal framework, the Health and Safety Commission and the Health and Safety Executive. Healthy workplace initiatives lead us to the subjects of benefits and facilities, managing stress, including employee assistance programmes and occupational support schemes, coping with stress, the cost of stress to employees and the organisation, the law on employee well-being and risk assessment. Again there are examples which include explanations of the causes and symptoms of stress and how they were handled.

Chapter 14 Diversity and equality

This is an examination of the current situation in British industry on this important and sensitive front. Legislation does feature here although much of the emphasis is on the effectiveness of policies on such matters as the management of diversity, including the moral and the business case for actively pursuing equal treatment. *Inter alia*, the chapter explains and discusses the variety of definitions of discrimination, and well-known cases are cited as examples. There is also a brief section on the social aspects of political correctness.

Part 3 Contemporary issues in HR

Chapter 15 Aspects of culture

The aim of this chapter is to provide an understanding of organisational culture, what it is, how it develops and its importance as the organisation's most powerful determinant of behaviour. To assist your understanding of what is meant by *organisational culture*, the chapter includes an account of how culture is perceived in the societal context. Reading about culture in extra-organisational contexts should help you to understand behaviour that occurs in a diverse workforce.

Chapter 16 Work–life balance

This chapter is concerned with the role of work in relation to the other aspects of a person's life. These include attending to responsibilities and obligations at home and in family life, marriage, what people do to relax and the time they need to pursue personal interests. Additionally, it examines and discusses:

- the role that employers have in providing practical support to employees with their need to balance their commitments at work with those at home
- the business case for encouraging employees to achieve work–life balance, including the benefits to employers from doing so
- the legislation that is relevant to work–life balance.

Features

To assist your learning, the chapters include activities, real-life case studies, hypothetical scenarios of organisational situations, mini cases and examples, which you are encouraged to work through; students usually find this to be most effective when carried out informally in small groups. Systems and techniques that are used in practice are clarified using charts, tables and figures. There are examples of essay questions and assignment topics and all chapters include a set of self-test questions.

To accompany this book there is a companion website at **www.cipd.co.uk/tss** in which items from the content are discussed further. The website also includes answers to the end-of-chapter self-test questions which are explained and discussed.

Glossary of terms

annual general meeting A meeting at which the directors of a company report on the company's financial performance to the shareholders and announce their plans for the future. Where relevant, new directors are elected by the shareholders.

annualised hours An employment contract in which there is a fixed annual number of hours an employee is expected to work. It is a very flexible scheme in which the hours that an employee works can be changed at short notice and, for example, he or she may be asked to work any number of hours in a week, from zero upwards. The total number of hours worked must not exceed the agreed annual number.

assessment centres These are not places, as the name may imply. Rather they are assessment situations in which participants undertake a series of tests and exercises under observation. The results of the tests and exercises are normally used for selection purposes.

Bradford factor A mechanism used for calculating and recording absenteeism.

classical conditioning An association of one event with another that leads to a particular pattern of behaviour (see also *operant conditioning*).

collective bargaining A system through which employers and employees, by negotiation, jointly establish, maintain and amend terms and conditions of employment and attempt to resolve disagreements.

competence The ability to perform the activities within an occupational area to the levels of performance expected in employment (Training Commission 1988). Also may be defined as 'the ability to apply knowledge and skills with understanding to a work activity'.

competence gap The difference between what a job holder is supposed to be able to do and what he or she is actually able to do.

competitive advantage Where an organisation serves the needs of its customers and clients in ways that give it an advantage over its competitors, putting itself in a position of advantage in the market.

continuing professional development (CPD) In which individuals have a personal commitment to keep their professional knowledge up to date and improve their capabilities throughout their working lives.

continuous change Refers to the long-term effect of the gradual, almost imperceptible daily and weekly changes that take place, such as minor changes to work systems or the gradual intake of different ethnic groups.

corporate strategy The process through which an organisation decides on its objectives and formulates a set of strategies and sub-processes which are designed to meet those objectives.

culture shift The ability of a human being to temporarily put aside the values and norms of his or her societal culture in order to conform to the values and norms of an organisation's culture.

delayering Reducing the number of staff at managerial levels, including middle managers and supervisors, in order to reduce costs. This results in a flattened structure in which a greater number of employees report to a smaller number of managers.

direct discrimination – marital status Occurs when a person, because of his or her marital status, is treated less favourably than a person of a different marital status, or would be treated less favourably in a similar situation. *Example:* a married woman is denied financial sponsorship and day release for a long-term training course because it is assumed she might leave to raise a family.

direct racial discrimination Occurs when an employer treats an employee or potential employee less favourably than it treats, or would treat, other employees, on the grounds of his or her race. Racial grounds are defined as colour, nationality or ethnic and national origin. *Example:* an up-market department store refuses to allow an Asian person to serve in the store on the grounds that the customers would prefer to be served by a white person. The candidate is offered a job in the stock room, even though the job that was advertised was for someone to serve in the store.

direct sex discrimination Occurs when a person is treated less favourably on the grounds of his or her sex than a person of the opposite sex would be treated in the same circumstances. *Example:* advertising that states or implies a preference for one sex or the other, eg using terms like headmistress, headmaster, Girl Friday.

discontinuous change Occurs when sudden 'one-off' or so-called 'overnight' changes take place, such as the implementation of a new policy.

downsizing Reducing the number of employees at operational levels and reorganising the work system in order to attain greater productivity.

employee assistance programme (EAP) An external agency, commissioned by the organisation, through which the employees have access to experts on stress, general well-being, and other matters on which they might need advice, support and assistance. The underlying idea is to reduce or eliminate distractions that might disrupt the employees' well-being and performance.

equity payment system Reward is determined by what it is worth to the organisation to have the job done, in relation to the worth of other jobs (see also *job evaluation*).

exit interview An interview, the purpose of which is to establish the reasons why a person is leaving the organisation of his or her own accord. The information gathered is used to identify possible shortcomings in the organisation's employment policy.

external labour market The local, regional, national and international pools of prospective employees (see also *internal labour market*).

externalisation Also referred to as 'outsourcing' or 'contracting out', refers to activities that the organisation needs to have carried out but may not be at the core of the main functions, and which it therefore subcontracts to another organisation.

flexi-time Not to be confused with *labour flexibility,* a system of attendance in which employees are required to work a preset *core time,* but can vary their attendance at other times, as long as their total attendance equates with the contracted working time.

genuine occupational qualification (GOQ) Where the person specification of a job includes a genuine requirement that the job can only be carried out satisfactorily by a member of a particular sex, race or ethnic background or religion, it is legitimate for the employer to discriminate against anyone who does not match the requirement. Typical types of work include entertainment, artistic or photographic modelling, specialised restaurants and community social workers.

hard HRM In which the needs of the organisation predominate; human resources are employed and dispensed with according to the demands of the corporate strategy (see also *soft HRM*).

health and safety audit An examination of the whole organisation in order to test whether it is meeting its safety aims and objectives. It examines hierarchies, safety planning processes, decision-making, delegation, policy-making and implementation as well as all areas of safety programme planning.

horizontal differentiation This can be seen in the way that the managers each take responsibility for a different department or function (see also *vertical differentiation*).

horizontal integration The term used to describe the relationships between employees at a similar level in the organisation (see also *vertical integration*).

human resource development (HRD) A strategic approach to investing in human capital. It draws on other HR processes, such as resourcing and performance assessment, to identify actual and potential talent.

human resource planning A strategic management function, the aim of which is to ensure that the organisation will have the human resources it needs currently and in the future, to realise its strategy and achieve its business objectives (see also *manpower planning*).

incentive system of payment A system in which the worker's pay is tied directly to his or her actual performance; eg the more you produce the more money you earn.

indirect discrimination – marital status The grounds for this are similar to those for indirect sex discrimination except that the requirement or condition is loaded against married employees, thus placing them at a disadvantage. *Example:* an employee's promotion is bypassed because one of the requirements of the job is to be abroad for long periods of time, which it is assumed a married person would not be able to do.

indirect sex discrimination This occurs when a requirement or condition is applied equally to men and women but disadvantages a significantly larger proportion of one sex than the other.

induction The period of time from when a new employee first joins the organisation until he or she reaches a satisfactory standard of performance.

internal justice system (IJS) A system through which on the one hand, the organisation takes action against employees who misbehave, and on the other, individual employees are able to seek a solution to perceived injustice, such as unfairness or ill-treatment.

internal labour market Regarding the current workforce as a prospective source of human resource supply (see also *external labour market*).

job analysis A data-gathering process that involves reducing every job to its constituent parts, including the nature of the activities, the task-related responsibilities the job entails, the knowledge and skills that are required to carry out the work, the reporting responsibilities and the level of the job.

job description A document containing the title of the job, the department in which it exists, a list of the main duties and responsibilities, the salary and other main terms and conditions, the performance requirements and the career prospects.

job evaluation A system of payment in which the worth of jobs is established by comparing them with each other.

job requisition A document in which a line manager states his or her HR requirements in terms of a job. This includes the nature of the tasks that make up the job, the priorities and the key tasks, the knowledge, competences and other personal qualities that a prospective job holder should possess.

job simulation An exercise in which a job applicant is required to deal with situations which typically represent the content of the job for which he/she has applied (see also *work sampling*).

labour flexibility (flexible working) Although this concerns attendance times, it is not to be confused with *flexi-time*. Employer and employee agree a pattern of attendance which is mutually acceptable and written into employment contracts such as those for part-time, occasional and zero-hours. Labour flexibility reduces costs and leads to a competitive advantage by allowing the organisation to continuously adjust the size and competences of the workforce in order to respond rapidly to customer demands.

learning Learning takes place when an individual has understood and internalised new information and/or has developed a new skill as a result of an experience. Evidence that learning has taken place may be inferred from a change in the individual's behaviour. Learning is an active process which may take place socially, systematically or experientially.

managerial judgement One of the techniques used in human resource planning, in which the organisation's managers estimate their future workloads and decide how many people they will need to employ in the future. The managers' decisions are based on their knowledge of past trends and forthcoming changes.

manpower planning The first attempts (in the 1960s) to develop a systematic method of ensuring that the organisation will have a continuous supply of the kinds of people it needs, now and in the future, in order to carry out the tasks that lead to the achievement of objectives. See also *human resource planning*.

matrix organisation A form of structure that may be introduced in organisations in which there is a need for teams to work on projects. Authority and responsibility operate laterally as well as vertically, and a project manager may call on the specialised services in the main organisation. The structure itself is typified by a grid indicating the lateral and vertical routes.

measured daywork A system that fixes the employee's pay on the understanding that he or she will maintain a pre-specified level of performance; the pay does not fluctuate in the short term as it would with an incentive system such as piecework.

national minimum wage A national, hourly-based and age-related level of payment that indicates the minimum rate of pay any worker should receive. The rate is regularly updated under the provisions of the National Minimum Wage Act 1998.

norm A tacit guideline that determines an individual's behaviour in particular situations, eg conforming to group or societal norms.

occupational test A portmanteau term covering all types of selection test that may be used for initial selection or selection for promotion or transfer.

operant conditioning A process in which the learner provides a response to a stimulus before that behaviour (the response) is reinforced or rewarded (see also *classical conditioning*).

organisation development The planning and implementation of programmes designed to improve organisational effectiveness.

performance appraisal The process through which an employee's standard of work is assessed in terms of previously agreed outputs and objectives.

performance-related pay A system in which the employee's performance is appraised and there is a mechanism in which overall performance levels are identified.

person specification A document containing an outline of the ideal candidate for a job, including qualifications, experience, skills, knowledge and attitude.

personal data Any information about a living person which enables the individual to be identified.

PESTLE analysis A process in which the organisation focuses upon the external pressures that impinge upon it with a view to planning responses to those pressures.

pluralistic perspective The view that employees should be facilitated to express themselves freely and engage in collective representation. In such organisations, several sources of power emerge (see also *unitary perspective*).

private sector organisations Organisations that are accountable to their shareholders for the efficiency and effectiveness of their decisions and actions.

psychological contract A contract that is based on an unwritten employee relationship in which the employer and the employee have a set of subjective expectations of each other.

public sector organisations Organisations which, directly or indirectly, are accountable to central government for the efficiency and effectiveness of their decisions and actions.

ratio-trend analysis One of the techniques used in human resource planning. The technique is based on the future stability of the relationship between productivity volumes and number of employees. The managers do not assume that this relationship remains constant.

risk assessment The task of identifying current and potential hazards, analysing the possible attendant risks and making recommendations for the removal or reduction of the risks.

sensitive data Defined by the Data Protection Act 1998 as information about an individual's (i) racial or ethnic origin, (ii) political opinions, (iii) religious or similar beliefs, (iv) membership of trade unions, (v) physical or mental health, (vi) sexual orientation, (vii) commission or alleged commission of offences, (viii) data relating to criminal offences, ongoing proceedings, or the decision of courts in respect of proceedings.

SMEs Small to medium-sized organisations.

socialisation The process through which individuals, in the early part of their lives, become familiar with their environment, adapt to the culture and learn about the kind of behaviour that is expected of them.

socio-technical system A model of the organisation which describes the interrelationship of the technical aspects and the human and social aspects.

soft HRM In which all human potential, regardless of the nature of contracts, will be nurtured and developed in order to achieve a competitive advantage (see also *hard HRM*).

span of control The number of employees that falls directly under the control of one manager. The term also refers to the shape and size of the structure in terms of its tallness or flatness.

stressors The factors that cause an individual to experience the effects of pressure imposed, for example, by particular situations, the state of relationships or simply by being aware of an impending situation that promises to be threatening.

SWOT analysis A process in which the organisation's strengths, weaknesses, opportunities and threats are examined with a view to making improvements in its current and future situation.

telecottage A centre containing equipment that is shared by people who work at a distance from their employer, or are self-employed. In some cases, the owner of the telecottage manages it.

training needs analysis (TNA) A technique for identifying training needs at individual, group and corporate levels. Usually, this is carried out through a training survey.

unitary perspective The view that the managers are the only legitimate source of power in the organisation. Managers see their role as controlling the activities of the employees, and assume that all employees are loyal, committed to the organisation's goals. Views that appear to conflict with this are regarded (by the managers) as communication failures or employees' foolish temperaments.

values An ideal to which an individual subscribes; it is what the individual has learned to be good and desirable. Values are developed as the individual is socialised (see also *socialisation*).

vertical differentiation Describes the differences between the roles of employees and managers at different levels within a department or section, such as the role of the employee resourcing manager and that of the recruitment manager.

vertical integration Describes the relationships between employees and managers at different levels in the organisation, such as the relationship between the general manager and the managing director.

VET Vocational education and training.

work sampling This involves placing a job applicant or a candidate for promotion in the actual role for a limited period of time and assessing his or her performance (see also *job simulation*).

The role of HR in the organisation

1

Organisations

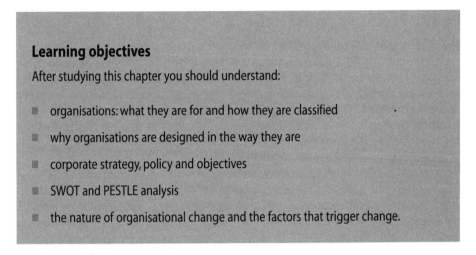

Learning objectives

After studying this chapter you should understand:

- organisations: what they are for and how they are classified

- why organisations are designed in the way they are

- corporate strategy, policy and objectives

- SWOT and PESTLE analysis

- the nature of organisational change and the factors that trigger change.

Introduction

The organisation provides the background within which the HR function works, so if you are studying HR for the first time, you need to develop a clear understanding of the context in which it is set. In other words, you need to have a sound understanding of organisations. The purpose of this chapter, therefore, is to help you to develop that understanding so that you can operate efficiently and effectively.

Using this chapter

This is a chapter which (I hope) you will find yourself dipping into from time to time for information about organisations. Different categories of organisation are explained, and how their purposes vary from one to another. The explanations of corporate strategy, policy formulation and objective setting will help you to understand how the organisation assesses and reviews its past performance, how it plans its long-term future and operates in the day-to-day context. Additionally, the factors that have triggered the significant changes that organisations have experienced in recent years are considered, as is the involvement of HR in the formulation of strategy.

Why organisations exist

We live in a society that is dominated by organisations. All of the major factors of our lives – our birth, health, education, marriage, employment, even our death – are influenced or handled by one kind of organisation or another. So why do we create organisations? The fundamental answer is that we do so in order to survive. Unlike other living creatures, human beings are rational and are therefore able to reflect upon their past, assess their current situation and make plans for the future. Since we are aware of our survival needs of the future, we create organisations to ensure that those needs will be met.

There are therefore vast industries involved in producing our basic needs, such as those for food, drink, shelter, security and a host of essential services; and on the lighter side, there are travel and entertainment companies. In fact, organisations are set up to serve us, not solely in order to survive, but to survive for longer, in greater comfort, and so that we may lead an interesting and pleasurable life. Organisations are the infrastructure of modern civilised societies.

Public sector organisations

The UK has a *mixed economy*, which means that some organisations are managed by central government. For example, government departments and local authorities provide us with essential services such as those for health, education, highways, policing, social services and dealing with emergencies. These organisations are said to be in the *public sector*. The provision of such services as drinking water, drainage, gas, electricity, and public transport used to be in the public sector, but privatisation towards the end of the twentieth century, transferred them to what we call the *private sector* (see later).

Ultimately, all public sector organisations are responsible to central government, and those who run them, the politicians, are accountable to the public. They derive their authority to make decisions and take actions on our behalf from what we call *public trust*. If the public is not satisfied with the way the politicians are managing, they can replace them at the next election through the voting system. Usually, politicians are amateurs in terms of the specific responsibilities they are given, and the policy decisions they make are based upon advice from employed experts, who also have the decisions implemented. These experts, who are senior civil servants, remain in their positions regardless of any political changes that the electorate makes, hence the term *permanent secretary*.

Private sector organisations

The *private sector* is made up of industrial and commercial companies that have evolved to respond to the stable and changing demands of the market. Each company exists to make a profit and is owned by its *shareholders* who are the prime beneficiaries. The members of the *board of directors*, who are responsible for managing the company, are elected to their positions by the shareholders. In the private sector, therefore, it is said that directors' authority to make decisions and take actions is derived from the *ownership* of the organisation.

The directors on the board are employed experts who formulate and implement policy. If the shareholders do not approve of the way the organisation is being managed, they can vote for changes in particular decisions, and when they think it is necessary, they may vote directors out of office. The shareholders' opportunity to vote arises at the organisation's *annual general meeting (AGM)*, where the directors report on the past year's performance, particularly the financial performance, and state their plans for the future. In reality, shareholding has become scattered widely among individuals and institutions, and many shareholders never attend AGMs.

Definitions of organisations

There have been many definitions of organisations, mostly drafted by academics. How an academic defines an organisation is usually determined by why he/she is defining it in the

Example 1

In 2004, the shareholders of a large public limited company (plc) voted down a board's decision to pay a large severance fee to a departing director. They did this because they considered that the director in question had failed in his job and did not, therefore, deserve to receive a reward for his performance.

first place. Economists, management scientists, social scientists and organisational psychologists have produced new and different ways of looking at organisations, while other definitions have been produced by working managers.

Theorists study organisations through the framework of their own particular science; each will study different aspects and not surprisingly, they all define them differently. Academics and practising managers have been studying organisations and how they should be managed for more than 100 years, and some of them say that the study of organisations and the study of 'management as an organisational process' are inextricably linked. Indeed, E.F.L. Brech (1965), a management theorist, defines organisations as 'the framework of the management process'.

Schein (1980) defines the organisation as:

the planned coordination of the activities of a number of people for the achievement of some common, explicit purpose or goal, through division of labour and function, and through a hierarchy of authority and responsibility.

As well as defining organisations, theorists also classify them. Above we described organisations as *public* and *private* sector undertakings. In 1966, Blau and Scott classified them in terms of who are the prime beneficiaries of the organisation. They proposed four types:

- *Mutual benefit organisations*, in which the members are the prime beneficiaries. A trade union is one obvious example. Others include sports and social clubs, some building societies and professional institutions, such as the Chartered Institute of Personnel and Development (CIPD).
- *Business concerns*, in which the shareholders are the prime beneficiaries. These are commercial and industrial profit-oriented organisations. Examples are motor car manufacturers and supermarkets.
- *Service organisations*, in which the prime beneficiaries are its users, such as its customers and clients. Examples of such organisations are health and educational institutions.
- *Commonweal organisations*, in which the public are the prime beneficiaries. Examples are the armed services, central and local government and the United Nations Organization (Blau and Scott 1966).

Charitable organisations in the UK have grown considerably since Blau and Scott proposed their classification. It was claimed then that any organisation would fit into one of their four categories, but it is difficult to see how any of them could accommodate a charitable organisation; perhaps there is room for a fifth category.

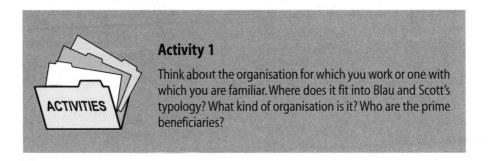

Activity 1

Think about the organisation for which you work or one with which you are familiar. Where does it fit into Blau and Scott's typology? What kind of organisation is it? Who are the prime beneficiaries?

Mechanistic and organic organisations

Burns and Stalker (1966) after extensive research into organisations defined them according to the degree to which they were mechanistic or organic. The research was related to the marketing function.

Mechanistic organisations

The researchers said that mechanistic organisations are those that have been serving a stable market for many years; that is to say that the demand for their products has consolidated, the assumption is made that things will not change significantly, and therefore the product demand, in terms of quantity and quality, can be predicted with a reasonable degree of accuracy. Internally, the result is a highly structured organisation with centralised policies, rigid hierarchical ranks, a strong emphasis on administration and tightly drawn boundaries between the departments and functions.

Organic organisations

Conversely, where customer demands are ever-changing, a mechanistic approach would seriously inhibit the organisation's ability to remain in the market. This kind of market situation, say the researchers, demands a flattened structure, *colleague*, rather than *command and control relationships* as the predominant mode, short-lived and flexible administrative systems and fuzzy departmental boundaries.

This is not to imply that industry is a dichotomy in which some organisations are totally mechanistic while others are totally organic. Organisations may be more or less mechanistic or more or less organic, which is best thought of as a dimension:

Mechanistic ⟷ movement ⟷ *Organic*

All organisations can be found somewhere on this dimension. Also, as market demands change and new products are developed, organisations are seen to shift to the left or right as they become more organic or more mechanistic.

Sizes of organisations

Finally, organisations may be classified by their size. They may range from the sole proprietor type of business to vast international and multinational undertakings employing hundreds of thousands of people. Curran and Stanworth (1988) identify three categories of size:

1. *Small to medium-sized enterprises (SMEs)*, which are subdivided by the European Commission into:
   (i) micro-enterprises, with less than 10 employees
   (ii) small enterprises, with between 10 and 99 employees
   (iii) medium-sized enterprises, with 100–499 employees.
2. *Large commercial enterprises* with over 500 employees.
3. *Public sector organisations*, such as those described earlier in this chapter.

Within this wide variety of sizes, the way in which HR is managed varies in style and sophistication. In micro-enterprises, for example, HR is dealt with by the owner/s, as are all of the management functions. Inevitably, in some cases, professional standards and legal requirements may be questionable, yet the employee relationship can be positive. The larger organisations, on the other hand, use systems and procedures that are based on sophisticated strategies and policies.

Small to medium-sized enterprises

There has been considerable growth in SMEs in recent years, and their importance to the economy has grown commensurately, employing collectively large numbers of people. The owners of such enterprises are usually busy people and are reluctant to allocate time to academics who wish to carry out research. Price (1997), however, says that smaller companies should be fruitful subjects for study because many conduct people management in the direct fashion advocated by HRM models.

Future growth

SMEs are a dynamic force in any country's economy; they are tomorrow's large organisations. They tend to start up on the basis of a single idea, and those that succeed go on to diversify and grow further. While it is clear that they do not all succeed and grow, many do, which is when they introduce the professional element into their internal systems, such as marketing, management and HR.

The purposes of organisations

The main purposes of all organisations are to survive and develop. To survive, the organisation must continue to provide the kinds of goods and services demanded by its customers and clients, bearing in mind, of course, that such demands change. Organisations also stimulate demand by creating and marketing new products and by modifying existing ones. The mobile telephone is an example of continuous modification.

Corporate strategy

Everyone wants the organisation to succeed and achieve its purposes of survival and development, and it is the responsibility of those at the very top, the board of directors, to ensure that this happens. Someone has to be at the steering wheel making decisions about the direction that the organisation should take; such decision-making is complex and sometimes involves considerable risk. The people at the wheel, making the decisions that shape the future direction of the organisation, are engaged in *strategy*. We discuss strategy in greater depth later in this chapter. Suffice to point out at this stage that strategy exists at corporate and functional levels.

Key concept 1: corporate strategy

Corporate strategy is a decision-making process by which the organisation attempts to meet its objectives. It is the way in which the organisation plans its long-term future.

Objectives and policies

For the organisation to reach its strategic goals, *objectives* are set, which are targets that need to be achieved by pre-specified dates. The achievement of objectives is a critically important factor in which appropriate timing is vital. The work that leads to the achievement of objectives has to be carried out within the limits of the organisation's *policies*. Policies are statements of intent about how the organisation proposes to conduct its business and achieve its strategic objectives. The organisation's specialists draft procedures that describe how policy decisions are to be carried out.

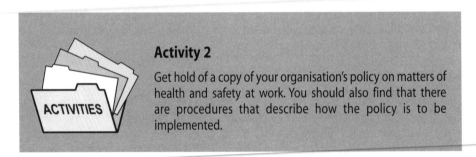

Activity 2

Get hold of a copy of your organisation's policy on matters of health and safety at work. You should also find that there are procedures that describe how the policy is to be implemented.

When the organisation knows where it is going (it has a *strategy*), what it has to do to get there (it has *objectives*) and how and when it is going to achieve those objectives (it has *policies and procedures*), attention may be turned to *resources*. The organisation needs resources in the form of money, materials, machinery and, of course, the human resource.

Survival and development

As we have seen, the main purposes of any organisation are to survive and develop, and to do this it has to continue to supply the types of goods and services demanded by its customers and clients. It is vital for a business to keep a keen eye on the activities of its competitors, changing market demands and the nature of internal and external pressures. The senior managers and specialists, therefore, carry out an *annual review* of the organisation's performance, and at the review, questions are asked about the internal and external situations. In today's fiercely competitive markets and rapidly developing innovation, such monitoring is a continuous, day-to-day process, since the rate of change in today's businesses is greater than ever before. Annual reviews are still held, especially in *public limited companies* (plcs), but what is discussed there now is the cumulative product of continuous monitoring. The organisation's current situation is discussed and strategic decisions are made about the future. In short, the process appraises the organisation's past performance and makes plans for the future.

Example 2

When the Corporate Strategy Section of J.K. Jones Ltd were conducting their annual review of the company's performance, it came to light that while the objectives they had set in the last period had been achieved in principle, there was room for improvement in certain areas. Productivity, for example, had experienced difficulty in keeping pace with sales, so the meeting decided to have the problem investigated with a view to improving productivity for the forthcoming year. The investigative report showed that investment in new technology would facilitate increased productivity, and thereby solve the problem.

Strategic planning techniques

Two main techniques have been developed to provide a structure to the strategic planning process, and it is vital for the aspiring HR practitioner to understand and be able to use these techniques.

The first was developed by Ansoff (1987). It focuses on an organisation's *strengths, weaknesses, opportunities* and *threats* and is usually referred to by the acronym SWOT. The second technique focuses on the internal and external *pressures* that impinge upon an organisation and these include such factors as *political, economic, social, technological, labour-related* and *environmental* pressures. The acronym PESTLE is used to refer to this technique.

SWOT analysis

Of the two techniques, this is the most well known. What follows is an analysis of the process that demonstrates the extent of the detail that goes into its application.

- **S**trengths are the valuable and successful aspects of the organisation, such as having ample resources, highly skilled people, and appropriate technology for achieving the objectives. Being good at product design, quality assurance and customer care are also examples of strengths, since they help to sustain and improve the organisation's position in the market. The organisation may also be doing well in some particular function, and it is a good idea to analyse this to see if lessons may be learned for other functions.
- **W**eaknesses are the organisation's negative features such as financial or skill deficiencies, out-of-date work systems or poor employee relations. The identification of weaknesses is essential since areas for improvement have to be addressed urgently.
- **O**pportunities are events or openings that may arise from the market or other areas

of the business environment. Perhaps the need for a new or modified product is identified, or it may be that the organisation's unique skills can be applied to a new venture or diversification.

- **Threats** can arise from the business environment. For example, an aspiring competitor may be about to invade the market and endanger the business. Competitors are also a threat when they modify standard products in order to achieve a market advantage. In this analysis, threats are usually thought to be external, but of course, threats may also arise from poor internal relations in which the employees are dissatisfied with the terms and conditions of employment and are threatening to interrupt business progress by taking industrial action.

Activity 3

Examine your own organisation and assess how it would stand up to a SWOT analysis. Make a list of what you regard as (i) its strengths and (ii) its weaknesses and think about how they might be capitalised on and improved respectively.

PESTLE analysis

Organisations have to keep abreast of, and respond to, the internal and external pressures that impinge upon them.

- **Political interventions** are pressures that appear in the form of new legislation, particularly on business practices, employment, health and safety, taxation and many other factors. In today's global market, however, pressures may also relate to overseas trading, for example, in the form of European policies on agriculture and regulations relating to commercial fishing. New employment legislation carries implications for the organisation, and these are discussed in Part 3. In the wider overseas trading context, internationally agreed sanctions may curtail, or even outlaw, our trading with particular countries which, for example, may be involved in terrorism or human rights abuses.

- **Economic changes.** The influence of regional, national and international economic conditions plays a large part in the fortunes of organisations. Sometimes the economy is buoyant and in a state of boom and plenty, unemployment is low, industrial and high-street spending is high and property values soar. At other times the economy dips and the 'highs' that are mentioned above go into reverse. Organisations have to adjust to the alternate peaking and dipping of the economy, and internally, they must prepare themselves accordingly. In a global economy, competition is very fierce, and organisations take steps to ensure that they remain competitive. HR specialists keep an eye on the changing economy, since in a good economy when the organisation is expanding, there are usually staff shortages, especially of rare technical skills, but when it is bad and the organisation has to contract, redundancies may have to be made.

- **Social trends**, in which market demands change according to changes in cultures, values, fashion, and even mere whim. The rate at which social preferences change can limit or extend product life cycles and internally, the need to keep pace will create the need for more frequent changes to be made.

■ *Technological innovation.* This occurs on two broad fronts. The first is in terms of process innovation, which includes modifying or replacing machinery and the production and administrative systems because new and better systems have been developed, giving greater productivity, cost efficiency and effectiveness. The second is in terms of product innovation, in which new products and services are developed and/or modifications to existing ones made. Organisations tend to develop their own product innovation. So far as process innovation is concerned, they are largely 'users' of technology that has been developed by manufacturers of capital equipment and computer software.

■ *Labour-related* pressures are applied in several ways; first, in terms of availability. The organisation may need to expand if, for example, an increased demand for its products or the development of a new product requires more staff. Second, pressure is applied where new technology produces the need for staff with skills that are hard to find, which can put pressure on productivity, or at least on the smooth running of the new systems. These pressures are examined further in Chapter 4.

■ *Environmental factors.* People are now extremely concerned about the effect that industrial activity is having on the environment, and pressure groups monitor and frequently demonstrate against particular business and scientific activities. Pressure groups such as Greenpeace monitor oil spills, deforestation and a host of other effects upon nature. Animal rights activists apply considerable pressure to organisations that carry out biological and cosmetic tests on living creatures, and sometimes even make physically violent, attacks on the premises of such organisations and on the people who work within them.

Using SWOT and PESTLE analyses

The information that is derived from carrying out SWOT and PESTLE analyses, including the facts that have accumulated as a result of continuous monitoring, provides a basis for the decisions that are made about the organisation's future. Where problems have come to light, the strategists look for causes with a view to resolving the problems, and where strengths are identified, they examine the possibilities of improving on those strengths in the future. This results in organisations formulating new policies in order to respond to the influences of legislation and other pressures.

ACTIVITIES

Activity 4

It has been noticed that some students confuse these two analytic techniques. Consider your own organisation in the light of both, and note the different answers that emerge from your analysis. While both are used to assist the strategic planning process, they should be kept apart conceptually because they serve different purposes. SWOT analysis is a reality check on the organisation's internal and external situations and its past performance, while PESTLE analysis focuses on the internal and external pressures that impinge upon the organisation. Looking at your own organisation in this way will enable you to remember which is which.

Organisational structures

Most of us are familiar with the conventional shape of an organisation's structure. It has a hierarchical design with descending levels of authority. Viewed vertically, we can see how the various departments and specialisms are separated, while laterally, we can see the layers that indicate levels of authority and responsibility.

Key concept 2: corporate structure

Commonly referred to as the 'organisational chart', the corporate structure is a hierarchical design (like a family tree), which may be 'tall', meaning that there are many layers of authority and responsibility, or 'flat', meaning that there are fewer layers. Tall structures are generally bureaucratically managed, while with flatter structures managers and employees usually work together in a 'colleague' type of relationship, in which communication is eased and more direct.

The structure shows the relationships that exist between the employees at *vertical* and *horizontal* levels, which are referred to as *vertical* and *horizontal integration*. The structure also outlines what we call *vertical* and *horizontal differentiation*. Vertical differentiation can be seen in the different roles of people within a department or function, such as in the roles of the employee resourcing manager and, say, the recruitment manager. On the other hand, horizontal differentiation can be seen in the way that each manager takes responsibility for separate departments and functions, such as the roles of the marketing manager and the finance manager. (You will find that some writers use the word *lateral* instead of *horizontal*.)

Case study 1: Something Afoot

Jane Firmstone is a regional sales manager for Something Afoot, a company providing tough footwear for agricultural workers and climbers, etc. Jane has divided the region into three districts and John Glass, Jim Ford and Sue Wilson are her district representatives. Before leaving home, John telephoned Jane to say that he would be calling in to the regional sales office on his way home to let her have a detailed breakdown of his sales figures for last month. This pleased Jane because she is about to compile the regional sales report for that month and she is anxious that her figures stand up well in the light of those from other regions with which her figures will be compared.

Just before ringing off, Jane wished John luck with Grays, an awkward client that she knew he was seeing that day, 'and don't go giving them discounts above the company norm, you know it annoys them at head office'. John is worried about his call on Grays. It is his district's largest shoe store and at one time was Something Afoot's biggest retail outlet. Over the past year, however, Grays has stocked fewer and fewer of Something Afoot's products and replaced them with imports from Poland. John believes that the problem lay in his company's introduction of a standard discount policy a year ago. Previously, the sales staff had been free to determine the discounts they offered, and major clients were able to obtain larger discounts than are possible under the company's new standard discounts policy.

John cheered up as he thought of lunch. He had arranged to eat with Sue Wilson. She had promised to bring samples of some of the company's latest designs which John thought would be of particular interest to Grays, whose customers are particularly fashion conscious. John reflected that working with the sales team was not so bad. They really are a team and their monthly meetings are one of the best parts of the job.

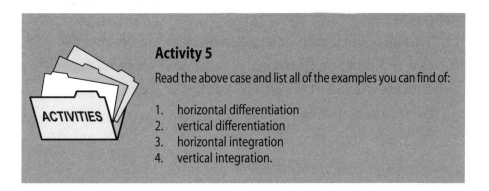

Activity 5

Read the above case and list all of the examples you can find of:

1. horizontal differentiation
2. vertical differentiation
3. horizontal integration
4. vertical integration.

Designing the structure

Designing a structure is not a simple task. Before embarking upon such a project, the needs of the organisation have to be identified. Child (1988) says that most of the information one needs can be found in the answers to five key questions:

1 Should jobs be broken down into narrow areas of work and responsibility so as to secure the benefits of specialisation, or should the degree of specialisation be kept to a minimum in order to simplify communication and to offer members of the organisation greater scope and responsibility in their work?

2 Should the overall structure of an organisation be 'tall' rather than 'flat' in terms of its levels and spans of control? What are the implications for communication, motivation and overhead costs of moving towards one of these alternatives rather than the other?

3 Should jobs and departments be grouped together in a 'functional' way according to the specialist expertise and interests that they share? Or should they be grouped according to the different services and products that are being offered, or the different geographical areas being served, or according to yet another criterion?

4 Is it appropriate to aim for an intensive form of integration between the different segments of the organisation, or not? What kind of integrative mechanisms are there to choose from?

5 What approach should management take towards maintaining adequate control

over work done? Should it centralise or delegate decisions? Should a policy of extensive formalisation be adopted in which standing order and written records are used for control purposes? Should work be subject to close supervision?

If we examine these questions, we see that Child presents us with alternatives, implying that each organisation has its own specific structural needs. The questions have very strong human resource implications in terms of 'greater scope and responsibility' (Question 1), 'communication and motivation' (Question 2) and 'sharing specialist expertise and interests' (Question 3). According to the principles of HRM, these advantages are best achieved by introducing a flattened, rather than a tall structure, so that managers and employees can work closely together, and the integrity of formal, vertical communication is improved, since it passes through fewer hierarchical levels.

Organisational structures are designed to reflect the roles and relationships of the various positions and employees. The structure should show the logic underlying the division of the organisation's expertise and how functions are placed to work in a co-ordinated way.

Structure makes possible the application of the process of management and creates a framework of order and command, through which the activities of the organisation can be planned, organised, directed and controlled.

(Mullins 1993)

Restructuring may be seen as a reflection of the need to make internal changes in order to continue to complement external changes. In the early twentieth century, academics and practising managers produced theories that have come to be known as classical approaches to management, which were succeeded by the human relations approach, management by objectives, system and contingency theories, and more recently, human resource management.

While some of these ideas remain relevant for particular organisations, the adoption of the principles and techniques of human resource management (HRM) has significant implications for structures (see Chapter 2).

Span of control

This term relates to the number of employees that falls directly under the control of one manager. Given that the organisation has a particular number of employees, the number of layers in the overall structure will be determined by the sizes of the spans of control within it. Organisations with tall spans of control will have many layers (as in Figure 1.1), and those with flattened ones will have fewer layers. Structures are referred to as 'tall' or 'flat' and the advent of HRM in the 1980s brought with it a tendency for organisations to flatten their structures (see Figure 1.2).

One of the effects of the trend towards flattened structures was to reduce the number of managers and increase the number of employees reporting to each manager. This changed employees' working situations in that in addition to having to adapt to changes in the work itself, they found themselves reporting to different managers and working with different colleagues.

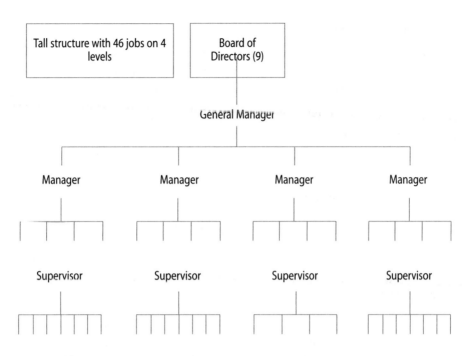

Figure 1.1 A conventional organisational structure

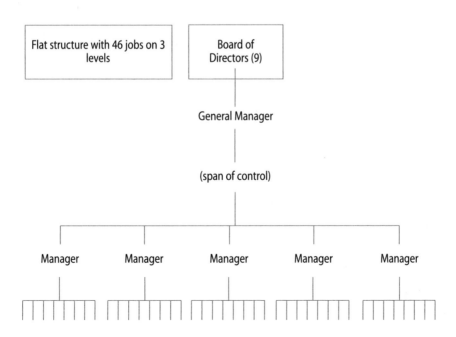

Figure 1.2 Span of control influencing structure

Matrix organisations

This form of structure may be introduced in organisations in which there is a need for teams to work on projects, such as those in the construction industry, civil engineering and other types of commissioning firms. Matrix structures may also be found in an enterprise in which there is a need to set up a temporary unit in order to carry out a specific project. Managers and specialists are seconded from different parts of the organisation for the duration of the project. On completion, the team may be disbanded and reintegrated into the main structure, or may move on to another new project; an organisation may have several projects running concurrently. A civil engineering concern, for example, may, *inter alia*, be carrying out such projects as building a bridge in the Midlands, a tunnel in Scotland, a high-rise building in Belfast and a road in East Anglia.

A matrix design is typified by a grid which depicts a two-dimensional track of authority and responsibility. Authority and responsibility in the functional departments track downwards, while from the project manager, authority and responsibility track laterally across the main structure. In this way, project managers may look across the organisation to access its resources, a concept that produces economic as well as practical advantages (see Figure 1.3).

Matrix structures have drawn criticism from employees. They say they become frustrated as a result of working for two bosses: first, the functional heads to whom they report, and second, the project managers who make demands on their services. Such frustrations usually arise from conflicting time constraints and priorities.

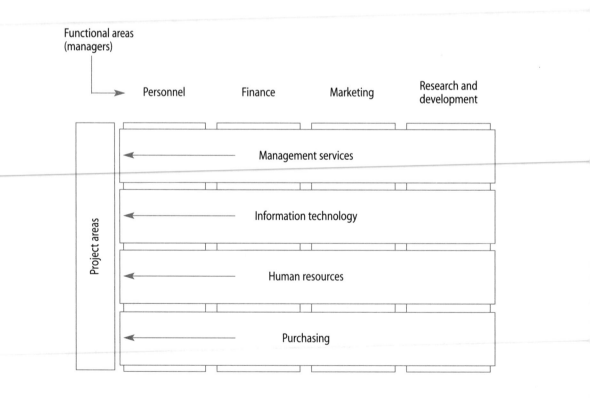

Figure 1.3 How a matrix organisation works

The flexible organisation

The need for senior managers to focus on survival and development while remaining competitive in a fierce global market has caused them to review their attitudes towards employment, and *flexible working* (not to be confused with 'flexi-time') is one of the ideas that has emerged. Flexible working was first introduced in the early 1970s, when it was referred to as *core staff theory*, but did not become widespread until the 1980s. Within this concept, the notion that the organisation needs to access particular skills no longer implies that it has to offer a conventional full-time contract of employment. The nature of the contract offered to the person is determined by the rarity and availability of his or her skills and the amount of time for which those skills are needed. For these reasons, the terms and conditions of employment vary from one category of employee to another. Organisations distinguish between *core* and *peripheral* workers (see Figure 1.4).

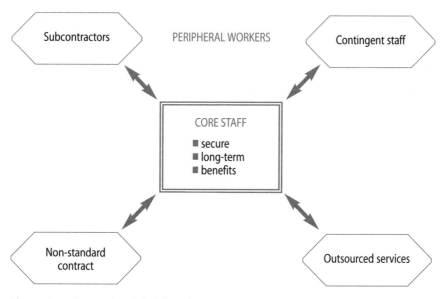

Figure 1.4 Core and peripheral workers

Source: Price (1997).

Core and peripheral workers

Core workers are those who are regarded as critically important to the organisation and who are, therefore, encouraged to stay by virtue of attractive prospects and rewards. Core staff are recognised as highly skilled and motivated technical, scientific or professional people without whom the organisation cannot optimise performance. Positive retention planning, therefore, has become an integral part of HR strategy. Peripheral workers on the other hand are not treated so generously, and in some cases are actively encouraged to seek employment elsewhere.

This attitude towards different categories of worker is reflected in the *reward management* structure. These ideas have grown in popularity for several reasons:

- operation of new technology which demands higher skills
- need for greater economic efficiency
- need to improve upon and sustain the quality of the organisation's product
- need for a more flexible and speedy response to external demands
- need for a greater degree of involvement and, thereby, satisfaction on the part of valued employees.

The virtual organisation

A futuristic example of the flexible organisation is summarised by Price (1997), in which he describes the 'virtual organisation'. Price represents the organisation as a network which is composed of expert nodules; a virtual organisation:

Advances in new technology allow the firm to extend the network concept to form enterprises with no permanent structures. They bring people together for specific projects. Teams dissolve on completion, to reappear in combinations for other tasks. The teams are made up of people who add value through their knowledge and traditional hierarchical structures have no role in this model. Departments, divisions and offices disappear, leaving an amorphous mass of people connected electronically and meeting only when required.

(Price 1997)

Organisational change

Lecturing at Manchester in 1832, Ralph Waldo Emerson said, 'The willingness to change is the most essential ingredient to success in any walk of life.' We create original concepts that bring about change, but we also adapt to changes that others have created. Emerson was referring to the latter when he made his famous comment at Manchester and many years later, he included it in his paper, *Conduct of Life* which was published in 1860. In fact he was talking and writing about the conduct of individuals, but the principle is equally relevant to organisations today.

Change factors

Inside the organisation, three of the major factors that have influenced and will continue to influence change, particularly as they affect HR, are:

- new and amended laws that affect employment, many of which, to a significant degree, have their origins in European directives
- the continuous advances in technology; especially in information technology
- human resource management (HRM), as a system that influences how the whole organisation is run; especially in terms of the internal structure, culture, development, human performance and the general working climate within organisations.

We discuss the first of these new and amended laws throughout the book, since they affect a variety of HR issues and activities. The ways in which new technology has instigated change in organisations are discussed later in this chapter, and HRM is the subject of Chapter 2. From your study of all of the foregoing, you should gain an understanding of how organisations operate and respond to the internal and external environments.

Evolution and revolution

The three change factors that are mentioned above are probably the most visible to those who manage organisations, but change has several perspectives. Charles Handy, for example, talks about two types of change: *continuous* and *discontinuous*. In his analogy that describes continuous change, he says:

> **If you put a frog in cold water and gradually turn up the heat, the frog will eventually let itself be boiled to death. Similarly, if we don't actively respond to the radical way the world is currently changing we will not survive.**
>
> **(Handy 1989)**

In organisations today, minor, day-to-day changes take place that are made as a result of 'on-the-hoof' decisions by managers and others. These changes go unnoticed at the time, such as a minor modification to a work system or a gradual change in the style of communication. This is evolutionary change in which organisations change gradually and evolve in ways that enable them to continue to meet the needs of the internal and external environments. It is also one of the ways in which organisations respond to the factors that are brought to light by a SWOT or PESTLE analysis.

Activity 6

How long have you been with your current employer? Look back to when you first joined and reflect upon what it was like to work there then. Now compare that with the way things are now. Try to identify exactly what has changed.

What Handy describes as *discontinuous* change is more revolutionary than evolutionary. This type of change imposes sudden, large-scale changes that seem to take place overnight, such as the implementation of a major new policy, a merger with another organisation or the privatisation of a public authority; but there are yet other evolutionary changes. Champy and Nohria (1996) claim that three major drivers stirring organisational change faster than ever before are:

- *technology:* particularly IT, which is transforming businesses in dramatic ways
- *government:* rethinking its role in business, with all governments on a worldwide basis initiating deregulation, privatisation and increasing free trade

- *globalisation:* where companies from all parts of the globe are competing to deliver the same product or service, any time, anywhere at increasingly competitive prices, which is causing organisations and companies to organise themselves in radically different ways.

On the other hand, Hussey (1996) identifies four major long-running forces of change as:

- competition
- more demanding customers
- accelerating pace of technological obsolescence
- pressure to deliver shareholder value.

Technology

Introducing new technology into the organisation produces both positive and negative outcomes. On the positive side, it enables the organisation to:

- enhance the productivity rate and the quality of its goods and services
- broaden and deepen its range of goods and services
- increase the efficiency and effectiveness of administration and the speed at which administrative tasks are carried out
- communicate internally and externally almost instantaneously
- carry out some of its functions more cost-effectively by transferring them to overseas locations: eg, call centres.

On the negative side:

- The initial capital outlay for new technology can be prohibitively high.
- The rate at which technology is developing means that further advances are made before the organisation has had a full return on its capital outlay.
- Advances in technology affect the types of knowledge and skill requirements, and often require costly wide-ranging training and retraining programmes.
- Its installation may cause the organisation temporarily to lose its day-to-day effectiveness.
- Employees may be negatively affected by the 'threat' of technological change.

Resistance to change

The chief preoccupations of managers when they are planning and implementing change are usually related to the cost and technical aspects of the change process. Truly, this can be a complex and testing set of disciplines to handle. Mistakes can be costly, but the key factor and certainly the most essential ingredient to a successful change process is the way in which the employees are taken through it. It is hard to imagine a more stringent test of managers' leadership skills.

When, for example, technological innovation triggers change, many of the long-serving employees fear it. Their skills have served them well in terms of their performance and earning capacity, but they feel abandoned and redundant when their previously valued abilities are no longer needed by the organisation. They might resist change for several reasons since to them it might mean:

- a threat to their stability and may make their jobs redundant
- a change of routines, which can be frustrating
- being moved into jobs they fear they may not understand
- a change in status
- a change in pay structure and other rewards
- having to work in a new area with previously unknown colleagues
- having to work for a new and unknown boss
- having to work for a boss who is known, but is generally not liked
- a change in working hours
- changing to a job that is insufficiently challenging.

Change is continuous; it affects the environment in which organisations operate and it exists within organisations themselves. Employees are affected by change and they must adapt, learn new skills, cope with different pressures, acquire new knowledge and forge new relationships.

(Martin and Jackson 2003)

Not all employees respond in the same way to change. Individual differences have a profound effect on how employees perceive change. Intelligence and motivational factors may frustrate retraining, and age differences may inhibit more mature employees when it comes to disrupting their routines and separating them from their long-term work colleagues. For these reasons, therefore, change may raise the staff turnover rate and lead to redundancy and recruitment programmes. Change therefore has significant implications for the HR role.

Dealing with resistance

Encountering resistance may be used as an opportunity to examine how the change proposal is being handled. If the nature of the change has not been fully explained to employees, the prophets of doom will step forward and rumours about the proposed change will become widespread. Resistance, however, can be turned around and made constructive if it causes managers to interact more frequently with their staff, for example, when they explain the nature of the proposed change in detail.

The proposed change should be explained to employees right from the outset. If it is not, it will create uncertainty among employees about what their future holds, which may lead to personal feelings of insecurity on the part of individuals. The approach to delivering news of change to employees should be a consultative one, in which the managers elicit employees' feelings and opinions. This kind of approach has been known to cause managers to explore alternative ways of meeting the desired objective. It may be that the alternatives proposed by the employees represent an improvement on the original proposal. If the employees are asked to think about the change, they will get to know more about it, which will serve three possible ends: first, to allay any rumours; second, to produce an improved proposal; and third, to reduce or even eliminate the resistance. A positive outcome to a consultative approach may confer upon employees feelings of 'ownership' of the change process, which naturally leads to their commitment to it.

A change process that has the backing and commitment of employees is far more likely to succeed.

Self-test questions

1. What are the main purposes of all organisations?
2. Name the four categories into which Blau and Scott classified organisations.
3. From where do those who manage public and private sector organisations derive their authority to make decisions and take actions?
4. What are the main differences between the two main techniques that senior managers use to assist the strategic planning process?
5. What HR implications arise from the five questions posed by Child (1988) when considering the design of an organisation's structure?
6. What do we mean by 'flexible working'?
7. What major factors have influenced organisational change?
8. What are the differences between evolutionary and revolutionary change?
9. Why might an employee choose redundancy rather than retraining?
10. How would you respond to resistance to change?

Human resource management | CHAPTER 2

Learning objectives

After studying this chapter you should understand:

▪ human resource management (HRM) in the traditional and modern contexts

▪ the various approaches to HRM

▪ strategic HRM

▪ the impact that HRM has had upon organisations' approach to management since the 1980s

▪ the influence of HRM on the management of people

▪ the differences between modern HRM and personnel management.

Introduction

There is a wide variety of views about HRM. The concept has been variously interpreted, and the style with which its principles and practices are applied varies among academics, practitioners and indeed, from one country to another. There is neither the space nor the need in a book of this size and level to venture deeply into a discussion of the philosophical pronouncements about HRM, but it is necessary to provide an understanding of how it has influenced not only the management of employment, but the management of the whole organisation.

This chapter offers some of the insights of academics and practitioners, and we hope you will attain an understanding of HRM that you will be able to take further in your later studies. If, however, you wish to look into the concept more deeply at this stage, the references that are cited here will lead you to a comprehensive account of the HRM debate: the philosophies underlying the various interpretations and how the principles and practices upon which HRM is founded are applied.

In addition to developing a sound understanding of HRM, you also need to be aware of the management systems that emerged earlier in the twentieth century. This is because many organisations have not fully adopted HRM and still adhere to the traditional practices of personnel management.

What exactly is HRM?

The history of management thought, which began in earnest in the early twentieth century, produced theories which contain allusions to what we now regard as HRM principles and practices, (Taylor 1947, Burns and Stalker 1966) but they were not introduced into British organisations as a totally new management system until the 1980s. At the time, people became confused about what the term meant, and this was understandable since the words 'human resource' caused people to think of personnel. Sisson (1995) says that in the late 1980s, there was much debate among practitioners and academics alike about the implications of HRM for the personnel function. He said that even if some found it difficult to understand what the fuss was about (HRM looked very much like the personnel management they thought they were practising), many practitioners welcomed the new paradigm (Armstrong 1987, Fowler 1987).

Ideal type of organisation

The main question became, what is the difference between HRM and personnel management? Indeed, is there a difference or was it just that the term personnel management had lost credibility and needed a new label? A second question is, how can you so dramatically introduce a new way of managing employment without affecting the ways in which the whole organisation is managed? On the basis of studying organisations in a series of case studies, Storey (1992) created an 'ideal type' of organisation in order to clarify and simplify the essential features that distinguish HRM from other forms of people management. His classification shows 27 points of differences in practice between personnel and industrial relations and HRM practice (see Table 2.1, overleaf).

It has to be understood that the comparative model illustrated in Table 2.1 is purely theoretical and that no single organisation conforms to all of the conditions within it.

What can be seen from the model is that those who have adopted the principles and practices of HRM, have shifted from what was regarded as standard practice in personnel and industrial relations terms (the middle column in Table 2.1), to the generally more flexible, open and mutually cooperative standard of HRM (the right-hand column of Table 2.1).

Research shows that HRM has been *more* or *less* adopted by organisations (Beardwell *et al* 2004, p26). British managers, however, have a record of reluctance to adopt new ideas in the comprehensive sense; they are very financially orientated and change, which is always a costly process, is usually carried out in a cautious and piecemeal fashion.

Sisson (2001, pp80–81) identifies two main explanations for this cautious reluctance. First, he says that they are inclined to 'try one or two elements and assess their impact before going further, even though this means forgoing the benefits of the integration associated with bundles of complementary practices'. The second, and in Sisson's words 'less comfortable', explanation is that 'HRM is not the only means of achieving competitive advantage and other methods, adopted by organisations … do not involve a change in the way that people are managed.' 'Other methods' refers to adaptations of the tried and tested management systems of the twentieth century. In many cases, this involves the use of an eclectic mix of the elements of earlier theories.

Capon (2000) draws a distinction between personnel management and HRM by saying that:

personnel management is directed very much towards the personnel or workforce and the personnel department managing their work-related

needs. In comparison the HR department considers the strategic contribution that employees make to the organisation. Issues concerning the number of employees, the skills required and the cost to the organisation of employees with the required skills are of prime importance to the HR department.

A large number of organisations, however, do use HRM terminology. Gradually, since the 1980s, 'personnel departments' have become 'HR departments' and the same staff working in those departments have become 'HR specialists' or 'HR advisers', regardless, it seems, of whether or not the organisation has formally adopted the principles and practices of HRM itself.

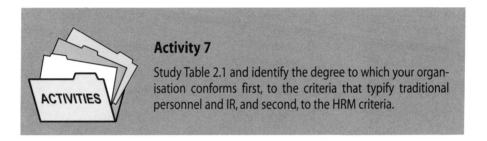

Activity 7

Study Table 2.1 and identify the degree to which your organisation conforms first, to the criteria that typify traditional personnel and IR, and second, to the HRM criteria.

An important point that should be made here is that the personnel and industrial relations activities that indicated good practice before the 1980s are still practised today using the same methods and techniques, but within HRM a new style of thinking underlies the practices and affects the degree to which the outcomes serve the purposes of overall corporate strategy.

HRM and traditional management

So far in this chapter the discussion has been about the history, principles and practices of HRM, without significant reference to the theories of management that were widespread before 1980. Academics and practitioners have been studying organisational management for more than 100 years, resulting in several generations of different approaches (see Table 2.2, overleaf).

The *human relations* approach emerged in the 1930s. While the classical theorists were concerned with structures, physical working conditions, work methods, measurement and proposing formal 'rules' of management, it became evident in the late 1920s that attention should be paid to the social aspects of workplace life. It was the study of employees' social interactions, their attitudes and values that gave rise to the human relations approach. One study in particular that stimulated academic and practitioner interest in the motivations of people at work is the Hawthorne study, which took place between 1924 and 1936 at the Hawthorne Plant of the Western Electric Company in Chicago. This was when the importance of peoples' motivations, in the social as well as the technical aspects of being at work, became evident.

Bureaucracy

The main theorist that followed these early researchers was the sociologist Max Weber (1964), whose most well-known work, *The theory of social and economic organisation*, was the

Table 2.1 Twenty-seven points of difference

Dimension	Personnel and IR	HRM
Beliefs and assumptions		
1 Contract	Careful delineation of written contracts	Aim to go 'beyond contract'
2 Rules	Importance of devising clear rules/mutuality	'Can do' outlook; impatience with 'rule'
3 Guide to management action	Procedures	'Business need'
4 Behaviour referent	Norms/custom and practice	Values/mission
5 Managerial task vis-à-vis labour	Monitoring	Nurturing
6 Nature of relations	Pluralist	Unitarist
7 Conflict	Institutionalised	De-emphasised
Strategic aspects		
8 Key relations	Labour management	Customer
9 Initiatives	Piecemeal	Integrated
10 Corporate plan	Marginal to	Central to
11 Speed of decision	Slow	Fast
Line management		
12 Management role	Transactional	Transformational leadership
13 Key managers	Personnel/IR specialists	General/business/line managers
14 Communication	Indirect	Direct
15 Standardisation	High (eg 'parity' an issue)	Low (eg 'parity' not seen as relevant)
16 Prized managerial skills	Negotiation	Facilitation
Key levers		
17 Selection	Separate, marginal task	Integrated, key task
18 Pay	Job evaluation (fixed grades)	Performance-related

19 Conditions	Separately negotiated	Harmonisation
20 Labour management	Collective bargaining contracts	Towards individual contracts
21 Thrust of relations with stewards	Regularised through facilities and training	Marginalised (with exception of some bargaining for change models)
22 Jobs categories and grades	Many	Few
23 Communication	Restricted flow	Increased flow
24 Job design	Division of labour	Teamwork
25 Conflict handling	Reach temporary truces	Manage climate and culture
26 Training and development	Controlled access to courses	Learning companies
27 Foci of attention for interventions	Personnel procedures	Wide-ranging cultural, structural and personnel strategies

Source: Storey (1992, p38). Reproduced by kind permission of Blackwell Publishers.

Table 2.2 Early management theories and theorists

Classical theorists		Classical theories
H. Fayol 1949	Management practitioners	General principles of management
F.W. Taylor 1947		Scientific management
F. and L. Gilbreth 1917	Academics	The science of management
E.F.L. Brech 1965		The framework of management

result of his study of the German civil service. In that book he first used the term *bureaucracy* and said that to some extent, bureaucracy existed in all organisations, in the private as well as the public sector. Weber drew distinctions between three types of organisation in terms of the kinds of authority that existed within them, which he described as *traditional, charismatic* and *legal-rational*. Bureaucracy is a frequently found form of organisation. Many writers believe that to some degree, all organisations are bureaucratised.

Table 2.3 Twentieth-century theories and theorists

Human relations approach	Systems and contingency approaches
Elton Mayo and the Hawthorne studies (1930s)	Trist *et al* (1963) Organisational choice
A.H. Maslow (1954–72) Motivation and personality	Burns and Stalker (1966) The management of innovation
F.W. Herzberg *et al* (1957) Work and the nature of man	Joan Woodward (1980) Industrial organisation
D. McGregor (1960) The human side of enterprize	

These were all different approaches to managing, and they were based on academic research (eg McGregor 1960, Weber 1964) and the experience of practising managers (eg Taylor 1911, Fayol 1949). Throughout the classical and mid-century studies of management the accepted managerial skills were described as planning, organising, directing and controlling; the four functions being linked together through co-ordination.

- *Planning.* This includes setting objectives and making decisions about how objectives are to be achieved.
- *Organising.* In this context, organising means developing a structure through which the work may be carried out, allocating the work to various staff members, delegating tasks and giving people commensurate authority to have them carried out.
- *Directing.* Within this function, the manager 'gets things done' through people. It means actually directing, or 'showing the way' (Taylor 1947). Directing therefore includes the use of such skills as leadership, motivation, communication, coaching and counselling employees.
- *Controlling.* The manager monitors and assesses the degree to which predetermined objectives have been met. This involves identifying any shortfalls between the work that was planned and the work that was actually carried out. Decisions then have to be made about how to head off those shortfalls in the future.

Control and compliance

Clearly, from the use of words such as 'command' and 'control' we can see that before HRM, work was carried out because managers 'controlled' everything and issued orders while employees complied by applying their knowledge and skills to the tasks. As far as history shows, it was not until the Hawthorne study that employees were consulted about their physical working conditions and their attitudes towards their supervisors. Even after that, control and compliance still prevailed.

The socio-technical system

An important discovery made by Elton Mayo at the Hawthorne plant was that employees made decisions and took actions that were not planned or in any way determined by the managers. Previously, it had been assumed that productivity levels were the result of managerial exhortation and the fact that the employees were skilled enough to do the jobs. Now, however, it was apparent that organisations have a social as well as a technical side. It had become clear to Mayo that the work groups, which had been put together for technical reasons, had developed socially. It had been thought that variations in productivity at the plant were attributable to problems with the physical working conditions, but Mayo realised that the groups, in the social role, were making productivity decisions that were different from those demanded by the managers. This was a second source of power in the organisation, and the question of what to do about it became important (Mayo 1933).

What became known as the socio-technical system (the organisation has a social as well as a technical side) was taken a step further by Trist and other researchers at the Tavistock Institute of Human Relations in London in 1963 by bringing into fuller realisation the interaction between a work group and the task it has to perform. The organisation was really a social system and a technical system; the two systems interacted and this had to be taken into account since it was realised that there would always be an interaction between the methods of work, technology and social relationships. Earlier approaches had concentrated on either technical aspects (eg scientific management), or the social aspects (eg the human relations approach) (see Tables 2.2 and 2.3).

Human resource management

Few would argue with the notion that it was the success of Asian industry in the 1970s and 1980s that gave rise to the development of HRM; it was one of the reactions of the West to the Asian invasion of European and US markets. Indeed, according to Goss (1996) it was a little more than that:

> **The development of HRM as a body of management thought in the 1980s can be linked to a conjunction of socio-economic factors – in particular, changes in international competition, the restructuring of industrial sectors and organizations, and a rise of a new confidence in the power of managers to manage.**

Undoubtedly, the Thatcher years restored managers' confidence, and this was achieved in part by waging war upon the militant trade unions which were considerably weakened in the 1980s.

A new perspective

At the time, most managers had 'cherry-picked' past theories and were managing through an eclectic mixture of ideas drawn from past theories, ideas and concepts. Indeed, some are still doing that today. But there was an urgent need to reorient industry's focus away from the traditional view of management and towards a new perspective. The nature of business was changing rapidly, new technology had increased the speed at which business was carried out and competition had already become fierce in the global context.

Definitions

David Goss (1996) treats HRM as:

a diverse body of thought and practice, loosely unified by a concern to integrate the management of personnel more closely with the core management activity of organisations.

Armstrong (1999) defines HRM as

a strategic and coherent approach to the management of an organization's most valued assets – the people working there who individually and collectively contribute to the achievement of its goal.

According to Storey (1995):

Human resource management is a distinctive approach to employment management which seeks to obtain competitive advantage through the strategic deployment of a highly committed and skilled workforce, using an array of cultural, structural and personnel techniques.

While it is clear that these three definitions have similarities in that they all refer to the importance of people, the emphases are different. Goss emphasises the need to integrate people management more closely with the core management activity of the organisation. Armstrong, on the other hand, says that it is an approach to the management of people, whereas Storey says that it is an approach that seeks to obtain a competitive advantage. Armstrong says what the employees do (they contribute to the achievement of goals), while Storey says what HRM does with the people (it strategically deploys a highly committed and skilled workforce). Storey (1992) says that HRM can be regarded as a 'set of interrelated principles with an ideological and philosophical underpinning'. It is concerned with the employment, development and reward of people in organisations and the conduct of relationships between management and the workforce. It involves all line managers and team leaders but human resource (HR) specialists exist to make important contributions to the processes involved.

Krulis-Randa (1990, p136) says that in contrast to the 'control and compliance' models (see above), HRM is typified by the following characteristics:

- A focus on horizontal authority and reduced hierarchy; a blurring of the rigid distinction between management and non-management.
- Wherever possible, responsibility for people-management is devolved to line managers; the role of personnel professionals is to support and facilitate line management in this task, not to control it.
- Human resource planning is proactive and fused with corporate-level planning; human resource issues are treated strategically in an integrated manner.
- Employees are viewed as subjects with the potential for growth and development;

the purpose of human resource management is to identify this potential and develop it in line with the adaptive needs of the organisation.

- HRM suggests that management and non-management have a common interest in the success of the organisation. Its purpose is to ensure that all employees are aware of this and committed to common goals.

With regard to the second point, it is not difficult to criticise the notion that devolving responsibility for managing people to the line managers is 'something new'. For example, line managers have been responsible for people management since industry's earliest days; certainly long before personnel management was conceived as a discrete function. Personnel management as a profession that offers expert advice and assistance to line managers is an early twentieth-century phenomenon. What is now the CIPD began life in 1913 as the Industrial Welfare Society. In fact, HRM, along with legislative changes has added to rather than conferred people responsibilities upon line managers.

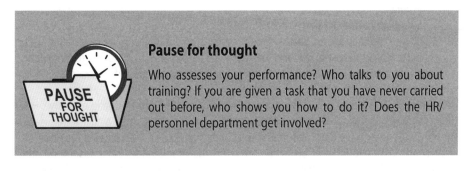

Pause for thought

Who assesses your performance? Who talks to you about training? If you are given a task that you have never carried out before, who shows you how to do it? Does the HR/personnel department get involved?

Two further HRM principles are:

- a recognition of the strength of the relationship between human performance and organisational success, producing the need to develop people to their ultimate potential as contributors to the realisation of the business plans
- the notion that there is a mutuality of interest between the organisation and its managers and employees in the survival and development of the organisation.

Doubts may surround the second point, which calls for the need for employees to be committed to, and involved in, the success of the organisation. Undoubtedly there is a 'feel good factor' that typifies employees' experiences of their organisation's successes and clearly, this has a visible, positive effect on them. However, one would suggest that this is far more frequently due to the enhanced feelings of job security that are produced when employees learn of the organisation's successes, rather than to feelings of personal involvement that might include, say, endorsement of the nature of the organisation's goals per se, feelings of personal achievement, or that for the enterprise to have achieved its objectives is a 'good thing'.

Hard and soft HRM

An analysis of HRM in terms of the style with which it is employed may be regarded in two ways: whether or not it may be regarded as hard or soft. According to Foot and Hook (1999):

- *Hard HRM*: The primacy of business needs means that human resources will be acquired, deployed and dispensed with as corporate plans demand. Little regard is

EXAMPLE

Example 3

When Rover Cars was saved from extinction by a financial angel, the workers came out on to the streets to express their delight and relief. However, in the period before their salvation was announced, all of the emphasis in the politicians' and trade union leaders' pronouncements was on securing continued employment for the Rover workers. Nobody mentioned commitment or involvement.

paid to the needs of those human resources and the emphasis is on quantitative aspects.

■ *Soft HRM*: In order to gain a competitive advantage through the workforce, regardless of whether they are full or part-time, temporary or contract staff, all potential must be nurtured and developed, and programmes which pay due notice to knowledge about the behavioural aspects of people at work are developed.

However, Legge (1995, pp66–67) points out that the two are not mutually exclusive. Hard HRM is sometimes defined in terms of the particular policies that stress a cost-minimisation strategy with an emphasis on leanness in production, the use of labour as a resource, and what Legge calls a 'utilitarian instrumentalism' in the employment relationship. At other times, hard HRM is defined in terms of the tightness of fit between organisational goals and strategic objectives on the one hand and HRM policies on the other. By contrast, soft HRM is sometimes viewed as 'developmental humanism' (Legge 1995) in which the individual is integrated into a work process that values trust, commitment and communication.

Allusions to these two features of how HRM may be interpreted and applied may be found in the theoretically diverse approaches to management that were expressed earlier in the twentieth century. For example, John Bramham's 1988 version of *manpower planning* adopts an approach that may be regarded as hard HRM because the demand and supply of human resources is calculated using statistics, employee numbers and costs (see also Chapter 4), while the ideas of the human relations school (Mayo 1933, Maslow 1954, McGregor 1960) may be regarded as soft HRM because they take the human factor into account.

From the employee's point of view, HRM has its disadvantages as well as advantages. Obviously flattened structures, which produce a greater number of employees reporting to each manager, restrict the scope for promotion since each worker has a longer line of competitors. To some extent, therefore, the message that is communicated to ambitious, career-minded employees has shifted from aspiration to inspiration, and the importance of their performance in their current positions.

Also, there is at least as much evidence of hard as there is of soft HRM. The culture that is found in some companies is far from benign. UK employees work the longest hours in Europe and workplace stress is more widespread than ever before. The nature of employment contracts has changed; one managing director was heard to say, 'just because you need to access someone's skills doesn't mean you have to offer a contract of employment in the conventional sense' (see Chapter 11).

On the positive side, HRM has actually achieved the integration of HR strategy and corporate strategy, and perversely, in terms of its unitary perspective, has managed to replace the *command–compliance* type of manager–worker relationship with a more colleague type of relationship, meaning that the employee works with, rather than for, the manager.

Strategy and operations

The hierarchical nature of the traditional organisational structure may be used to demonstrate the difference between strategy and operations. To the traditionalist, management is strictly a top-down function in which the strategic decisions about the future of the organisation – what needs to be done in order to survive and develop – are made by those at the top. This implies that an understanding of the purpose of a strategy need be known only to those at the top, and the workforce is there to carry out the operational tasks that lead to the success of the strategy.

Strategic human resource management

Strategic human resource management on the other hand integrates, rather than separates, strategy and operations. In this chapter we have seen that the nature of strategic decision-making has changed in order to remain competitive with a new and greater emphasis on:

- the importance of having a structure that is flexible enough to respond adequately in a variety of circumstances
- the price and quality of goods and services
- the organisation's speed of response to customer demands.

In fact today, all of the functions within the organisation have to be able to show how well they contribute to the success of the organisation; and this, of course, includes the functioning of the HR department.

The notion that the organisation's activities are contingent upon the strategy, however, is not new. If you read the earlier texts on 'management', you could be forgiven for concluding that the functional heads were sitting around strumming their fingers, waiting for Moses to come down the mountain bearing the tablets so that they could then get on with drafting their own plans. One of the CIPD national examination questions that was asked in the 1980s read, 'Is it possible to develop a manpower plan in the absence of a corporate plan?' Thankfully, things are different today. Strategic human resource management (SHRM) advocates say that HR planning should be integrated with corporate strategy which, simply as a concept, makes more sense and many organisations now do that. Indeed, academics and personnel practitioners had been campaigning for such integration for decades.

In terms of the management of personnel and industrial relations, SHRM blurs the distinction between strategy and operations. There is a 'wave of strategic human resource management literature focusing on the link or *vertical integration* [see Chapter 1] between human resource practices and organisation's business strategy in order to enhance performance' (Golding 2004). We saw in Chapter 1 that the organisation's strategy is described in its plans, and that all of the activities or operations that are carried out internally and externally by the employees of the organisation are designed to contribute to the success of the strategy. It is, therefore, essential for those at the operational level to understand the strategy. It has long been known that employees derive a great deal of satisfaction from understanding how their work contributes to the achievement of corporate objectives.

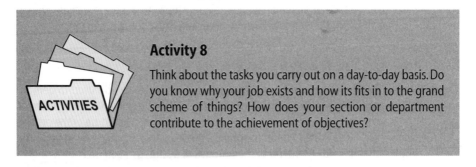

Activity 8

Think about the tasks you carry out on a day-to-day basis. Do you know why your job exists and how its fits in to the grand scheme of things? How does your section or department contribute to the achievement of objectives?

Achieving a competitive advantage

We saw above that Golding (2004) refers to vertical integration as a means of enhancing performance, but what actually happens? One view of SHRM that is taken by some academics and practitioners is generally referred to as the 'best-fit school of SHRM', which assesses the degree to which there actually is vertical integration between business strategy, policies and practices and activities. This implies 'the notion of a link between business strategy and the performance of every individual in the organisation' (Golding, 2004).

Vertical integration therefore ensures an explicit link or relationship between internal people processes and policies and the external market or business strategy, and thereby ensures that competences are created which have a potential to be a key source of competitive advantage.

(Wright *et al* 1994)

Restructuring the organisation

One of the most visible features of the introduction of HRM in Britain resulted from the depression of the 1980s. In order to compete effectively in a global market, organisations had to become more flexible and responsive and one of the approaches to achieving these qualities was the restructuring of the organisation. The objective was to create a 'leaner and fitter' organisation that could achieve similar or even greater productivity using a smaller number of employees. 'Increasingly, organisations have sought to cut costs by reducing the number of employees who are not contributing directly to production or service delivery' (Claydon 2004, p138). The restructuring techniques that are used to achieve the leaner and fitter organisation are as follows:

Downsizing, also referred to as *rightsizing*. This means reducing the number of employees at operational levels and reorganising the work system in order to attain greater productivity.

Delayering. This means reducing the number of staff at managerial levels, including middle managers and supervisors, in order to reduce costs. The result of this is a flattened structure in which a greater number of employees report to one manager. By doing this, the structure of a small production team might move from this:

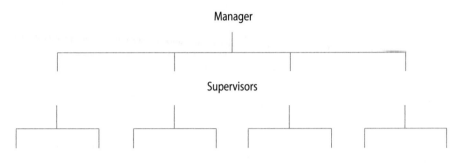

Manager

Supervisors

Employees

Figure 2.1 Tall or 'house of cards' structure with 12 employees reporting upwards

To this:

Manager

Employees

Figure 2.2 Flattened or 'garden rake' structure with nine employees reporting upwards. This structure has only nine employees since downsizing would also have reduced the number reporting upwards.

Clearly, if such a change is made, communication between the workers and their supervisor would flow more freely but the same types of tasks would have to be carried out, which implies that a training programme would be necessary in order to ensure that the employees possessed all of the necessary skills. In a larger and/or more complex situation a programme of multiskilling would have to be introduced. Also, the work methods would have to be changed to accommodate this.

Externalisation – often referred to as *outsourcing* or *contracting out* – refers to activities that the organisation needs to have carried out but are not at the core of the main functions. Outsourcing is a means of reducing employee numbers by having selected activities carried out by external specialist organisations, thus saving on employment costs and work space. The most frequently found examples of 'contracting out' are catering, cleaning, transport and security. Increasingly, some of the organisations' administrative tasks, such as computer maintenance and payroll, are now being contracted out.

Significant changes such as those discussed above have further implications in terms of employment. A variety of the techniques for creating a flexible workforce, for example, have to be applied when the market is volatile. The instability (ups and downs) of the market means that the organisation has to be flexible enough to vary the size and skills of its workforce according to demand. We discuss this in more detail in Part 2, particularly in Chapters 6, 7 and 9.

Summary

- There is a wide variety of views about human resource management. The concept has been variously interpreted and the style with which its principles and practices are applied varies among academics, practitioners, and indeed from one country to another.
- The history of management thought, which began in earnest in the early twentieth century, produced theories which contain allusions to what we now regard as HRM principles and practices (Taylor 1947, Burns and Stalker 1966), but they were not introduced into British organisations as a totally new management system until the 1980s.
- Research shows that HRM has been *more* or *less* adopted by organisations (Beardwell *et al* 2004, p26). British managers, however, have a record of reluctance to adopt new ideas in the comprehensive sense; they are very financially orientated and change, which is always a costly process, is usually carried out in a cautious and piecemeal fashion.
- Differences between the underlying philosophies and practices in personnel and industrial relations and those of HRM have been postulated by Storey (1992), who clearly outlines 27 points of difference showing how those who have adopted HRM have shifted towards a more open and flexible approach.
- Throughout the *classical* and mid-century studies of management the accepted managerial skills were described as *planning, organising, directing* and *controlling*; the four functions being linked together through co-ordination. By contrast, HRM engages the employee by changing the nature of the manager–worker relationship away from the *control* and *compliance* model towards a *colleague* relationship, meaning working *with*, rather than working *for*.
- There is a variety of definitions of HRM, each stressing at least one main feature that differentiates it from other approaches to managing the personnel and IR functions. These main features range from 'integrating the management of personnel with core management activities', 'moving towards a more flexible organisation in order to achieve a competitive advantage' to 'a strategic and coherent approach to the management of an organisation's most valued assets the people working there'.
- Distinctions have been drawn between hard and soft HRM, in which *hard* HRM is typified by an emphasis on numbers of people, while little regard is paid to their needs. *Soft* HRM, on the other hand, is typified by a flexible workforce whose talents are nurtured and developed further to enable them to make contributions to the achievement of a competitive advantage.
- Strategic human resource management integrates organisational strategy with operations whereas previously they were regarded as separate entities. In this way employees' understanding of the strategy means that they can see how the nature of their work contributes to the success of the strategy. This, in turn, influences employees' attitudes to their jobs and encourages commitment to and involvement with the all-round success of the organisation.

Self-test questions

1. If you were asked, 'What is the difference between personnel management and human resource management?' what would be your interpretation?
2. How might the introduction of HRM into an organisation affect how the non-personnel functions are managed?
3. Why has British industry been slow to take up HRM?
4. It has been said that the adoption of HRM is not the only way to achieve a competitive advantage. To what does this statement refer?

5. What is meant by the terms 'hard' and 'soft' HRM?
6. What are the four main managerial skills associated with earlier theories of management?
7. What is the main reason why an organisation would take up HRM?
8. Why do you think organisations that have adopted HRM aim to reduce the size of the workforce? Which employees did they not keep?
9. What events brought about the rise of HRM?
10. Why does the 'best-fit school of strategic human resource management' measure the degree to which there is vertical integration?

Assignment

Write a 1000 word report on why it is not possible to replace your current personnel system without influencing how the rest of the organisation is managed.

The role of the HR practitioner | CHAPTER 3

Learning objectives

After studying this chapter you should understand:

- the responsibilities of the various grades of HR practitioners

- the distinction between operational and strategic HR activities

- the range and scope of the activities of the HR worker

- the structure and uses of HR information systems and records

- the principles and the law relating to data protection

- the performance standards that are expected of the HR professional

- the code of conduct to which the HR professional is expected to adhere.

Introduction

This chapter examines and discusses the functions and activities in which the HR practitioner becomes involved and the variety of roles in which he/she may be seen. A section on data protection law and the steps that organisations might take in order to ensure compliance is also included. The chapter concludes with an explanation and discussion about the performance standards that are expected of the practitioner and the code of conduct to which he/she is expected to adhere.

In the HR field, practitioners operate at several levels, and the tasks and responsibilities vary according to the level and status of the practitioner. For example, those who occupy the senior positions – HR managers – are involved in departmental management, corporate strategy and HR policy formulation, while those in the middle ranks may be specialists with sectional responsibility. HR officers and administrators carry out tasks at operational level. The range and scope of HR activities is wide, and different individuals may aspire to become specialists in one of the main functions, while others may prefer to operate as generalists and work in several of the functions.

How HR practitioners operate in this respect determines, to some extent, the structure of the HR department. If practitioners operate as specialists the department is divided into sections according to the main functions and activities. Where practitioners are generalists, the structure is divided into *parishes*, in which each practitioner is responsible for all HR requirements in a particular department or area of the organisation. There are, however, wide variations in the ways that organisations structure their departments. What HR people actually do depends on the needs and HR policies of the particular organisation in which they work, and of course on their own individual capabilities. Table 3.1 is an analysis of the levels at which HR practitioners normally operate and their duties and responsibilities.

Table 3.1 Example of an analysis of HR responsibilities	
Level	**Responsibility and specialism**
Senior HR managers	Participation in corporate-level strategic decision-making
	Formulation of HR strategy and policies
	Advising other managers on the implementation of HR policies and procedures
Middle-level HR managers and specialists	Managing specialist sections including:
	HR planning
	Recruitment and selection
	Employee development
	Performance and reward
	Employee relations
	Health and safety management and welfare
HR officers and administrators	Day-to-day administration of the HR department
	Updating and maintaining secure and confidential records
	Ensuring efficient organisation of events including: interviews, induction and training, liaising with colleges and universities, attending career conventions.
	Maintaining and updating HR plans and producing data for such purposes
	Maintaining and updating HR systems and procedures

It has to be stressed that Table 3.1 is only an example, since organisations vary in how they deploy their HR staff. It does, however, give a broad indication of the kinds of responsibility and tasks that are carried at each level.

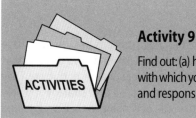

Activity 9

Find out: (a) how the HR department in your organisation (or one with which you are familiar) is structured, and (b) how the duties and responsibilities are allocated to the HR staff.

Pause for thought

Notice how the structure of Table 3.1 separates HR strategy from operational matters. It is customary to do this if the organisation is governed in accordance with traditional management principles. Modern management, however, integrates strategy and operations by encouraging the operational employees to develop an understanding of the organisation's overall objectives and to become involved in their achievement.

In this context, 'modern' management includes human resource management (HRM). Additionally, however, there are businesses which have adopted some of the principles of HRM and mixed them with traditional styles to form a kind of hybrid system of overall management. Your organisation, therefore, may or may not be one that integrates strategy and operations (see Chapter 2).

The range and scope of HR activities

From what has been said in the introduction to this chapter and from Table 3.1, it can be seen that the functions in which HR practitioners become involved are well known. There is, however, a wide range of activities that are related to these functions which require both personal experience and specialised knowledge and skills.

In fact, the actual management of human resources and employee relations is primarily the responsibility of the line managers. It is line managers who – with the advice and assistance of HR specialists – make the initial employment decision, manage and lead people, allocate their work, assess their performance, guide and counsel them in their jobs, make decisions about their training and development, and handle employee relations problems such as matters of grievance and discipline.

Key concept 3: line manager

A line manager is a senior employee who is responsible for ensuring that all of the tasks necessary for the achievement of the objectives of an operational department or section are carried out on time and to the required standard.

Working with line managers

Line managers, however, have usually been appointed to their positions because they have shown proficiency along some non-HR professional or technical line and have qualities that indicate their suitability for adopting particular functional or sectional responsibility. They may be regarded as the media through which the top managers have their strategy and policies implemented operationally. In many cases, there is little or nothing in their background or training to indicate that they have the appropriate *knowledge* and *expertise* to handle HR matters unaided. Such knowledge and expertise resides within the HR department, and it is the HR practitioner's job to work with line managers, team leaders and staff specialists assisting, advising and generally guiding them through the HR aspects of their jobs.

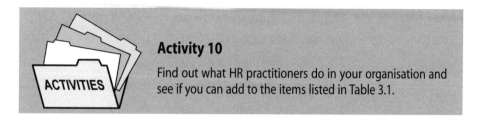

Activity 10

Find out what HR practitioners do in your organisation and see if you can add to the items listed in Table 3.1.

The full range of HR activities, therefore, is not confined to the main functions that are referred to above; there is a range of related activities which are listed in Table 3.1.

According to Armstrong (1999) the activities carried out by HR practitioners 'vary widely according to the needs of the organisation, the job they carry out and their own capabilities. In general, however, they provide services, guidance and advice.'

Services

These are specialist services provided for all levels of staff, and these may include any or all of the items mentioned in Table 3.2 (overleaf). For example, at an individual level, a line manager may need to recruit a new member of his or her staff, in which case the service provided is to activate the recruitment process on behalf of the manager and then to advise and assist him or her with the processes that lead to a new appointment. In the organisation-wide context, a service such as the management of health, safety and welfare is essential; for example, the service might be to develop and maintain accident records or to advise and assist with the implementation of health and safety policy. A further service might be to provide access to specialised counselling where employees are stressed or where they have a problem that is not related to work.

Guidance

Demands for guidance from HR vary from one organisation to another depending on business needs and the status of the HR function in the general scheme of things; that is to say, the degree of importance that is attributed to the HR function by the top managers. HR managers and practitioners offer guidance at all levels. Table 3.1 shows the ideal situation, in which senior HR managers are involved at the top level. They formulate HR strategy and policies, have them integrated into the overall corporate strategy and offer guidance to other senior managers on the implementation of policy.

Top-level managers rely on the expertise of HR managers for guidance on such matters as the availability of particular knowledge and skills in the internal and external labour markets (see Chapter 5), since the employment of people with appropriate knowledge and skills is essential for the achievement of objectives. The HR manager's contribution is also based on his or her knowledge of current and forthcoming employment legislation, since policy has to comply with legal requirements.

Line managers turn to HR practitioners when they need guidance on such matters as policies and procedures in relation to remuneration, absenteeism, grievance and discipline and areas of

Table 3.2 List of HR activities

Services	Activating main HR systems as and when required
	Providing access to employee counselling services
	Providing contracts of employment
	Providing welfare services
	Negotiating terms and conditions of employment
	Systems of payment and other forms of reward
	Management of health and safety at work
Guidance and advice	Implementation of policies and procedures at all levels
	Advising on redundancy and other forms of separation from the organisation
	Implementation of systems of performance management
	Forecasting future HR requirements
Administrative	Recruitment and selection procedures
	Induction processes
	Training events
	Employee development activities
	Meetings relating to matters of grievance, discipline, dismissal, etc.
	Establishing and maintaining HR records
Monitoring	Fairness, equal opportunities and diversity at work
	Working time
	Absence management and control
	Family-friendly policies
	Health and safety at work
	Legal compliance and ethical standards

employment policy such as managing diversity, equal opportunities, fairness and family friendliness. In fact guidance may be provided on many such matters at all levels. When giving guidance, the HR practitioner may need to draw upon several of his or her personal skills. since providing guidance in such areas 'means taking on the roles of business partner, strategist, innovator, interventionist, internal consultant and monitor' (Armstrong 1999).

Advice

HR practitioners may offer advice to line managers on a wide range of issues that are relevant to their expertise: for example, when line managers need to forecast their future HR requirements, interviewing and employment decision-making, systematic skills auditing, appraising performance, handling grievances and disciplinary procedures, and other legal aspects of employment. Individual employees may also need advice on legal matters, solving workplace problems such as bullying and sexual harassment, and personal problems and issues such as coping with stress, career prospects and personal development planning.

Mediation

Conflict at an individual level may occur between a manager and an employee or between two employees. In such situations, an HR practitioner may be asked to intervene and try to resolve the conflict. Interventions of this nature should be made by those who:

- have had wide and relevant experience of organisational life
- have developed good listening skills
- can hear both sides of a story without prejudice
- can remain objective enough not to become involved in the altercation
- are skilled enough in the general sense to steer the meeting towards a successful resolution.

The structure and uses of HR information systems

Now that corporate and HR strategists work together, it is clear that managers, team leaders and specialists, as well as the HR people need access to particular information.

Confidentiality

While managers, team leaders and specialists need access to HR information, control should be exercised over the type of information that is released. Confidentiality is an extremely important issue and is discussed later in this chapter.

The need for information has been steadily increasing over the past 20 years. With the advent of the Internet, the world's advanced economies have now entered the information age and the basis upon which management decisions are made has shifted from the 'educated guess' and the 'seat of the pants' method, to become more systematic, factual and information-based. Legislation also demands information, and the amount of research carried out by educational and industrial organisations grows larger by the day. The amount of available information, therefore, has grown considerably.

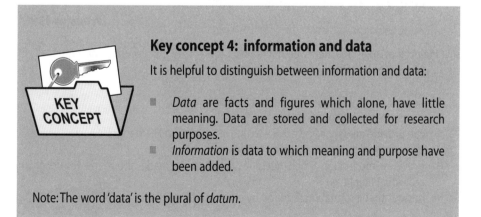

Key concept 4: information and data

It is helpful to distinguish between information and data:

- *Data* are facts and figures which alone, have little meaning. Data are stored and collected for research purposes.
- *Information* is data to which meaning and purpose have been added.

Note: The word 'data' is the plural of *datum*.

Peter Drucker, the US writer on management, said that 'information is data endowed with meaning and purpose' (Drucker 1988). Armstrong (1999) says that knowledge is the key. In HR terms, he defines knowledge as the application and productive use of information:

> **It provides personnel specialists with the ability not only to administrate their functions effectively but also to contribute to strategic decision taking on matters affecting people. It enables the responsibility for personnel to be increasingly devolved to line managers who, with the knowledge acquired through a computerized human resource information system, can be powered to make decisions related to their team management responsibilities.**
>
> **(Armstrong 1999)**

Manual versus computerised systems

In a medium-sized or large organisation the quantity of information that is stored and used is immense. Even most small enterprises, such as the corner shop, the local tennis club and the modern cottage industries, now use electronically stored information. There are still a few small set-ups, however, that rely on information that is kept and handled manually and keep their records in filing cabinets.

In this section of the chapter, the main concern is with computerised information systems, although it is worth bearing in mind that all organisations, regardless of the size and informational needs, still have manual systems for the storage of particular documents, such as employees' original application forms, contracts of employment and any other documentation – letters, references, etc – that relate to employment. Such records should be systematised for security purposes and ease of access to authorised users.

Computerised HR information systems

Richard Wheeler says that:

> **a computerised human resource information system functions as a repository of critical information and an enabler of change. .... The key to obtaining knowledge and understanding of human resources is being able to access and manipulate information.**
>
> **(Wheeler 1995)**

This means that an established, well-maintained, up-to-date and accurate computerised HR information system (CHRIS) has many advantages. It:

- provides a reliable basis for strategic decision-making
- supports services to line managers
- can provide guidance and advice to line managers on HR matters
- gives immediate access to policy statements
- provides information when decisions need to be made about the future of an individual employee
- ensures that information required by law is readily available.

At the strategic and policy-making level, managers turn to the HR department when they need particular information, for example when HR practitioners and the organisation's managers meet to make decisions about the organisation's future which inevitably affect employees at all levels.

Pause for thought: are you computer literate?

The HR records in virtually all organisations are computerised and to be effective as an HR practitioner, you need to be computer literate, at least to the stage at which you can use HR packages. Additionally, it is sensible to learn how to carry out a variety of other tasks such as report writing, preparing a presentation and generally using the creative and mathematical software that is built into modern computers.

Most universities and colleges provide free tuition in IT to their students. Enrolment details may be found in the library or information centre.

Using and maintaining HR records

One of the most important administrative duties of the HR practitioner is keeping records. 'HR records and statistics provide the information that is an essential part of a system for effective personnel management' (Tyson and York 1996). From the records, the HR department can provide strategic planners and other managers with information that will enable them to make good-quality decisions about people. In fact it is continuously necessary as a basis for decisions affecting major HR functions at an organisational level, such as human resource planning, recruitment and selection, performance management, succession planning and health and safety.

HR records should be seen as a useful and lively tool of management, and maintaining them can be a full-time job. Well-maintained records are up to date, accurate and secure, yet easily accessed. If they are neglected, especially in terms of keeping them up to date, they do not become merely useless, they can become dangerous. Clearly, poor decision-making will result from the use of out-of-date records as a source of information for matters of importance.

What the records contain

Information about the human resource is vital to the successful management of the whole organisation. The HR department keeps and maintains records that include the personal details of all employees and the events and activities in which they become involved during their period of employment. For example, a personal history is kept on every individual employee from when he/she first joined the organisation. The details that are held include:

- the employee's original application form
- copy of the contractual arrangements
- job title on joining (updated with any changes)
- date on which employment commenced

- background and previous employment history
- department in which the employee works
- employee category (staff or hourly paid, etc)
- state of health on joining
- National Insurance number
- date of birth
- sex
- ethnic origin
- marital status
- salary/wage details and other rewards
- hours of work
- record of attendance and absences
- personal contact details
- academic achievements
- training and further education undertaken before and since joining
- performance assessments
- suitability for transfer and promotion
- career interviews with managers and HR staff
- pension contributions
- trade union membership.

Activity 11

If you work in HR, have a look at the records and see the types of information that are held. Examine how they are recorded and think about how you might retrieve information from them for an HR purpose.

Uses of individual information

From what is said above, it can be seen that when individual information is held on all employees, collectively, it represents an extremely useful data bank for management and planning purposes. But the individual records themselves are also valuable. If, for example, a case arises that concerns an individual's current employment or future position, his or her personal history will provide background information that will assist in managerial decision-making. Similarly, when people are being considered for further training and development, promotion or special assignment work, their personal records provide an ideal basis upon which good-quality decisions can be made, which would be to the benefit of the individual and the organisation.

Statistical information

Organisational statistics serve two very important functions:

- They provide essential information about main areas affecting the general state of the organisation at a particular time.

- They also indicate trends that need to be made apparent so that timely measures may be taken to improve conditions of work and performance.

HR-related statistics can be drawn from accumulated individual records which have been collated, such as those for attendance management, accident rates and wages and salaries. Statistical information may also be drawn from accumulated records relating to staff turnover, workforce stability, sickness absence, skills inventories, deployment, job analyses, recruitment trends and employment costs. Externally gathered data may also be added to provide information on the availability of labour, including special or rare skills, local, regional, national and international employment trends, and average earnings. Information of this type and quantity is indispensable to senior managers and HR strategists.

Legal aspects of record keeping

On the one hand, many managers are reluctant to allow employees access to the information about them that is on record, while on the other, most employees feel that they are entitled to have access, even if only to check that the information is correct. The Data Protection Act 1998 (DPA98) provides a legal entitlement for employees to access their own personal records and, indeed, any information about them.

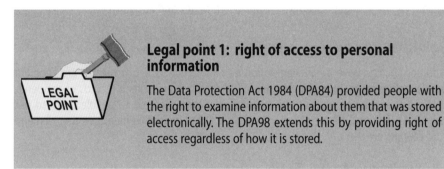

LEGAL POINT

Legal point 1: right of access to personal information

The Data Protection Act 1984 (DPA84) provided people with the right to examine information about them that was stored electronically. The DPA98 extends this by providing right of access regardless of how it is stored.

Data protection is a critical aspect of record-keeping, and this is discussed later in this chapter.

Confidentiality

Confidentiality is a two-way issue. Most people would object to their personal information being disclosed to others unless it was clear that it was needed for legitimate purposes. However, there can be little harm in communicating collective and anonymous data in statistical form to internal and external third parties who, for example, are generally looking for information such as absence or accident rates, which is normally acceptable. The really sensitive area is in passing on information from which people can be identified.

As a broad rule, therefore, the release of blocks of statistical data is normally acceptable, while the release of personal information about individual employees is not; at least not without the express permission of the employee concerned.

Authorised access to information

With properly run computerised systems it is difficult for an unauthorised person to access information to which he/she is not entitled, although illegally 'hacking in' to systems – a

Legal point 2: releasing information

The release of personal information without the express permission of the employee concerned is actionable in law. HR records are confidential and should be kept under very tight control. A 'safety first' maxim in this respect is: if in doubt, hold back.

process whereby unauthorised users gain access – obviously is always possible. There is a variety of ways in which systems may be made secure from 'intruders'. The most frequently used of these is the 'password' system, in which authorised employees are given a personal password, which is unknown to others and which will provide them with access to the information to which they are entitled.

Legislation provides for the protection of individuals, and usually relates to information rather than the keeping of records, but if the data is kept in secure systems, maintained and updated regularly, the information that results is more likely to be lawful, accurate, useful and reliable. It can be accessed speedily, and presented clearly and attractively.

Legislative requirements

In addition to the above details, legislation demands that particular records are kept. For example, under health and safety law, there is a requirement to keep records of accidents, injuries sustained by employees, the training they have received to enable them to use equipment safely, and a host of other measures. Other legislative measures that demand record keeping are the:

- Race Relations Act 1976 (RRA76)
- Sex Discrimination Act 1975 (SDA75)
- Employment Rights Act 1996 (ERA96)
- Working Time Regulations 1998 (WTR98)
- National Minimum Wage Act 1998 (NMWA98)
- Health and Safety at Work Act 1974 (HASAWA)
- Data Protection Act 1998 (DPA98)
- Equal Pay Act 1970 (as amended).

Bearing in mind the provisions of the legislation listed above, organisations feel the need to protect themselves and the records include accounts of relevant incidents and events that might lead to complaints of:

- race or sex discrimination (see Chapter 14)
- unfair dismissal (see Chapter 11)
- imposing unreasonable working hours on employees (see Chapter 11)
- offering wages and salaries which are below the legal minimum limit (see Chapter 12)
- breaching health and safety regulations
- refusing to allow justifiable access to individual records
- failing to provide equality with employment contracts.

HR records contain information that may be used in evidence if an employee's claim leads to an employment tribunal or other legal proceedings. Employers try to avoid such circumstances, not only because of the cost but also because the organisation's reputation as an employer may be at stake.

Data protection

This part of the chapter is largely about the law on data protection. Data protection is a legal issue that has been under close scrutiny, not only in employing organisations, but in many areas of our lives, for at least two decades and certainly since the period before 1984, when the DPA84 came into effect.

The DPA98 – which has its origins in the European Union Data Protection Directive – came into effect in March 2000, replacing the DPA84. The DPA98 has many provisions in common with the DPA84, but there are also significant differences. Space prevents us from going into the greater detail of the DPA98, but there are points of which the personnel practitioner should be aware, especially since this is an area of the law which is having an important impact on how organisations are managed, although data protection is yet to become an issue at the management/trade union negotiating table.

Those who are familiar with the vocabulary of the DPA84 will need to understand two minor points on which the new Act differs from the old one.

1. The DPA98 changed the Data Protection Registrar's title to Data Protection Commissioner.
2. The *'registration'* system under the DPA84 is replaced under the DPA98 by the *'notification'* system.

Individual rights

In the DPA98, the person about whom the information is held is referred to as the *data subject*. This Act defines data and refers to a *relevant filing system*.

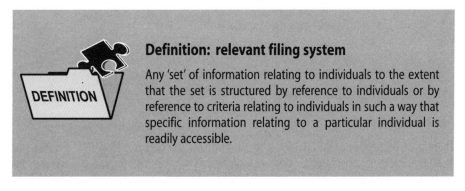

Definition: relevant filing system

Any 'set' of information relating to individuals to the extent that the set is structured by reference to individuals or by reference to criteria relating to individuals in such a way that specific information relating to a particular individual is readily accessible.

Any information falling into the category of a relevant filing system constitutes data. The new Act also distinguishes between *personal data* and *sensitive data*.

Personal data

Any individual employee is entitled to:

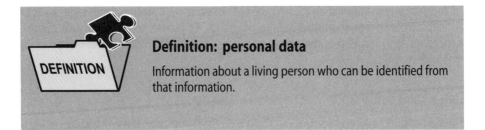

Definition: personal data

Information about a living person who can be identified from that information.

- receive a copy of any data – including manually stored data – processed by reference to them
- know what data is being processed
- know why the data is being processed
- know who might receive the data
- be told the source of the data – except in limited circumstances
- where data is processed automatically, and is likely to form the sole basis for any decision significantly affecting the individual, the right to know the logic involved in that decision-making and not to have significant decisions based on results of automatic processing
- prevent processing likely to cause damage and distress.

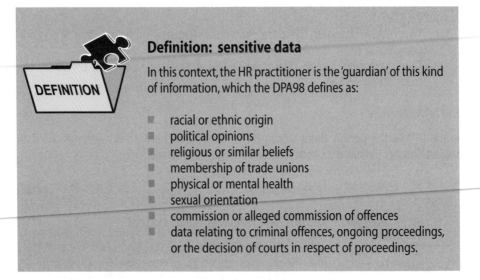

Definition: sensitive data

In this context, the HR practitioner is the 'guardian' of this kind of information, which the DPA98 defines as:

- racial or ethnic origin
- political opinions
- religious or similar beliefs
- membership of trade unions
- physical or mental health
- sexual orientation
- commission or alleged commission of offences
- data relating to criminal offences, ongoing proceedings, or the decision of courts in respect of proceedings.

Sensitive data

There are other types of data which it is inadvisable (although not illegal) to process. For example, results of occupational or psychological tests may be misinterpreted if accessed by someone who is not an expert in testing and does not understand how and why particular inferences are drawn from test results. Most employers provide the test subjects with hard copies of their results.

Incidentally, a word of caution to all aspiring HR practitioners who may believe that the records they hold in the department are the only records that refer to employees: they are not. Many line managers keep private notes about their staff, some of which are very

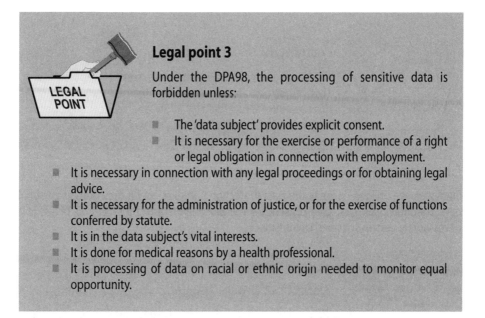

Legal point 3

Under the DPA98, the processing of sensitive data is forbidden unless:

- The 'data subject' provides explicit consent.
- It is necessary for the exercise or performance of a right or legal obligation in connection with employment.
- It is necessary in connection with any legal proceedings or for obtaining legal advice.
- It is necessary for the administration of justice, or for the exercise of functions conferred by statute.
- It is in the data subject's vital interests.
- It is done for medical reasons by a health professional.
- It is processing of data on racial or ethnic origin needed to monitor equal opportunity.

personal. One manager, for example, was found to have information – which would be classified as 'sensitive data' – about his staff stored in his new electronic diary which he was showing off to a colleague!

Case study 2: Know what you are doing

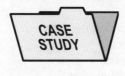

Along with two of his colleagues, Ahmed, an employee in a Birmingham company, was being considered for an important promotion. As part of the selection process, they were all subject to a psychological test, which was conducted by properly trained and qualified people. The test results were stored electronically.

The general manager of the company, a very authoritarian person who had no training or background in psychological testing, accessed the results, after which he told Ahmed that rather than being promoted, he should be dismissed. Obviously this caused Ahmed great concern, and he feared for his future with the company. Despite this, Ahmed appeared before the selection panel and got the job. On hearing this, the general manager took the matter to the managing director, who had chaired the selection panel, and demanded an explanation for 'this very unwise promotion'.

On hearing what the general manager had to say, the managing director held a meeting with the HR manager, the general manager and the people who had conducted the tests. It became clear that the general manager had completely misinterpreted the test results and that Ahmed's appointment was fully justified.

Task: You have been asked to ensure that this kind of misunderstanding does not occur again. Write a brief paper outlining the action that you would take.

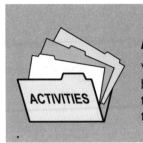

Activity 12

You work as an HR administrator and have been approached by a supervisor in the marketing department's administrative section. He has asked for information concerning one of the employees. How would you deal with his request?

Employers' obligations

Employers are obliged to notify the Data Protection Commissioner if they process personal data. The individual must give consent for the personal data to be *processed*, unless it is necessary for certain specified circumstances.

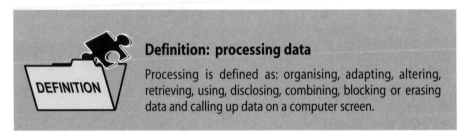

Definition: processing data

Processing is defined as: organising, adapting, altering, retrieving, using, disclosing, combining, blocking or erasing data and calling up data on a computer screen.

There is a list of eight criminal offences which are:

- processing without notification
- failure to notify the commissioner of changes to notification register entry
- failure to comply with an enforcement or information notice
- making a false statement in response to an information notice
- obstructing or failing to assist with the execution of a search warrant
- obtaining or disclosing personal data without permission from the data controller
- selling or offering to sell unlawfully obtained data
- making a person supply a copy of their personal data, unless required or authorised by law or in the public interest.

Data protection policy

Managers are advised to formulate and actively implement clear policies and procedures that will ensure that all employees understand the organisation's approach to compliance with the data protection laws. Employers may be confident that they are conforming to the data protection laws if they follow the eight data protection principles, which state that data should be:

- processed fairly and lawfully and shall not be processed unless certain conditions are met
- obtained only for specified and lawful purposes
- adequate, relevant and not excessive in relation to the purposes for which it is processed
- accurate and up to date
- kept for no longer than is necessary
- processed in accordance with the rights granted under the DPA98

- kept securely
- not transferred to a country without adequate data protection.

This might necessitate programmes of training for particular employees, such as personnel practitioners, middle managers and team leaders. Also, there should be a system for monitoring the effectiveness of the procedures, which will be designed to ensure that the Data Protection Principles are followed.

What steps might organisations take?

The CIPD has developed an extensive *Factsheet* which includes a list of statutes that are concerned with the privacy of the individual, and access to and disclosure of information in the public interest that employers need to consider. All those collecting data have to ask themselves why it is being collected, how it is going to be used and who will have access to it. The statutes include:

- the Public Interest Disclosure Act 1998
- the Human Rights Act 1998
- the Telecommunications (Lawful Business Practice) Regulations 2000.

The *Factsheet* also contains an action plan that suggests 10 steps organisations might take to ensure compliance:

- Organisations should consider the appointment of a person to be in charge of all aspects of information, including, when it comes into effect, the Freedom of Information Act.
- Audit information system – find out who holds what data, and why.
- Consider why information is collected and how it is used. Issue guidelines for managers about how to gather, store and retrieve data.
- Ensure that all information collected now complies with the Data Protection Act 1998.
- Check the security of all information stored.
- Check the transfer of data outside the European Economic Area.
- Check the organisation's use of automated decision-making.
- Review policy and practice in respect of references.
- Review or introduce a policy for the private use of telephones, e-mail and post.
- Review or introduce a procedure for reporting under the Public Interest Disclosure Act.

Professional competence

This refers to the standards of work that are expected of an HR practitioner. Competence as a concept is defined and discussed in detail in Chapter 8. Levels of competence may refer to what you are expected to be able to do because of the level or HR position that you occupy, but they may also mean the level at which you have achieved excellence in your job. Your own personal professional standards, however, mean more than task-related competence.

Professional standards

The standards to which you are expected to adhere as a qualified and chartered HR practitioner are set out in the Chartered Institute of Personnel and Development (CIPD) Code of Professional Conduct. This refers to competence by stating that its members:

are expected to exercise relevant competence in accordance with the Institute's professional standards and qualifications. CIPD members provide specialist professional knowledge, advice, support and management competence in the management and development of people.

Additionally, however, Section 4 of the Code goes on to state that in all circumstances they (the members) must:

1. Endeavour to enhance the standing and good name of the profession; adherence to this code of professional conduct is an essential aspect of this.
2. Seek continuously to improve their performance and update and refresh their skills and knowledge.
3. Within their own or any client organisation and in whatever capacity they are working, seek to achieve the fullest possible development of people for present and future organisational needs and encourage self development by individuals.
4. Within their own or any client organisation and in whatever capacity they are working, seek to adopt in the most appropriate way, the most appropriate people management processes and structures to enable the organisation to best achieve its present and future objectives.
5. Promote and themselves maintain fair and reasonable standards in the treatment of people who are operating within the scope of their influence.
6. Promote and themselves seek to exercise employment practices that remove unfair discrimination including but not limited to gender, age, race, religion, disability and background.
7. Respect legitimate needs and requirements for confidentiality.
8. Use due diligence and exercise high standards of timeliness, appropriateness and accuracy in the information and advice they provide to employers and employees.
9. Seek to recognise the limitations of their own knowledge and ability and must not undertake activity for which they are not yet appropriately prepared or, where applicable, qualified.
10. In the public interest and in the pursuit of its objects, the Chartered Institute of Personnel and Development is committed to the highest possible standards of professional conduct and competency. To this end members:
    (i) are required to exercise integrity, honesty, diligence and appropriate behaviour in all their business, professional and related personnel activities
    (ii) must act within the law and must not encourage, assist or act in collusion with employers, employees or others who may be engaged in unlawful conduct.

Section 4 of the Code, therefore, focuses upon honesty, integrity and competence. Additionally, the fact that self-development appears in the Code demonstrates its importance. This is a recognition of two important factors: first, change and the need to keep abreast of the implications of change, a significant proportion of which is triggered by employment legislation; and second, the need for the pursuit of excellence in one's own performance. The CIPD itself encourages its members to adopt *continuing professional development* (CPD) and to urge organisations to encourage their employees to engage in *personal development planning*. These are discussed in greater detail in Chapter 10.

Activity 13

Do you keep a log of your activities and what you have learned from them? Do you have a plan outlining your future development? Why not start now? How do you go about doing it? See Chapter 10.

Self-test questions

1. What is the difference between an HR specialist and an HR generalist?
2. Who is responsible for managing, leading and developing people?
3. How would you distinguish between data and information?
4. What are the indicators of well-maintained HR records?
5. How do the uses of individual and statistical information differ?
6. Under what circumstances would you release individual information?
7. What kind of information does health and safety legislation require to be kept?
8. What is the difference between personal and sensitive data?
9. What steps might the organisation take to ensure compliance with the Data Protection Principles?
10. In the term 'professional competence' what two meanings might the word 'competence' imply?

Human resource planning

Introduction

More than ever before, human resource planning plays an essential and integral role in the achievement of the overall business strategy. The purposes of this chapter are to explain and discuss the techniques that are applied to human resource planning (HRP) and to demonstrate how the HR plan relates to the organisation's overall business plan. First, there is a brief history of its background, including definitions of traditional and modern systems. Second, we detail the ideas and theoretical concepts that form the basis upon which traditional and modern HRP activities are founded. Third, we examine and discuss the activities in which you become involved when you are operating as an HR planner. Fourth, there is guidance on how the activities themselves may be carried out.

The chapter contains case studies and activities for you to work through, and to aid your understanding there are examples based on organisational situations, some of which are hypothetical while others have been taken from real life.

A brief history

From the very early days of industrial activity, organisations have tried to ensure that they would have people coming up to succeed longer-serving skilled employees. Apprenticeship, for example, in which young people learn the skills that will be needed in the future, dates back to the 'cottage industries' that preceded the Industrial Revolution. It made sense for master craftworkers to take on apprentices and train them in their crafts.

It is important to bear in mind that these arrangements for continuity of the crafts were made in the days when change was slow; the craftworkers could rely on their skills remaining useful long into the foreseeable future, and they could safely pass their industrial genes down to the rising generation. With the Industrial Revolution came the development of factories and larger-scale industries which created a demand for a more organisation-wide approach to planning the future workforce.

The growth of planning for the future workforce

By the twentieth century, apprenticeship was widespread across a broad range of skills and crafts. Modern apprenticeships, which fall within the government VET initiative (see Chapter 9) are 'mainly for 16 and 17 year old school leavers and training includes at least an NVQ at level 3, showing that the apprentice can do the job to the standard that industry and commerce require' (Holden 2004). As you will see in Chapter 9, all of today's HR development systems are more sophisticated than they were in the very early days.

Manpower planning

The *manpower planning* process first appeared in the 1960s. This was the first attempt to develop a systematic method of ensuring that the organisation would have a continuous supply of the people it needed now, and would need in the future, in order to carry out the tasks that led to the achievement of objectives.

Definition: manpower planning

This was defined by Department of Employment in 1974 as 'a strategy for the acquisition, utilisation, improvement and retention of an enterprise's human resources'.

When manpower planning was first proposed, manufacturing represented 60 per cent of jobs and the planners relied on the availability of traditional skills. The process was analytic, and it was comprehensive in the sense that it set out to provide the staffing needs of the whole organisation. This approach was fine for the purpose it served, since the demand was for traditional knowledge, skills and competence across the total spectrum of organisational activities. By today's standards, change was still relatively slow, large-scale change was rare, and innovation was limited to little more than the modification of current methods and techniques.

Few organisations, however, developed and maintained manpower plans. In the absence of computers the related tasks were found to be cumbersome and time-consuming, and many organisations thought of it as an unwarranted cost. It was a paper exercise in which the need to maintain and keep the plan up to date included a set of tasks that could be likened to painting the Forth Bridge.

Manpower planning and HRP

The term *human resource planning* came into being in the 1980s, when human resource management (HRM) first appeared. Around the same time, political correctness was introduced and it was inevitable anyway that an alternative term to *manpower* planning would have be found. Modern human resource planning is different from manpower planning. Attempts to define them show there are areas that are common to both, but they differ markedly in the strategic approach and purposes. Definitions of processes, however, say more than simply what a process is; they also indicate the thinking that underlies the approach to its implementation.

For example, the original thinking behind defining manpower planning was that it was a strategy that '*secured the enterprise's human resources*', which amounted to acquiring the right number of appropriately skilled people when they were needed. The central idea was to achieve a match between manpower demand and manpower supply. *Demand* means the organisation's current and future human resource requirements, while *supply* refers to the degree to which the demand may be met, from the current workforce and externally. Cost and statistical analysis was central to the whole process.

Definitions

Julie Beardwell and her colleagues define modern HRP as 'the process for identifying an organisation's current and future human resource requirements, developing and implementing plans to meet these requirements and monitoring their overall effectiveness' (Beardwell *et al* 2004). According to Bulla and Scott (1994), it is the process for ensuring that the human resource requirements of an organization are identified and plans are made for satisfying those requirements.

Key concept 5: human resource planning

Human resource planning (HRP) is a strategic management function, the aim of which is to ensure that the organisation will have the human resources it needs currently and in the future in order to realise its strategy and achieve its business objectives.

The nature of planning

Before giving in-depth consideration to such a specialised area of planning as HRP, it is essential for you to develop a clear understanding of what we mean by planning. All organisational processes are planned to serve the overall corporate strategy.

An imprecise process

Organisational planning is not a precise activity. Indeed the question has been asked, 'If it is an imprecise process, then why do it?' Truly, the predictions and demands that form essential components of a plan are seldom precise, but having some information with which to work is better than having no information. The rigorous application of related skills can produce a plan that is manageable, and in terms of precision, one can actually come close. In fact, all of business planning is like that; after all, few strategists would try to predict the precise nature of the business environment of the medium or long-term future.

This is not to say that the future is a complete mystery to the strategist, since the organisation itself, by developing and marketing new products and new and creative ways of serving its customers, does have an influence on what happens in the future. There are, however, many external factors that are beyond the organisation's control; competitors' activities and the vagaries of the economy are two examples of this.

Planning periods

Plans are normally divided into short, medium and long terms. The period over which business plans extend varies from one organisation to another, depending on the type of organisation, the type and state of market it serves (see Example 4), the rate of internal change and its financial situation. Since we cannot predict all of the future, long-term plans have to be fairly vague in their content and direction. Medium-term plans, on the other hand, are slightly easier to specify; clearly, we can forecast more accurately what will happen in the forthcoming, say, two to five years. Short-term plans, which might range from the present day to two years hence, need to be precise and crystal clear; they are plans that demand more or less immediate action.

EXAMPLE

Example 4: Factors influencing planning timescales

Sugar is a *stable product*, a product for which the demand is steady and long term. There is no *product innovation* and there are few companies in the industry at primary level. With such a dependable market, the companies can draw up marketing plans that stretch far into the future and invest in capital equipment, confident that since there will not be a significant reduction in demand, they will get a return on their investment.

Software, on the other hand, is a an *unstable product*, the demand for which changes rapidly and continuously. Product innovation is the main route to survival, and there are many companies in the industry. Few such companies have a long-term plan. To them, the medium term might be 18 months and the short term is in real time, depending on the rate at which the specifications of their products change. Mobile telephones and computer products fall into this category.

The planning process

All types of planning have a set of features in common. For example, according to Maund (2001) there are five stages in the planning process:

1. Identification of the goal.
2. Clarification of the present position.
3. Consideration of the range of strategies that could be used to achieve the set goal.
4. Choice of the most appropriate strategy.
5. The breaking down of the chosen strategy into smaller, more manageable steps.

Example 5: A simple analogy: planning

All five of these stages are interrelated, and in the simplest of terms, the process is no different from that of planning a journey. Suppose for example you wanted to drive from London to Exeter. Your goal (Stage 1) is to get to Exeter. You know that London is your starting position (Stage 2). Then you consider the variety of routes that would enable you to achieve your goal and arrive in Exeter (Stage 3). After that, you select the route that you think is best suited to your purpose (Stage 4). Clearly, there will be grounds upon which you selected the route; for example, the time you need to be there will be an important factor in making this decision. Finally, if you break the route down into its natural geographic stages, allowing yourself times and places for rests, you will be able to manage the trip more easily (Stage 5).

Certainly, business planning is more complex than planning the journey as described in Example 5, but the simplicity of the analogy is intended to clarify the nature and sequence of the stages in the process.

Activity 14

Think of three companies that you think would plan for the very long term and three that would have to be short term. Write down a justification for your selection.

Case study 3: The importance of planning

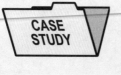

Two weeks ago, Alan submitted an assignment report and was glad to have seen the end of it; he had found it particularly arduous. Now, he has been notified of the grade and it is much lower than he had anticipated. Reflecting upon how he went about this task, Alan concluded that his poor performance was due to his lack of planning.

1. He failed to clarify his true goal.
2. In terms of other commitments, he had not assessed his position in terms of time management before he had started.
3. He had launched himself in at the deep end without considering alternative methods of approach to the task.
4. He could not, therefore, select an appropriate method.
5. He carried out the work randomly, as and when he felt like it.

Task: Draw up a plan for carrying out your next assignment.

Reflection: What have you learned from Alan's experience? How will you approach your assignments in the future?

Plans are a very important part of business and have a number of uses:

- They give an opportunity for individuals to give serious thought to what they want.
- They allow people a better opportunity to achieve what they want.
- They give managers an opportunity to calculate the resource available to achieve the plan: for example, financial, equipment supplied and human resources (Maund, 2001).

Traditional and modern HRP

At this stage it is necessary to draw a distinction between what many writers refer to as *traditional* and *contemporary* (or *modern*) HRP. In Chapter 2 we drew a distinction between hard and soft HRM. The approach that is taken here is that traditional HRP largely follows the 'hard' approach, while contemporary HRP equates with the 'soft' approach. Most writers would agree that the elements of manpower planning are indicative of hard HRP.

It is important to note that while modern HRP has found a firm foothold in British industry, one should not assume that it is widespread. Many HR planning specialists are still using traditional systems, largely because their organisations have not adopted the principles and techniques of HRM. In the rest of this chapter, therefore, it is necessary to explain and discuss traditional and modern approaches to HRP.

HRP has grown in importance in recent years, and in well-run organisations it is firmly integrated with business planning. Advances in information technology (IT) have eased the tasks that industry used to complain about and added impetus to the formulation and maintenance of HR plans. Now, with the right software, the computer has eliminated the tedious pen-pushing element and turned HRP into a dynamic, interesting, and at times exciting function.

HRP as a competence-centred function

In modern management terms the human resource is the most important resource in the organisation, which means that HRP is one of the most important processes. Human resource planning is a *competence-centred* activity, since its central purpose is to match the knowledge and skill *supply* to the organisation's knowledge and skill *demand*. To this end, HR specialists study and analyse business plans, consult the business's managers to obtain information about their HR needs, make decisions about the nature of the HR requirement in terms of competence, and identify the most appropriate sources of supply.

Shadowing the business plan

The best HR plans are produced by those who understand how their particular organisations interact with their total business environment, since this enables them to understand the thinking that underlies the business plans. It is essential for the HR plan to complement the business plan. To meet the needs of an ever-changing business environment, business plans are continuously monitored and updated to ensure that the organisation competes effectively and continues to serve the needs of its customers and clients. This means that those who create, maintain and update the HR plan appreciate that both business and HR plans are interdependent living entities which are continuously changing. The business plan changes in order to continue to reflect and create external market demands, while the HR plan changes in order to complement the business plan. The HR planner, therefore has to shadow and keep pace with the business plan in order to maintain this complementary relationship.

Traditional approaches to HRP

There are four main activities involved in the HRP process:

1. Forecasting HR demand.
2. Identifying sources of HR supply.
3. Producing the HR plan.
4. Activating and maintaining the plan.

In 1975, John Bramham devised a model depicting the HRP process which he modified in 1994. This was adapted by Pilbeam and Corbridge in 2002 and was adapted yet again by Beardwell *et al* in 2004 (see Figure 4.1).

According to the model, the HRP process goes through four main stages:

1. Analysis and investigation.
2. Forecasting.
3. Planning.
4. Implementation and control.

Analysis and investigation

This first stage is concerned with analysing and investigating the condition of the internal and external labour markets and the current capability of the organisation in terms of knowledge, skills and competence. The corporate strategy also has to be scrutinised for details of any future changes that would affect the HR requirement.

Internal labour market

Qualitative and quantitative information has to be gathered about the current workforce in terms of the kind of work that is carried out by each individual; the qualifications, experience, skills and competence they need in order to do the job and the level at which they operate. When you assess the current workforce as a source of supply, you do so within the context of continuous movement and activity. It may be that a large proportion of the employees will remain in their present positions, but there are always people leaving and joining the organisation, being promoted, transferring, and so forth. From your HR records you should be able to assess:

- how many employees there are

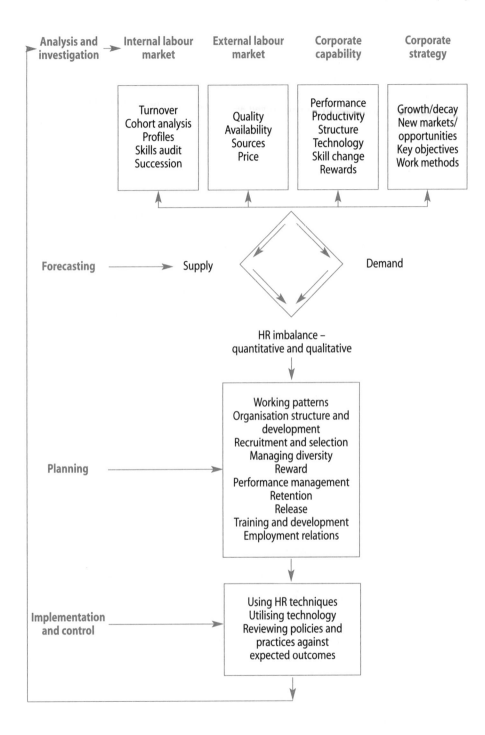

Figure 4.1 The process of human resource planning

Sources: adapted from Pilbeam and Corbridge (2002) and Bramham (1994), in Beardwell *et al* (2004).

- the nature of their skills and other qualities
- their level or status in the organisation
- the standards of their performance
- their attitudes and versatility
- their potential for promotion or other movement
- how many are likely to go sick, and when
- how many are likely to resign or be dismissed
- how many will retire, and when.

External labour market

Where the results of the HR demand analysis produces shortfalls in staff numbers and required competences, we gather and assess information about the external pool of potential future employees. The nature and levels of the jobs that are, or will be, affected by the shortfall means that the HR planner needs to search the labour markets at three levels: locally, nationally and internationally.

It also has to be borne in mind that other organisations will be searching at the same three levels and competing with your organisation for the same people. To compete effectively with other organisations, you must develop and keep up to date records of terms and conditions of employment that are offered at regional and industrial levels. This is often referred to as the *going rate*.

Corporate capability

Information is gathered about the performance of the organisation, its structure, the technology it uses and intends to use in the future. You need to gather information about the organisation's strengths and weaknesses; the results of a recent SWOT analysis will provide much of this data (see Chapter 1).

Activity 15

Obtain a copy of your organisation's annual report and compare what is said about the degree to which past objectives were achieved with what is said about how any problems with achieving future objectives might be overcome in the future. Find out where the information for this prediction came from.

Corporate strategy

This is where the focus is on the organisation's future direction. Strategy is seldom a 'more of the same' process; in today's business environment strategic planning, for most organisations spells change. The organisation's current capability, therefore, may not totally match up to the requirements that are laid down in the strategy and you need, therefore, to compare this with the capability it will need.

Forecasting HR demand

Looking again at Figure 4.1, you will see that at the second stage, the planner studies the data gathered from the analysis and investigation in order to identify, and thereby forecast, the HR demand and supply.

Forecasting HR demand is a data-gathering process. It involves identifying the kinds of knowledge, understanding, skills and competences that will be required, where in the organisation the requirements exist, when they are needed, and in what quantities. The data must be gathered in an organised and systematic way.

According to Armstrong (2001) there are four basic demand forecasting methods for estimating the numbers of people required:

- managerial judgement
- ratio-trend analysis
- work study techniques
- modelling.

Managerial judgement

This is a subjective technique and is not renowned for its accuracy. It is, however, the most commonly used. It is most effective in small organisations and those whose structure, technology and productivity remain relatively stable. What happens is that the organisation's managers estimate their future workloads and decide how many people they will need. The managers' decisions are based upon what they know about past trends and forthcoming changes. Managers sometimes do this under the guidance of their seniors who, in turn, are probably acting on the advice of specialists, such as those in the HR department. The information they are given may include:

- replacements for retirements, leavers, transfers and promotions
- possible improvements in productivity
- redeployment of existing staff
- planned changes in output levels
- planned reorganisation of work
- the impact of changes in employment law or collective agreements.

Armstrong (2001) refers to this *top-down* approach and suggests an alternative and additional *bottom-up* approach, in which the line managers submit staffing proposals for agreement by senior managers. He further suggests the use of both approaches in which, in addition to being given guidelines, line managers are encouraged to seek the help of the *HR, organisation and methods (O&M)* or *work study* departments. Staffing targets are usually set and while the line managers are producing their departmental and functional forecasts, HR, work study and O&M get together to produce an organisation-wide HR forecast.

The use of this technique draws on the contents of the business plan in that guidelines are issued to the managers indicating which of the organisation's future activities will be most likely to affect their departments.

Both forecasts (the line managers' and the HR version) are then reviewed

by an HRP committee consisting of functional heads. This committee reconciles with departmental managers any discrepancies between the two forecasts.

(Armstrong 2001)

Eventually agreement is reached and the forecasts are submitted to senior managers for approval.

Ratio-trend analysis

The effectiveness of this technique is determined by the future stability of the relationship between the productivity volume and the number of employees. It would, however, be risky to assume that this relationship will remain constant. Few organisations would survive without at least some element of growth and enrichment, and the technique, therefore, does emphasise the need to allow for foreseeable changes. This implies that the efficiency with which the technique is managed relies upon the planner's ability to handle (juggle with) changing ratios, a task that is made somewhat easier when the changes are planned, or at least foreseen.

There is a section on organisational change in Chapter 1, and by studying this you can see the factors that trigger change and the kinds of change they bring about. If, for example, the organisation plans to introduce new technology into the administrative and manufacturing processes, then demand forecasts would have to be based, *inter alia*, upon the need for new knowledge and skills. Additionally, however, the new technology may reduce the human resource demand, which would affect the balance of the relationship between the number of workers and the predicted productivity figures. In such a case, forecasting the demand for skill and competence requirements would probably be more appropriate through the use of managerial judgement.

Work study techniques

Work study techniques are used less frequently than they were in the twentieth century, largely owing to the decline in manufacturing. They are used to measure work in terms of how long it takes for operators to carry out particular tasks and how many operators would be required to carry out a total work schedule. The work study approach is most effective when it is used to forecast requirements on the factory floor and in administrative sections where the tasks are repetitive.

Modelling

This refers to mathematical modelling techniques in which spreadsheets are used in the preparation of demand and supply forecasts.

Forecasting HR supply

Forecasting HR supply involves using information from the internal and external labour markets. HR planners keep a monitoring eye on the staff turnover and workforce stability indices. The staff turnover index informs you of the turnover that is likely even when we discount any major or minor planned changes. The stability index gives you an indication of the degree to which long-serving employees remain with the organisation. You need to be able to calculate both of these indices.

Forecasting internal supply

Most of the employees who will be needed in the future are already in the workforce and many of them will stay in their current positions. Staff movements, however, have to be taken into account.

Calculating staff turnover

Staff turnover refers to the rate at which people leave the organisation. The turnover index is expressed as a percentage and is calculated as follows:

$$\frac{\text{Number of leavers in a year}}{\text{Average number of employees}} \times 100 = x\% \text{ turnover}$$

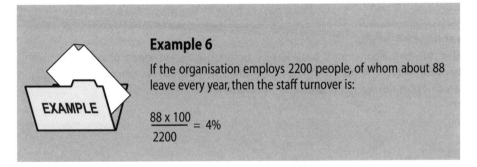

Example 6

If the organisation employs 2200 people, of whom about 88 leave every year, then the staff turnover is:

$$\frac{88 \times 100}{2200} = 4\%$$

Sectional distribution of turnover

The simple calculation in the example above is fine if we wish to compare the staff turnover with that of other organisations in the same industry, or against national trends. But the figure is of limited use to the HR planner in a medium-sized or large organisation. In such organisations the planner needs to identify the sectional distribution of staff turnover. To achieve this he/she has to calculate the turnover for every separate department and function in the organisation.

Calculating the sectional distribution of staff turnover is vital if your projection of future HR needs is to be useful. That is to say, if, as in the example given in the box above, the past turnover trend of 4 per cent is likely to continue, then you can be reasonably sure that the HR department will need to recruit at least 88 new employees in the forthcoming year. Furthermore, having completed the calculation in the departments and functions, you will know where the replacement staff will be needed and the kinds of skills and other qualities contained in the requirement. The results of this second calculation, however, have been known to unveil problems which are unrelated to the task in hand.

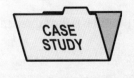

Case study 4: One problem leads to another

The organisation has a staff turnover problem. In Department A, turnover is 2 per cent, in Department B it is 3 per cent and in Department C it is 7 per cent, producing an average of 4 per cent across all three departments.

Clearly, however, there is a more significant staff turnover problem in Department C and rather than simply allowing for such a high figure when she was projecting HR requirements, Julie, the HR manager, decided to investigate the possibility of reducing it. She wanted to know why it compared so unfavourably with the figures for the other departments, not only because a high staff turnover is costly in recruitment terms, but because Julie suspected that there might be a deeper problem.

She assigned the task to Jack, who discovered that people were leaving because they were fed up with the communication style of the manager. This triggered further investigation after which the manager agreed to receive counselling.

This is an example of how a problem in one area of HR can uncover an entirely different kind of problem.

Staff turnover figures vary considerably between different kinds of organisation and between different industries. The type of organisation in which you work and the industry in which it operates will have national turnover averages.

Activity 16

Find out the national staff turnover average for your kind of organisation and the same for the kind of industry in which it operates. How does your organisation compare?

In Case Study 4 above, the point is made that recruitment is costly and a staff turnover that is too high can cause financial problems. Equally, however, a staff turnover that is too low may also cause problems. An organisation needs to maintain objectivity when it is assessing the efficiency and effectiveness of its operations and new people coming in bring good ideas; they can see things more objectively than those who have been with the organisation for many years.

Long-serving people fall into work routines that they perform out of habit; the habits become *activity ruts* and they fail to notice areas in which improvements could be made. New people will bring in a fresh perspective influenced by different experiences in other organisations. If a too-high or a too-low staff turnover rate can be problematic, then the aim is to achieve a healthy balance of in-house experience and incoming fresh ideas.

Calculating the workforce stability index

Just as important as staff turnover is the workforce stability index (WSI). This is also expressed as a percentage and is calculated as follows:

$$\frac{\text{Number of employees with more than one year's service}}{\text{Number of employees employed one year ago}} \times 100 = \text{Workforce stability}$$

Experience shows that people who are going to leave do so in their first year of employment, and that those who stay for a year will probably stay for much longer. The WSI, therefore, is useful in that it provides an indication of the percentage of people who will be unlikely to leave in the forthcoming year. In the above form, however, it does not take account of the number of people joining the organisation during the past year nor does it account for exact length of service, although there are techniques that can be used to obtain such information.

Analyses of labour turnover

As far back as 1955, Hill and Trist identified three phases in labour turnover, the *induction crisis, differential transit* and *settled connection*. I alluded to the induction crisis above by saying that people who are likely to leave do so in the first 12 months of employment. The reasoning that underlies Hill and Trist's analysis is discussed in greater depth in a section on induction in Chapter 7.

According to Julie Beardwell and her colleagues, 'the major drawback with all quantitative methods of turnover analysis is that they provide no information on the reasons why people are leaving. ... [Q]uantitative analyses can help to highlight problems, but they give those responsible for planning no indication about how these problems might be addressed' (Beardwell *et al* 2004).

Exit interviews

In addition to quantitative methods of calculating turnover and stability, data from qualitative methods may be gathered, for example, from exit interviews. These are most frequently carried out when the departing employee is leaving to join another employer. The main purpose of carrying out exit interviews is for the organisation to gather information about the reasons for leaving. For example, the pay and other entitlements may be more attractive elsewhere, or the prospects of training and promotion are better. The organisation may find the interviewee's responses valuable in the sense that it may consider using them to make improvements.

It should be remembered, however, that the responses to an exit questionnaire or a face-to-face interview may not be totally reliable, bearing in mind that the person leaving will be aware that his or her next employer might request a reference, and the interviewee's responses might be couched in terms designed to ensure that nothing is said that might diminish the value of the reference. You cannot make an employee submit to an exit interview, but most leavers will agree, if only on the grounds that a refusal might negatively influence the reference.

Planning

Dealing with deficits and surpluses

The third stage involves the planner in identifying imbalances between demand and supply. While this would have implications for recruitment, in terms of the geographic scope of the search for talent, it would also trigger a *skills audit* of the current workforce, and consideration of whether there are people who are retrainable (see Key concept 6 below). The planner has to take numerous factors into account, including future developments, work patterns and the structure, and such policies and procedures as those for managing reward, diversity, training and development.

Key concept 6: skills audit

This is a way of identifying the competence gap at departmental and sectional levels. The skills needed to carry out all of the tasks on time and at the required standard are listed and placed against the skills possessed by all of the members of the section or department. Where deficits are found, arrangements are made for the gaps to be filled.

This is a reconciliation process in which the solutions to problems may be hard or soft. Piercy (1989), writing about strategic planning in the general context, suggests a set of tools to help managers to work through the issues that may arise.

On the hard side, the feasibility of the plan may be focused on the supply forecast being less than the demand forecast. For example, the forecasts may have revealed a shortage of a particular skill in the internal and external labour markets, to the extent that it might be difficult to fulfil parts of the demand. Piercy recommends that you might:

- Alter the demand forecast by considering the effect of changes in the utilisation of employees, such as training and productivity deals, or high-performance teams.
- Alter the demand forecast by considering using different types of employees to meet the corporate objectives, such as employing a smaller number of staff with higher level skills, or employing staff with insufficient skills and training them immediately.
- Change the company objectives, as lack of staff will prevent them from being achieved in any case. Realistic objectives may need to be based on the staff who are, and are forecast to be, available.

When the demand forecast is less than the internal supply forecast in some areas – for example, the employees that are already in the organisation are capable, or would be in some areas with training – the possibilities are to:

- consider and calculate the costs of over-employment over various time spans
- consider the methods and cost of losing staff
- consider changes in utilisation: work out the feasibility and costs of retraining, redeployment and so on
- consider whether it is possible for the company objectives to be changed. Could the company diversify, move into new markets, etc?
 (Piercy 1989)

It is worth a reminder at this stage that HRP is a continuous process. Staff movements and changes to other plans trigger amendments to the plan in order to keep it up to date. On the soft side, however, there are factors that need to be taken into account, such as the degree to which the changes are acceptable to the senior managers and other employees who have their sights set on the vision of the future for the organisation, managing its culture and keeping abreast of environmental trends. Sometimes you will find yourself 'selling' the plan within the organisation, and you need to understand the people and the factors that could facilitate or hinder implementation.

What makes an HR plan?

Students often ask, 'What does the HR plan actually look like?' The answer is that it is virtually impossible, and not really advisable, to draw up a grand plan containing all of the necessary features. With the demand and supply situations reconciled, and feasible solutions decided upon, specific action plans are designed to include all of the organisational areas and activities. Rather than a single HR plan, therefore, there are a number of action plans.

Torrington and Hall (1998) for example, highlight several plans which are précised here:

1. *Human resource supply plans*: Plans may need to be made concerning the timing and approach to recruitment or downsizing. For example, it may have been decided that in order to recruit sufficient staff, a public relations campaign is needed to promote the company image. Internal movement plans would also be relevant here.
2. *Organisation and structure plans*: These plans may concern departmental structure and the relationships between departments. They may also be concerned with the hierarchy within departments and the levels at which tasks are carried out. Changes to organisation and structure will usually result in changes in employee utilisation.
3. *Employee utilisation plans*: Any changes in utilisation that affect human resource demand will need to be planned. Some changes will result in a sudden difference in employees' tasks and the numbers needed. Managers need to work out the new tasks to be done and the old ones to be dropped. Other plans may involve the distribution of hours worked: for example, the use of annual hours contracts or the use of functional flexibility, where employees develop and use a wider range of skills. All of the employees involved will need to be consulted about the changes and be prepared and trained for what will happen. A final consideration is: if fewer employees are needed, what criteria will be used to determine who should be made redundant and who should be redeployed and retrained, and in which areas?
4. *Training and management development plans*: There will be training implications for both the HR supply and utilisation plans. The timing of the training can be a critical aspect. For example, training for specific new technology skills loses most of its impact unless it is carried out immediately before installation. The organisation may wish to promote other training and development arrangements in order to entice candidates
5. *Performance plans*: These directly address performance issues: for example, the introduction of an objective-setting and performance management system, setting performance and quality standards, or culture change programmes aimed at encouraging specified behaviour and performance.
6. *Appraisal plans*: The organisation needs to make sure it is assessing the important things. For example, if customer service is paramount, employees need to be assessed on relevant aspects. This reinforces the importance of customer service and provides a mechanism for improvement in this area, and perhaps rewarding this, where appraisal is to be linked to pay.
7. *Reward plans*: It is often said that what gets rewarded gets done, and it is key that the rewards reflect what the organisation sees as important.
8. *Employee relations plans*: These plans may involve unions, employee representatives or all employees. They include any matters that need to be negotiated or areas where there is the opportunity for employee involvement and participation.
9. *Communication plans*: The way that planned changes are communicated to

employees is critical. Plans need to include methods for informing employees what is expected of them, and methods that enable employees to express their concerns and needs if implementation is to be successful. Means of eliciting employee commitment are also important: for example, communicating information about the progress of the organisation.

(adapted from Torrington and Hall 1998)

Job analysis

As a practitioner, your effectiveness in carrying out HR planning procedures will be influenced by the degree to which you understand the jobs: for example, in terms of their content, the required competences, where in the organisation they are situated, the degree to which they are subject to change and many other details. This information is obtained through the process of job analysis.

What is job analysis?

Job analysis is an operational, data-gathering process that involves reducing every job to its constituent parts including the nature of the activities, the task-related responsibilities that the job entails, the knowledge and skills that are required to carry out the work, the reporting responsibilities and the level of the job. Work methods sometimes change, perhaps through the introduction of new technology, and when this occurs parts of the job need to be updated, which means that the future job holder might use different work methods to achieve the same or modified ends. If the tasks and the skills needed to carry them out in the future are integrated into the final analysis, the process is referred to as *job modelling*.

Purpose

On the grounds that the products of job analyses are job descriptions and person specifications, books on this subject often discuss job analysis in a chapter on recruitment and selection. While personnel specifications certainly 'form the essential basis for recruitment and selection ... it is felt, however, that job analysis is an essential part of human resource planning activities' (Foot and Hook 1999). It is worth noting that job analyses that have been competently carried out are prerequisites for many decisions and activities that have a crucial influence on the lives of employees, including:

- designing systems of payment
- designing work systems
- designing and remodelling the jobs themselves
- assessing the competences that are required to carry out the job effectively
- training and longer-term career development needs
- building health and safety policies and procedures, and auditing health and safety practices.

Although not always evident in practice, there is an important distinction between *job-oriented* and *worker-oriented* procedures. As the terms suggests, job-oriented procedures focus on the work itself, producing a description in terms of the equipment used, the end results or purposes of the jobs, resources and materials utilized, etc. By contrast, worker-oriented analyses concentrate on describing the psychological or behavioural requirements of a job, such as communicating, decision-making and reasoning (Arnold *et al* 1991).

Activity 17

First, analyse your own job or a job that
past and arrange the tasks and respo
importance; compare what you have d
of your job description. Second, do the
colleague's job.

Job descriptions and role definitions

According to Michael Armstrong (1999), a job:

> **can be regarded as a unit in an organization structure that remains unchanged whoever is in the job. A job in this sense is a fixed entity, part of a machine that is 'designed' like any other part of a machine. Routine, or machine-controlled jobs do exist in most organisations but, increasingly, the work carried out by people is not mechanistic.**

Flexible approach

Many academics and managers take a flexible view of what a job actually involves, some even regard the job description as redundant. The reason for this is that the rate at which organisations are changing and developing is still increasing, and many line managers feel that job descriptions inhibit the flexibility that is needed to respond adequately to customer demands. The case they make is that:

> **inflexible definitions of jobs place limitations on change and development because they do not allow for changes in deployment or for multi-skilling and a wide variety of other factors that describe the reality of the ways in which the talents of the human resource need to be maximised in today's organisations.**
>
> **(Currie 1997)**

Defining the 'role'

One approach to resolving this dilemma is for the organisation to reach an agreement with the employee in which the role is loosely defined and there is mutual agreement that within the limits of the individual's capabilities – and trainability – the role may be flexible and subject to change. This approach has implications for the kinds of people the organisation prefers to recruit: those people who are sufficiently willing and motivated to accept the challenge of change. This also implies that the traditional approach to analysing jobs may, in some organisations, be inappropriate.

Pause for thought: job versus role

Stop and think for a moment. Would you prefer to have a job, which is described by Armstrong as a 'fixed entity, part of a machine that is "designed" like any other part of a machine'; or would you prefer to have a 'role' in the organisation, which means playing a flexible part in the changing organisation?

Information from a job analysis

The information that you obtain from a job analysis is may be summarised as:

- *The overall purpose of the job*: what the job is for and how it contributes to the achievement of the organisation's objectives.
- *The type of job*: the nature of the tasks and responsibilities; the duties to be carried out and the expected outcomes.
- *Professional jobs*: does the job holder need to be a member of a recognised professional institution such as those for law, accountancy, HR, etc?
- *Exclusivity*: is the job the only one of its kind in the organisation, or are there other similar jobs or jobs to which this one is related?
- *The location of the job*: in which department or functional area does it exist?
- *The status of the job*: where does the job stand in the departmental structure?
- *Reporting responsibilities*: to whom the job holder reports, such as to a line manager for his/her work performance and to an appropriate senior for specialised responsibilities like IT, marketing or finance.
- *Motivation*: the degree to which motivational factors and/or demotivators are built into the job.
- *Movement*: is the current job holder likely to move upwards or laterally in the foreseeable future?

Gathering the information: four steps

You need to gather as much relevant information as you can and you need to ensure that the information is correct. To achieve this the following four steps are suggested:

- *Step 1*: Examine documents that provide information about the job. These include the existing job description. Relevant information about the job may also be obtained from training manuals and the individual's records.
- *Step 2*: Interview the job holder. Here, you seek information about the activities that are involved in carrying out the job.
- *Step 3*: Talk to the manager to whom the job holder reports about the purpose of the job and to confirm the information that was provided by the job holder.
- *Step 4*: Observe employees while they are doing their jobs.

Examining documents

The important features of the existing job description are the date on which it was last reviewed and why it was reviewed. You need the job description so that you can see how well it matches up with the data you collect from the job holder. Training manuals will contain information about the knowledge and skills required to carry out the job effectively. Individuals' records include data about their performance standards and the training to which they have been exposed.

Interviewing the job holder

Depending on the scope and complexity of the job, it may be advisable, two or three weeks in advance, to ask the job holder to keep a diary or activity record of the tasks that he/she performs. Since this is done on a daily and weekly basis – as the job is being carried out – it avoids problems associated with faulty memory and so on. This may be difficult at times, and time-consuming.

As soon as you have decided to interview the job holder you should, as a matter of courtesy, tell his/her line manager about your intentions. In addition, it is essential to tell the interviewee the exact purpose of the interview. If this is not done the employee may become uneasy, thinking perhaps that the job is going to be redesigned or even worse, he/she might be made redundant.

Preparing for the interview

It is advisable to prepare for the interview by drafting a questionnaire which includes not only the basic elements of the job as described above but also further supplementary questions The questionnaire will act as a checklist and enable you to build a logical sequence into the interview (see Table 4.1 overleaf).

The questions listed in Table 4.1 are not exhaustive. Studying them, you will see that they may be asked about any job. It is an obvious advantage if the job has been analysed previously. The information that was gathered then – the answers to the questions – should have been stored on the computer in the HR department. By comparing the previously gathered information with what you have gathered, you will be able to assess the degree to which the job has changed.

Conducting the interview

While common sense tells us that the job holder should be able to give a good account of the information referred to in Step 2 (above), caution needs to be exercised since it sometimes happens that information obtained in this way conflicts with that provided by the manager. For example, when a job is first created it is the organisation that prescribes its content in terms the orders of importance in which the tasks and accountabilities are arranged. Experience shows that after individuals have settled into their jobs they unconsciously alter the task priorities to suit their own liking and abilities, favouring some tasks above others. Job holders have also been known to give an inflated account of the importance of what they do. Despite this, the job holder can provide some information, but it is always advisable to check it with the line manager, whom you interview after you have seen the job holder.

Interviewees are sometimes inclined to offer more information than you have asked for, and some of this may not be relevant. On the other hand, answers may be lacking in sufficient detail, especially when answering questions about items that the job holder appears to be unsure about or perceives to be at the bottom of his or her priorities. In such a case you have to probe more deeply to get the information you need.

Table 4.1 Job analysis interview – questionnaire

Questions

What is your job title?

What is the job title of your manager?

What is the purpose of your job?

Does anyone in the organisation do a similar job and if so, how many?

What do you actually do? (Here you ask the job holder to list the job-related duties)

Did you require training to enable you to do your job?

Would anyone require training regardless of their qualifications and experience?

What knowledge and skills are needed to do your job?

What qualifications and experience do you need in order to carry out your job?

Do you have people reporting to you and if so, how many?

What are their job titles?

How would you describe your responsibilities?

Do you have authority to make decisions and if so, what types of decision?

Do you have contact with others within the organisation and externally?

Does your job involve travelling and/or working unsocial hours on behalf of the organisation?

What problems do you encounter in your job?

What performance standards are required of you in your job?

Activity 18

First, think of the ways in which the information from a job analysis may affect peoples' lives at work. Second, think about how any significant changes might affect the status of the job itself.

Interviewing the line manager

The interview with the line manager should cover two main areas for discussion. First, it is to discuss the answers given by his or her staff member. For example, the manager may help you to sift out any irrelevant material – such as responsibilities that may have been inflated – or help with the technical detail that was not fully explained by the staff member. Second, it is to discuss what the manager knows about the future of the job. For example, technological change might be on the horizon which may have implications for the design of the job, including changes in the necessary competences.

Using observational methods

For this, *structured observational techniques* (see below) are used and those being observed should be advised that you are observing them at work and why you are doing it. The fact that they are aware of why you are observing them may cause them to modify what they would do in a normal unobserved situation, but it is still possible to gather useful information in this way from, say, office or factory floor workers.

Key concept 7: structured and participant observation

Observation may be *structured*, in which the observer simply watches and notes what the person does, or it may be *participant observation*, in which the observer works with the person and gathers *qualitative* rather than *quantitative* information. In both cases the person being observed must be told the purpose of the observation.

Modern approaches to human resource planning

This section of the chapter focuses on the principles of human resource planning in terms of the modern approaches that are taken by many organisations. It reflects how traditional HRP has been revised to produce differences in the aims of HRP and the thinking that underlies modern practices. Armstrong (2001) outlines these aims as:

- to attract and retain the number of people required with the appropriate skills, expertise and competences
- to anticipate problems of potential surpluses or deficits of people
- to develop a well-trained and flexible workforce, thus contributing to the organisation's ability to adapt to an uncertain and changing environment
- to reduce dependence on external recruitment when key skills are in short supply by formulating retention and development strategies
- to improve the utilisation of people by introducing more flexible systems of work.

As you will see, the first two of these aims are similar to those of traditional HRP. Largely, however, they are aims that redirect the focus away from the practices of traditional manpower planning and towards an emphasis on internal workforce flexibility. Problems of deficits and surpluses in the HR demand and supply situations are dealt with first through the development and redevelopment of the internal workforce. Where recruitment is necessary, part-time workers are brought in and short-term contracts are offered to people whose skills are needed for limited periods (see also 'Core and peripheral workers' in Chapter 1).

The underlying thinking here is that a more flexible workforce with a broad repertoire of skills and competences, available when needed, is more likely to be able to respond appropriately to the volatile demands of today's global market.

The influence of business strategy

The degree to which an HR strategist can operate effectively is determined by the clarity of the business strategy. Older business strategies worked because the market was more stable than it is today. Now, however, the objective is to achieve a competitive advantage, and the ability of business strategists to be precise about their requirements is governed by market forces that, in turn, govern the degree to which the HR strategists can be precise. Whittington (1993) points out that strategies may be deliberate or emergent.

> **Deliberate strategies assume a rational evaluation of external and internal circumstances and an identification of the best way to achieve a competitive advantage Emergent strategies, on the other hand, are the product of market forces.**
>
> **(Beardwell *et al* 2004)**

'The most appropriate strategies ... emerge as competitive processes that allow the comparatively better performers to survive while the weaker performers are squeezed out' (Legge 1995, p99).

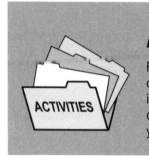

Activity 19

First, how does the content of the teaching on your course, or the HR strategy in your organisation, match up to the ideas that are expressed above? Second, how does the content of your teaching compare with the HR strategy at your workplace?

Summary

- Those involved in early industrial activity, even before the Industrial Revolution, tried to ensure that there would be people coming up to succeed longer-serving skilled employees. With the Industrial Revolution came the development of factories and larger-scale industries which eventually demanded a more organisation-wide approach to planning the future workforce.
- By the twentieth century, apprenticeship schemes were widespread and the demand was for the continuation of traditional skills to serve the purposes of a largely manufacturing economy. Manpower planning, now referred to as HR planning (HRP), appeared in the 1960s, and a modified version of it is still practised. Information technology has eased the activities related to HR planning.
- In the 1980s HR planning was revised to enable organisations to meet the demands of a rapidly developing and fiercely competitive global market. Many of the traditional practices are still used for HRP purposes, but new HR resourcing strategies have been introduced.
- Planning itself always was an imprecise process, but the rate of change that was necessary to sustain a competitive advantage shortened planning periods and

altered strategic emphases. The degree to which HR planners can be precise in their forecasts is determined by the business strategy which, in turn, is strongly influenced by market forces. The ideas underlying modern strategic developments in the management of employment and employee relations call for a workforce that is flexible and able to respond appropriately. Part-time working and access to skills via short-term contracts are now commonplace.

Self-test questions

1. What are the purposes of HR planning?
2. Why were organisations slow to adopt manpower planning when it was first introduced?
3. How would you define HR planning?
4. What factors influence the length of planning periods?
5. What are the five stages of the planning process?
6. Why is HRP said to be a 'competence centred' function?
7. What are the four main elements in the process of HR planning?
8. How might imbalances between HR demand and supply be reconciled?
9. What are the four steps you can take to gather information when carrying out a job analysis
10. How would you distinguish between deliberate and emergent strategies?

Recruitment

CHAPTER 5

Learning objectives

After studying this chapter you should:

- understand traditional and modern approaches to recruitment

- understand the context in which recruitment is set

- understand the effect of unemployment on the ability to obtain satisfactory outcomes from recruitment drives

- understand how demographic changes have affected the labour markets

- be able to develop and use appropriate documentation

- understand recruitment advertising and alternative methods.

Introduction

The main objectives of this chapter are to explain the purposes and the processes of recruitment. First, however, there is a discussion that is concerned with the traditional and modern perceptions of recruitment. Since the inception of HRM in the 1980s, perceptions of recruitment and the design of its related systems have been subject to significant change; advancing technology has facilitated new ways of recruiting. A large number of organisations have updated their systems, although others still use traditional systems. In the light of this, the discussion focuses on the current overall situation.

Definitions

In one sense, recruitment and selection may be regarded as separate functions in that selection begins where recruitment ends. In this context, recruitment commences when a genuine vacancy has been identified and ends when a list of candidates has been built from the applications that have resulted from making a vacant position known. The selection process then takes over. The applications are examined and sifted until a shortlist of the most suitable candidates is produced, after which the final elements of the process are activated, including arrangements for assessing the candidates. The selection process ends when a suitable candidate has been given and has accepted an offer of employment (see Chapter 6).

Dowling and Schuler (1990), for example, say that recruitment means 'searching for and obtaining potential job candidates in sufficient numbers and quality so that the organisation can select the most appropriate people to fill its job needs'. On the other hand Beardwell *et al* (2004) define recruitment and selection as integrated activities, in which, 'the recruitment and selection process is concerned with identifying, attracting and choosing suitable people to meet an organisation's human resource requirements', which seems to bind the two functions together. Yet again, 'where recruitment ends and selection begins is a moot point' (Anderson 1994).

Different methods and techniques are used in carrying out each of these functions, and for teaching and writing purposes, they are easier to understand if they are treated separately. In practice, recruitment and selection are a continuous process and the relevant HR practitioners are skilled in both.

The context of recruitment

Bringing new people into the organisation is an important function, especially now, when the focus is on people as the organisation's main means of achieving a competitive advantage. While organisations vary in the degree to which they have adopted the principles and practices of HRM (few have ignored it completely), there is a visible inclination towards designing recruitment systems that support the overall strategic intent of the organisation. Beaumont (1993) refers to this when noting the role of 'strategic selection' and the 'enhanced potential importance' of selection (see Chapter 6).

Fierce competition in a global market has brought with it the need for a multiskilled and flexible workforce recruited to cope with a strengthened customer focus. All of this has shifted the emphasis away from attracting people who are potentially capable of operating effectively within the confines of a clearly defined job, and towards adaptable people who are prepared to take on a flexible role. This means that recruitment is carried out in anticipation of change and with the organisation's overall strategy in mind. In the main, the basis for recruitment has moved away from the traditional 'person–job match' and towards a more behavioural and attitudinal justification, although traditional methods are still used in small to medium-sized organisations.

Diversity and flexibility

Another factor that has influenced change since the 1980s is the increased level of diversity in the make up of today's external labour market, from which, of course, new employees are drawn. This is reflected in the make-up of the workforce and has emphasised the importance of fairness in selection decision-making. There are, therefore, legislative measures that affect recruitment and which demand particular approaches. These are discussed later in this chapter.

The labour markets

Recruitment processes are carried out within the context of the *internal* as well as the *external* environments, both of which offer constraints and opportunities.

Internal labour market

Some writers say that when a vacancy or a new position arises, the internal labour market should be the first port of call. This is justified on the grounds that first, it offers opportunities to existing employees, especially those whose current positions have become vulnerable to redundancy, perhaps owing to technological change or a restructuring programme. To some employees a new position might be more interesting and/or more challenging, or it might be a more senior position enhancing their terms and conditions and providing an opportunity to raise the level of their contribution. In fact some organisations are well known for 'promoting from within'. Employees of the high street banks and all of the emergency services, where training is a long-established tradition, are promoted up through the organisation because they have shown proficiency in their jobs.

Second, from the organisation's point of view, recruiting from the internal labour market heads off the costs associated with recruiting externally; and third, it demonstrates to the workforce in general that the organisation regards upward internal movements as opportunities to develop its employees and encourage them to take on further responsibility. Conversely, a good case can be made for achieving a healthy balance in the use of both internal and external labour markets, since all organisations benefit from injections of 'fresh blood' (see Chapter 4).

External labour market

The external labour market can be viewed on four different levels: *local, regional, national* and *international*. The size and location of the area from which you need to recruit is determined first and foremost by the nature of the job in terms of its level in the organisation, its technical complexity and degree of specialism, the qualifications, competences and experience required. Further important considerations include the related costs compared with the potential benefits to the organisation of using particular markets, especially the international market.

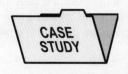

Case study 5: Searching for talent

Solent Toys Ltd is a new venture in the south of England which will manufacture four different categories of toy. The company will be made up of four divisions, each of which will be headed up by a project director who will also be a member of the board of directors.

1. *The Nursery Division,* making soft toys such as cloth dolls and teddy bears.
2. *The Educational Division,* making problem-solving toys in the form of games and puzzles.
3. *The Electronics Division,* making interactive toys, such as robots and 'talk-back' gadgets.
4. *The Musical Division,* making toy keyboards and other instruments.

The company already occupies a large site, an office block has been built and the total building programme will be completed in four months. The board of directors, including the project directors and the HR director, are already in their positions and to begin with, the HR director will have a small staff of specialists. The company now needs to embark upon a large-scale recruitment programme.

For each of the divisions the recruiters will be searching for managers, creative designers, quality inspectors, machine operators and administrative staff.

Think about the variety of competences, qualifications and experience that will be required across all of the divisions. For example, the company will need people who are skilled and experienced in designing and making soft toys, designing and making educational problem-solving toys, electronics experts to make interactive toys and people who are skilled and experienced in designing and making toy musical instruments. Just imagine the breadth of the range of knowledge and competences required to staff the whole organisation.

Task: Write down two categories of employee for whom you would search in each of the four main areas of the external labour market; that is: two from the local, two from the regional, two from the national and two from the international markets.

Factors affecting success

There are a variety of factors that can inhibit or facilitate an organisation's recruitment success rate:

- *Unemployment.* Unemployment fluctuates with the state of the economy. While in the UK, the economy is relatively stable, we should not assume that is the case globally, nor indeed that employment is evenly distributed across the UK. While low unemployment is regarded as a positive factor in economic terms, it does limit the availability of the 'right' people. On the other hand, when unemployment is high, job applications abound and the selection process has to be handled with great care if the organisation is to employ the kind of people it needs.
- *Diversity.* The increase in immigration rates in recent years has had a positive effect on recruitment in that it has raised the level of the availability of required knowledge and skills. In a moderate way, this has helped to alleviate the skill shortage. Among the overseas applicants for UK residency there are doctors, nurses, dentists, engineers and all of the trades and crafts.
- *Skill shortages.* Advancing technology has created a 'talent war' in the external market, in which organisations are competing with each other to 'capture' people who possess exceptional knowledge and rare competences.

Recruitment processes

This section explains the systems of recruitment and offers guidance on the related skills. The stages of the recruitment process may be depicted as the 'systematic recruitment cycle'. Once a genuine vacancy has been identified, the recruitment process can be activated. It is carried out systematically and is depicted in Figure 5.1 (overleaf).

Authority to recruit

When a line manager identifies a vacancy he/she normally has to complete an *authority to recruit* (ATR) form. The design of the form will oblige the line manager, and at least one senior manager, to review the situation. Typically, the job details appear on one side of the form, and on the other side, the manager makes a case in support of the need to fill a post, by justifying it in terms of practicality, cost and productivity benefits. The form is seen by a senior manager who comments on the line manager's case and gives or withholds the authority to make the appointment.

Example 7: Graduates have to be wooed

Engineering and manufacturing firms must work harder at recruitment if they want to attract the best graduates, according to a recruitment consultancy whose blue-chip clients include Rolls-Royce and Honda.

Emma Powers, a consultant at Jonathan Lee recruitment, said, 'There is an increased demand for engineering graduates with industrial experience or specific training, as firms become more concerned with adding value through their people.'

Powers said that companies needed to approach good candidates quickly and sell themselves before applicants were snapped up by competitors. 'Graduates need to be sold the benefits of taking a job and offered positions with a variety of projects,' she said.

Source: *People Management*. 17 June 1999, p21.

Before making a decision, the senior manager may consult other managers and the HR department. Eventually, the form is returned to the line manager concerned. If authority is given, the line manager, in consultation with the HR specialist, makes out a job requisition.

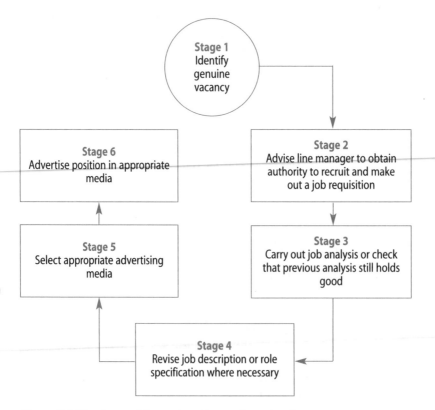

Figure 5.1 The stages of the systematic recruitment cycle

The job requisition

This is a document on which the line manager describes his or her requirements in terms of:

- the nature of the tasks that make up the job
- how the job has changed (if it has) since it was last analysed
- the priorities of the job and the key tasks
- the knowledge, understanding, skills, competence and other personal qualities needed for the job.

These factors are identified from a job analysis (see Chapter 4) and they are used to write up a job description or role definition (see Table 5.1, overleaf) and a person specification. In practice, these documents are usually stored on a computer but it is recommended that the HR practitioner and the line manager get together to agree on their contents in case there have been any changes since the documents were last drafted.

The job description

Every opportunity should be taken to keep job descriptions up to date. The fact that a specific vacancy has been identified provides an opportunity for the HR practitioner to make a further update, in consultation with the relevant line manager who will be aware of any changes to the job. In addition to their use in recruitment, job descriptions have a key role in other activities, such as identifying training needs, and introducing or reviewing a job evaluation scheme and other systems of payment.

The person specification

This document is alternatively referred to as a *recruitment*, or job, specification. Its purpose is to detail the particular qualities that match the profile of the ideal person for the job, and these may include education, qualifications, experience, competences, attitudes and any specific requirements that are exclusive to the job in question.

The expectation that the main duties and responsibilities that are detailed in the job description will be fulfilled at or above the required performance standards, and the nature of the duties and responsibilities themselves, will provide indications of the knowledge and competences that will be required of the prospective job holder. The person specification, therefore, may be regarded as a reflection of the main features of the job description in the form of personal qualities.

In the past, considerable time and ingenuity went into the development of person specification models. Each model presented a basic set of criteria, against which 'minimum/essential' and 'desirable' job requirements can be set. The contents of the job description (Table 5.1) provide the basic criteria for the person specification.

Three models that have, in part, stood the test of time are:

- The seven-point plan (Rodger 1952).
- The fivefold grading system (Fraser 1966).
- The eight-point plan (Plumbley 1976).

Rodger's model is the most well known and most frequently used.

Table 5.1 A typical job description

Organisation	Farm Fresh Foods Ltd Wheatsheaf Lane, Penyard, Wiltshire
Department	Accounts department
Job title	Financial accounts section leader
Main duties: *Report to the accounts* *manager*	1 Keep the accounts of the company's largest customers, ensuring their accounts are kept up to date and that invoices and statements go out on time
	2 Monitor credit limits, ensuring they are not exceeded without special permission
	3 Arrange that all credit limits above £2500 are insured
	4 Maintain liaison with credit reference agencies
	5 Allocate work to clerical staff
	6 Supervise the work of a team of eight accounts clerks, offering advice and guidance where necessary
	7 Monitor the performance standards of accounts staff
	8 Supervise the efficient and effective operation of the accounts office
	9 Maintain good customer relations when responding to their accounts queries
Salary and other main terms *and conditions*	Salary £20,000 p.a. plus company car. Relocation allowance, well-appointed office, situated pleasant rural area. Option to join pension scheme after two years. Must participate in formal appraisal scheme after expiry of a six-month probationary period.
Performance and career *prospects*	Possible promotion to assistant manager after two years. The critical performance standards relate to the maintenance of good customer relations and the degree to which invoice and statement deadlines are met.

While the structure of Rodger's model still holds good, the contents in their original form are not recommended for use today. They reflect the values that were held at the time of publication, which was 20 years before discrimination laws came into being. For example, items such as 'physical make-up' and 'circumstances' are potentially discriminatory. The model, however, provided a structure or 'checklist' that personnel specialists found useful in that it enabled them to place the requirements against the appropriate categories on the specification. The seven-point plan is laid out in Table 5.2 as an example of the content and form in which all three models were originally written.

The points used by the other two models (the left-hand column) are:

J.M. Fraser: Fivefold grading system	P. Plumbley: Eight point plan
Brains and abilities	General intelligence
Qualifications	Special aptitudes
Impact on others	Attainments
Adjustment	Physical make-up
Motivation	Disposition
	Circumstances
	Interests
	Type of person

Table 5.2 Structure for a person specification

Quality	Description
1 Physical	This covers health, physique, age, appearance, hearing, and speech. Physical attributes may be added or removed as necessary.
2 Attainments	Including academic attainments, training received, knowledge, skills and experience already developed.
3 Intelligence	The general intelligence, specific abilities and the methods for the assessment of these.
4 Special aptitudes	Any special aptitudes, such as mechanical, manual, verbal, numerical, creativity, etc.
5 Interests	Personal interests as possible indicators of aptitudes, abilities or personality traits (eg intellectual, practical/constructional, physically active, social, artistic).
6 Disposition	Personality characteristics needed (eg equability, dependability, self-reliance, assertiveness, drive, energy, perseverance, initiative, motivation).
7 Circumstances	Personal and domestic circumstances (eg mobility, commitments, family circumstances and occupations).

It was mentioned above that the contents of the three models are not recommended for use today but the structures are still useful. Staying with the job of financial accounts section leader, Table 5.3 is a general adaptation of the structure which, in the light of current legislation and modern approaches to recruitment, might prove to be legitimate and useful.

Making the vacant position known

Having gathered the necessary information and compiled or reviewed (as necessary) the documentation, advertising the position is the next step. However, depending on the nature and

Table 5.3 A typical person specification

Farm Fresh Foods Limited	Job title: Financial Accounts Section Leader	
Job requirements	**Essential**	**Desirable**
1 Qualifications	AAT and business studies	ACCA or accountancy degree
2 Knowledge	Good understanding of financial accountancy	Understand all aspects of financial and management accountancy
3 Skills	Ability to keep accounting systems. Able to handle accountancy IT packages.	Exceed minimum standard and maximise on use of IT software
4 Experience	Two years in a team leadership or supervisory role	4/5 years in a relevant team leadership role. Accustomed to dealing with supermarkets' accounts departments.
5 Management	Accustomed to leading a team of accountants. Able to monitor and assess performance standards.	Ability to exceed minimum requirements. Able to raise performance standards.
6 Personal qualities	Polite manner. Good oral and written communicator.	Good leadership skills and accustomed to pressure

ACTIVITIES

Activity 20

Draft a person specification for your own job, or one which you have held in the past, and another for a colleague's job which is different from yours.

level of the position, advertising may not necessarily be the best option and can be expensive. The word 'advertise' comes from the Latin *advertere*, which means to *make known,* and the fact that a position is vacant may be made known in several ways. For example, we can:

- *Advertise internally* on notice boards and in the company magazine, but check the frequency of the magazine, find out its closing date for the acceptance of advertisements and see how this matches up to the target date for filling the vacant position.
- *Search the HR records* for suitable internal candidates and scan the files on people who have previously sent in curricula vitae on speculation. The internal

advertisement should still appear, since everyone should have an equal opportunity to apply for the post.

- *Use general and specialist selection consultants.* Consultants are brought in when the organisation would benefit from their expertise in recruiting for positions in the higher levels of the organisation, and when vacancies occur in key specialisms, such as in certain aspects of engineering, IT, chemicals – whatever the organisation needs.
- *Use employment agencies.* People associate employment agencies with temporary and part-time staff, but most of them are extremely good at finding people for positions in other areas of the workforce. Their reputation is for finding administrative and clerical workers, but many specialise in particular kinds of function, such as finance, catering, the building trades, HR and IT.
- *Invite applications from 'work experience' students.* This can be quite a good source, especially since the managers have already met the candidate and seen something of his/her work.
- *Contact schools, colleges and universities,* support their career conventions and maintain good relations. These are opportunities to meet prospective employees and 'sell' the benefits of working in your organisation.
- *Use job centres.* People who register with job centres are usually unemployed, and some employers may see this as a disadvantage, questioning why the person is unemployed. On a more positive note, Torrington and Hall (1998) point out that job centres are socially responsible and secure, that they can produce applicants very quickly and the number of people who find employment through them has risen significantly. A further advantage that job centres have is that they can offer the facility of a locally situated national database on which one may carry out a trawl for suitable candidates. Also, it is worth noting that they do not charge fees.

External advertising

The benefits of using an advertising agency cannot be over-emphasised. An agency can provide expertise in copywriting, producing artwork and eye-catching captions and other forms of visual impact. It can advise on all aspects of advertising including the legal aspects (discrimination), media selection, placing the advertisements and working with you on response analysis. Agents can also provide anonymity, in which your advertisements appear under the name of the agency. The organisation may decide to do this when it is carrying out confidential marketing or developing a new product and does not wish the job titles in the advertisements to reveal the nature of the plans. All of this has a cost, of course, but the benefits usually outweigh it.

Philip Plumbley points to some of the advantages of using an advertising agent:

Only one copy of the text need be supplied no matter how many publications are to be used; the agency will book space; prepare the layout and typography; read and correct proofs; verify that the right advertisement has appeared in the right publication at the right time; and only one cheque has to be raised to settle the agency's monthly account.

(Plumbley 1985)

Types of recruitment advertisement

The most commonly used media for recruitment advertisements are newspapers and magazines in which the advertisements may be:

- *Classified*: sometimes referred to as lineage or run-on, classified advertisements appear in single columns and are a typical feature of newspapers, especially the local and regional papers.
- *Classified semi-display*: which also appear in single columns among the classified advertisements. The idea is to make the advertisement stand out from the ordinary ones by using bold captions to head up the advertisement, perhaps narrowing the body of the text or placing the advertisement in a single column box.
- *Displayed advertisements*: these have borders and contain artwork that is designed to project the organisation's corporate image, usually including a logo. They are the most expensive type of advertisement but they do produce a greater impact than classified ads and are ideal for advertising the more senior technical and professional jobs. They also create an image with which readers will eventually become familiar.

Placing an advertisement

Handling classified and semi-displayed advertisements is a fairly simple process, since they can be placed by telephone, letter or e-mail. There are, however, a few 'dos' and 'don'ts', given in Table 5.4.

Table 5.4 Dos and don'ts for placing advertisements

Do:	Don't:
Get the line manager to approve the advertisement.	Allow the 'tele-ads sales people to talk you into taking more space than you actually need.
Ensure that the copy you have written conforms to the provisions of the legislation on discrimination.	Place the advertisement by telephone and leave it at that. Always get written confirmation of: (i) *what* will appear, and (ii) *when* it will appear.
Ensure that your written material includes the date the advertisement will be published.	
Get written confirmation of the actual copy that will appear and the date.	

Full display

Handling a full display advertisement is best left to the experts. Few individuals have the capacity to, first, produce good copy, second, produce artwork that will be indicative of, and reflect well on, the organisation, and third, lay out an advertisement that will compel the attention of a serious potential candidate. Most display advertisements are designed and placed by advertising agents.

What the advertisement should contain

The advertisement should contain a caption, and usually this is the job title. On the other hand there may be something about the job which is more likely to 'draw the eye', such as the salary, prospects or the location. 'Come and work in the Lake District', for example, would make an attractive caption. On the question of the job title, it should be remembered that people who scan the recruitment section of a newspaper are looking for something familiar, so 'playing' with job titles in an attempt to attract is definitely out. The days of 'sales director elect' instead of sales representative, and 'head of development' instead of training manager ended in the early 1980s.

If the salary is to be included, John Courtis advises:

> **Don't weasel. If the market rate for the job, according to age, experience and skills, is £38,000 p.a. offer it unequivocally. Do battle with the Managing Director who looks at your copy and suggests that you advertise it at 'circa £35,000 p.a.' arguing that you can always negotiate upwards. True, but think about the ideal candidate you will miss, who is already sitting on £35,500. You'd have paid a little extra to get him or her, wouldn't you? But now you've missed the chance.**
>
> **(Courtis 1994)**

Include also a brief synopsis of the job content, its requirements, reporting responsibilities and benefits. Say something about the organisation itself, its status in the industry, employment policy, promotion prospects, etc. Obviously, advertising space is expensive and limited, so you cannot eulogise for too long! Finally, the advertisement should inform the reader how to apply for the job. This might be by submitting a letter of application, a curriculum vitae, by writing or telephoning for an application form. This last is seen by many organisations, especially those in the public sector, as an opportunity to send out 'further details' about the job, which may include a job description and person specification. Alternatively, many advertisements refer the reader to an application form on the organisation's website.

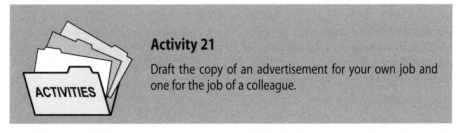

Activity 21

Draft the copy of an advertisement for your own job and one for the job of a colleague.

Other media

Large organisations, such as the armed services, the National Health Service and government departments, use television, often as part of a campaign which includes displayed advertisements in newspapers and magazines. Television is the most expensive medium to use, and advertisements in spoken and written media are transitory and therefore have to be repeated, but the impact cannot be matched through any other medium.

Recruiting electronically

There has been a significant growth in making vacant positions known by electronic means, largely through the use of the Internet and the organisation's own intranet, with responses by e-mail. Whether electronic usage is mostly designed to replace or supplement traditional methods is difficult to assess. Neither approach is exclusive, and traditional and electronic activities can be combined at almost any stage. For example, a press advertisement may direct readers to a website providing further information, or a corporate website may require applicants to request an application form via e-mail or telephone that will then be processed manually (CIPD 2002).

It has been estimated that about 75 per cent of employers now use some form of electronic recruitment, especially e-mail responses and the acceptance of curricula vitae via e-mail (Beardwell and Wright 2004). According to the CIPD, around 20 per cent of organisations accept completed application forms by e-mail (CIPD 2002).

Advantages and disadvantages of electronic recruitment

The advantages of using electronic media may be summarised as follows:

- It has a shorter recruitment cycle time.
- It can reduce costs if used instead of more expensive methods.
- It can reach a wider range of applicants.
- Organisations can display a more up-to-date image.
- It provides global coverage 24/7.

The disadvantages may be summarised as follows:

- It is most effective when used as part of an integrated recruitment process and many organisations currently lack the resources and expertise to achieve this.
- It is not yet the first choice for most job seekers.
- Not all potential applicants have access to the Internet, so using it alongside press advertisements might increase costs.
- It can lead to more unsuitable applications being received which have to be screened out, thus increasing costs.

The above material is taken from the CIPD website, 'Recruitment on the Internet: quick facts' (2002), and is included with the permission of the publisher, the Chartered Institute of Personnel and Development, London.

Application forms

The advantage of using application forms is that they set out the information you need in a standardised format. This speeds up the pace of manually sifting applications since, unlike curricula vitae, which may take many forms, you know where on the form to look for each successive item of information. One of the problems of application forms is that many respondents feel that they have to write something in answer to every single question.

Example 8: OCR or OMR forms

The form is designed so that the applicant is presented with a series of options, each of which has a tick box. For example if the person specification says that one of the minimum requirements is an HND while the desired requirement is a degree, the relevant section of the form would appear thus:

EXAMPLE

Higher National Diploma

Degree

The applicant is asked to fill in the relevant box in black and the system will pick up which box has been filled in. In this case, the applicant has a degree. The forms are passed through the machine at speed as it screens the applications.

Responses to advertisements

It was said above that information about how prospective candidates may register their interest in the job is part of the advertisement content itself, which means that applications will soon be received. It is at this point that recruitment ends and selection commences.

Self-test questions

1. How would you define recruitment?
2. What are the factors that have influenced change in approaches to recruitment advertising?
3. What societal factors have caused an increase in the importance of recruitment?
4. Why, when recruiting for a vacant position, might the internal labour market be your first choice?
5. Why, on the other hand, might the external labour market be your first choice?
6. In terms of its spread and scope, what are the four main dimensions of the external labour market?
7. What is a job requisition and who drafts it?
8. What is the purpose of a person specification?
9. What are the main benefits of using an advertising agency?
10. When making a vacant position known, what are the alternatives to advertising jobs in newspapers and magazines?

Selection

Introduction

Selection is one of the most important tasks of the HR practitioner, since it is vital to fill vacant positions with people who are not only suitably skilled for specific jobs, but flexible, and willing and able to cope with change.

Those involved in selection include HR practitioners and line managers in the sense that they actually organise the selection events and participate in them all the way through to the final selection decisions. Senior managers formulate selection policies, draw up the procedures and facilitate training for those involved at the interface.

Bringing in the right people

The modern perception of the objectives of selection means that selectors must exercise great care in ensuring that the 'right' people are employed. In order to achieve this, there is an increased emphasis on the use of assessment centres, which may include job simulation/work sampling. Selectors may also use occupational tests that are designed specifically to identify in candidates the necessary skills and competences that are required to carry out the work, and psychological tests that identify candidates' personality characteristics, intelligence, values and attitudes that are necessary for the appropriate adoption of the role. The job interview, which was once the central feature of the selection process, still has an important part to play, but the use of more sophisticated techniques has moderated its significance.

Traditional methods

All of this is not to say that traditional methods of selecting new employees have been completely abandoned. Most small organisations still have the interview as the main, and in many cases the only, selection method. Even in medium-sized organisations, traditional methods, in which the interview is the central feature, are still widely used.

Factors influencing the modern approach

Beaumont (1993) identifies three key issues that have increased the importance of the selection decision. First, the demographic changes in the labour market are reflected in the groups of job applicants and this has placed increased importance on fairness and equality in selection. Second, the demand for a multiskilled and flexible workforce and an increased emphasis on teamworking have meant that selection decisions are concerned more with behaviour and attitudes than with matching individuals to job requirements. Third, the emphasis between corporate strategy and people management has led to the notion of strategic selection, that is, a system that links selection processes and outcomes to organisational goals and aims to match the flow of people to emerging business strategies.

Selection policy

This is part of the organisation's overall employment policy, and should state how the organisation intends to go about the selection of new staff. The policy statement should relate the selection systems directly to the achievement of the organisation's aim to achieve a competitive advantage. The actual procedures, therefore, should be designed specifically to bring in people with knowledge, skills, competences and attitudes that will enable them to make appropriate contributions towards the achievement of that aim.

Equality and diversity

The policy should also state the approach to selection in relation to ensuring equal opportunities. Organisations vary in their approaches to formulating ethical and legitimate strategies and policies on discrimination. This is an extremely important section of the policy statement and is dealt with at greater length in Chapter 14.

The selection process

Selecting new employees is a critically important task. It is about predicting potential and in-job performance, and the final decisions should be based on data of the highest possible quality. 'People make the place, and people set the pace' (Herriot 1989, p1). 'Continued organizational survival and growth ... depends on attracting and retaining high calibre people, while motivating them to apply their talents for the benefit of the organization' (Cooper and Robertson 1995, p2).

Successful recruitment will have produced applications from qualified and experienced people from whom the best person for the job can be selected. The aim of this section is to review the principal features of the selection process and then to move on to discuss the purposes, principles and standards of selection. The sequence of the total selection procedure includes, first, screening the applications; second, developing a short list of candidates; and third, organising and conducting interviews.

Selection strategy

The selection strategy should be flexible enough to accommodate the selector's needs in respect of the variety of jobs that exist in the organisation. For example, the strategy that might be adopted to select, say, a maintenance engineer will be different from that for selecting a sales representative.

Screening applications

In many organisations this is still carried out manually, but computerised systems are available for use when the response material has been designed for this method. Used mostly by recruitment agencies and where large numbers of application forms are received, the forms can be processed electronically through the use of optical character recognition (OCR) or optical mark recognition (OMR) (see Chapter 5). When screening is carried out systematically, all of the applicants are subject to exactly the same process and are therefore all treated equally (see Figure 6.1).

Producing the 'long' shortlist

After making a list of the basic details of all of the applicants (name and contact details), read through the applications, comparing their contents with the demands of the person

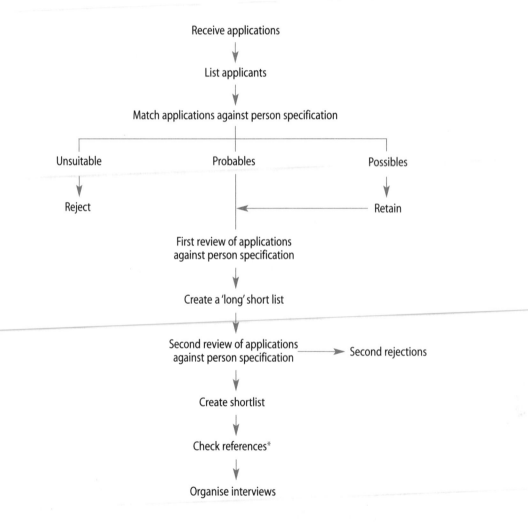

*Important: do not check references from current employers until after a job offer has been made and accepted.

Figure 6.1 Stages in the screening process

specification and sort them into piles under the headings of rejections, possibles and probables. Clearly, if OMR is used the number of applications to be studied is reduced. A
courteously worded letter is then sent to the rejected applicants and the 'long' shortlist is
made up of the remaining possibles and probables.

> If, at the advertising stage, a large number of applications is anticipated, a line may be
> inserted in the advertisement saying that only those who reach the minimum stan-
> dard will receive further correspondence, thus heading off the need to spend time and
> money on written replies.

Shortlisting

The next step is to re-screen the 'long' shortlist, and it is important to involve the line
manager at this stage. He/she will have had a hand in the development of the person specification, and understands the purposes of the job, the meaning and importance of any
technical aspects, and how the job might develop in the future.

The process begins by re-reading through the possibles, studying those that most closely
match the demands of the person specification and deciding, with the line manager, if any of
them could be moved into the probables file. With this task, it is best to err on the side of
caution and the rule is: *if in doubt, retain.* The remaining applications (the probables) are then
studied and finally checked to ensure that they are all genuine probabilities. Those that are
not rejected at that stage make up the shortlist. Rejection letters are then sent to all of the
remaining applicants and interview invitations are sent to the applicants who have been
shortlisted.

Organising interviews

The approach to this is determined by the selection strategy. In this context, the word
'interview' refers to all of the selection process, which may, of course – depending which
strategy has been decided upon – include a medical examination, occupational tests and
assessment centres, which can include job simulation/work sampling and/or group selection methods. The interviews may be held in one-to-one or two-to-one situations, panel
interviews, selection boards or a combination of these models.

Screening interviews

Sometimes the competition for the job is particularly tight, making it difficult to distinguish
clearly between the possibles and probables. One approach to this problem is to hold
preliminary interviews, in order to clarify specific points with the candidates, with the final
interviews following at a later date.

Administrative preparation

The arrangements, including the venues, timing and all who are to be involved, need to be
carefully co-ordinated. The answers to the following questions make a reasonable
administrative checklist:

- *Timing.* Have all relevant dates been set and agreed by everyone involved?
- *Venues.* Has all of the necessary accommodation been booked for:
    i. waiting area?
    ii. medical examinations?
    iii. interviewing?
    iv. selection testing?
- *Reception.* Have the people in reception been given a list of the candidates, the title of the job, the times and dates of their arrival, where they are to wait?
- *Personnel.* Has everyone who will be involved in the process been briefed on the timing and sequence of events?
- *Testing.* If testing is included, will a qualified test administrator be available?
- *Candidates.* Have all shortlisted candidates been advised of the relevant times and dates, and has their availability been confirmed?
- *Special needs.* Have appropriate arrangements been made for candidates, and members of your own staff, who have special needs? This should include access to the premises, car parking and physical assistance where required.
- *Medical examinations.* Have arrangements been made for any medical examinations that the organisation requires candidates to undergo?

Sequence of events

Figure 6.2 shows a recommended sequence of events, from the arrival of candidates to the selection decision itself.

Arrival and waiting

When candidates arrive, they should be shown to the waiting area and told approximately how long they will be waiting, which should not be so long as to give the impression of a

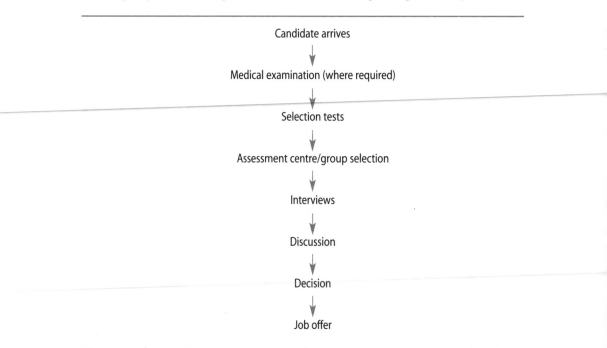

Figure 6.2 The interview process: sequence of events

poorly organised event. This stage can be handled by the receptionist, but some organisations, especially for important jobs, have one of the selection team ready to go out, greet the candidate and make him or her comfortable.

Reasonably comfortable chairs, coffee tables, recent editions of the company magazine, a copy of the latest annual report and accounts and any other relevant literature may be placed in the waiting area. Candidates will be keen to learn as much as they can about the organisation before the interview process starts.

Medical examination

Where a company's own clinician carries out a medical examination, it may be done on the premises shortly after the candidate arrives. If this is the case, the candidate should be informed of it in advance. Some organisations have a policy of getting a medical report on all new employees. Others retain the regular use of a doctor to carry out the examinations, in which case they may take place on the doctor's premises, in advance of the interview day. Yet others ask candidates to provide a written medical history, which is obtainable from their general practitioner and usually paid for by the organisation.

Occupational tests

Properly trained people are needed to carry out selection tests, and suitable accommodation has to be available. Large organisations are usually well provided for in this respect, although some tend to use local hotel accommodation.

Assessment centres

Where assessment centres or group selection methods are used, more time has to be allowed and the process may last more than one day, in which case candidates should be given advance warning of this.

Interviews

This is the final stage that involves all of the candidates. Depending on the interview strategy, sufficient time has to be allowed and the interviews have to be organised so that every candidate is allocated the same amount of time.

Candidate assessment methods

Figure 6.2 shows that in the sequence of events, the objective assessment methods precede the interview. Information about the candidates that is needed by the interviewers is gathered from tests and assessment centres. The following section describes, examines and discusses tests and assessment centres.

Use of occupational tests

If the candidate knows that the interviewer is in possession of the test results from the start of the interview, he/she will be more inclined to be frank about his/her strengths, weaknesses and any other qualities that the tests were designed to elicit.

What are occupational tests?

'Occupational tests' is a portmanteau term covering all types of test that are used in the selection process. Indeed, some writers refer to them as 'selection' tests. In general terms a test has been defined as 'a standardised measure of aptitude, knowledge, ability, personality or performance with fixed rules for administration and scoring' (Reilly and Chao 1982).

Psychometric testing

Definition: psychometrics

Psychometrics is the measurement of psychological attributes, including mental testing such as intelligence and personality, usually in the form of questionnaires. As the term implies, a psychometric test is one in which the outcome is analysed statistically.

Components of intelligence, such as verbal, spatial and numerical ability, are measured through cognitive tests. Personality tests are concerned with identifying a person's disposition to behave in certain ways in certain situations. Cognitive and personality tests are available commercially.

Who designs occupational tests?

Selection tests are not randomly designed by HR people, nor usually by anyone else in the organisation. Ideally, they will have been designed by psychologists employed by a firm of consultants who are experts in the field. The consultancies train their clients in test administration, which includes the use of psychometric techniques, through which the test performance of the candidate is elicited. Tests should be valid, which means that they measure what they purport to measure, and reliable, which means that they produce consistent results.

Why use such methods?

There has been a steady growth in the use of occupational testing in recent years, partly because of the doubt that research evidence has thrown upon interviewing, and partly because the principles and practices of HRM have highlighted the importance of people as the means of achieving a competitive advantage. Such emphasis has caused selectors to use the best means available in order to achieve this. Also, the use of evidence from tests supports the organisation's drive for fairness and equal opportunities, since all applicants for any one particular job undergo exactly the same test, and it is not a test that has been devised by the selectors.

The advantage of using psychometric testing techniques is that they produce corroborative and objective evidence, although an employment decision should never be made on the sole basis of test results. Some objective evidence, however, is better than none, especially if it supports what you subsequently learn about the candidate during the interview.

Who conducts the tests?

The British Psychological Society (BPS) now requires test users to be properly trained and certified. Any organisation considering the use of psychometric measures for selection purposes must ensure that properly trained personnel are available. For organisations that lack properly trained people, there are independent consultants who can provide the appropriate service.

Cultural differences

It is necessary to be careful with occupational tests, especially when putting newly arrived overseas people through psychometric tests. Those undertaking such tests need to have a reasonable command of the English language. Also, the tests may contain elements of culture that people from other parts of the world may fail to understand. Inferences that are drawn from the results of tests through psychometric techniques may not pick up the fact that, for example, someone who has failed a test of 'leadership ability' did so because he/she did not know how to take the test; he/she might well have good leadership potential.

Assessment centres

Definition: assessment centres

An assessment centre is 'a small group of participants who undertake a series of tests and exercises under observation, with a view to the assessment of their skills and competencies, their suitability for particular roles and their potential for development' (Fowler 1992). A number of trained judges and selectors are involved, and applicants are put through a number of 'hoops' designed to detect their strengths and weaknesses (Porteous 1997).

According to Beardwell and Wright (2004), assessment centres have a number of defining characteristics:

- A variety of individual and group assessment techniques are used, at least one of which is work simulation.
- Multiple assessors are used (frequently the ratio is one assessor per two candidates). These assessors should have received training prior to participating in the centre.
- Selection decisions are based on pooled information from assessors and techniques.
- Job analysis is used to identify the behaviours and characteristics to be measured by the assessment centre.

Job simulation

This is an exercise in which the candidate is required to deal with situations which typically represent the job for which he/she has applied. Often, in-tray exercises and role plays are involved.

Work sampling

This involves placing the candidate in the role for a predetermined amount of time and assessing his/her performance. Another example of work sampling is one is which the candidate is asked to carry out a number of the kinds of task that he/she would be required to carry out in the job itself. The candidate is observed throughout the process.

Further sources of information

There are several additional sources of information about candidates:

- *Biodata*, in which the data about the candidate is collected from the application form and/or from a biographical questionnaire. The data relates to criteria such as qualifications and experience. Predictions of work behaviour are based upon past achievements.
- *Peer assessment* is of little use in the assessment of external candidates. It can, however, have some predictive value when assessing internal candidates who are well known to their peers.
- *Graphology* is the study of a person's social profile through his/her handwriting. Its use in selection is based on the idea that handwriting reveals something about the individual's personality which provides the basis for making a prediction about work behaviour.
- *References* may be obtained from several sources including previous employers and academic tutors; also personal character references may be obtained from independent parties. The reliability of references is sometimes questionable; Armstrong (2001, p408), for example, maintains that factual information, such as nature of previous job, time in employment, reason for leaving, salary and academic achievement are essential, but opinions about character and suitability are less reliable. On the question of personal references, he says that they are, of course, entirely useless, since all they prove is that the candidate has at least one or two friends.

Interviewing

The selection interview has been defined as 'a controlled conversation with a purpose' (Torrington *et al* 2002 p242); also as 'the most used and least useful part of the selection process'. Research evidence tends to support this by casting doubt on its predictive power (Arvey and Campion 1982). By their very nature, interviews are subjective, although the need to treat all candidates equally has encouraged selectors to structure interviews, which also goes a little way towards reducing subjectivity. Having said all that, the absence of the interview from the selection process would be regarded as unusual and it is still widely used as a selection method.

Structured and unstructured interviews

It was mentioned above that interviews may be structured or unstructured. Much of the criticism mentioned above is levelled at unstructured interviews, in which the interviewer enters into a free-flowing conversation with the interviewee. Truly, there are some experienced people who can derive a considerable amount of information about a candidate in this way, but where this method is used, it is unlikely that all candidates will be treated in exactly the same way.

Structured interviews may take one of several forms, but they all tend to share common features (Anderson and Shackleton 1993, p72):

- The interaction is standardised as much as possible.
- All candidates are asked the same series of questions.
- Replies are rated by the interviewer on preformatted rating scales.
- Dimensions for rating are derived from critical aspects of on-the-job behaviour.

The following case study provides a practical example of the differences between structured and unstructured interviews.

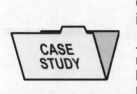

Case study 6: Structured versus unstructured interviews

Jennifer, an HR officer at Solent Toys, and Tony Jackson, the manager of the electronics subsidiary company, have short-listed 10 candidates for the job of electronics engineer. Ideally, they would have preferred about six candidates, but in the second screening process there was little to choose between the final 10. They agreed that they would each interview all 10 in order to create a final shortlist and then compare their choices.

Tony carried out his interviews sitting at his desk in his office with the candidate sitting opposite him. He established a rapport with the candidate by chatting generally, and at the same time, he was trying to gather an impression of what kind of person he had in front of him. Some of his questions were rhetorical, such as, 'You're probably OK at designing interactive toys, aren't you?', to which of course, the answer was 'Yes.' Most of the questions were about the candidates: availability, what they enjoyed about their work, leisure pursuits, etc.

Jennifer's approach was quite different. She began by showing all the candidates around the factory, so that they could see the work situations for themselves. She then used an interview room which had a few comfortable chairs and coffee tables. The atmosphere was relaxed and friendly but businesslike. Jennifer asked every candidate the same set of questions, which were mostly about the job. She asked open questions that began with phrases such as, 'Tell me about …' and 'Why did you decide …?', etc. She had designed a form (see Figure 6.3) on which she graded each candidate's interview performance, and as soon as each candidate left, she completed the form for that person.

When Tony and Jennifer compared their results, they found major differences in their choices. Only two of Tony's top six were in Jennifer's top six. Clearly their strategy had not produced the results they were expecting, and when they discussed this, it emerged that Tony's choices were influenced by the 'types' of people he had interviewed. He attributed importance to their qualifications and the personal impression they gave. Jennifer, on the other hand, had focused on the candidates' knowledge, experience and competences, and her questions were largely about the job.

Discussion of the case study

Clearly, Tony used an unstructured approach to the interview. He focused on the person rather than the job, which meant that each of the 10 candidates had a different interview experience with him. Jennifer, on the other hand, had prepared a structure, and had notes that she had made shortly after each interview, while the candidates' responses were still fresh in her mind. Since Jennifer centred her questions around the demands of the job, the data she had gathered about each candidate was objective and enabled her to predict each candidate's likely performance in the job.

Candidate name			Position			
Grade			Department			
Criteria	Poor	Fair	Adequate	Good	Excellent	Comments
Qualifications						
Experience						
Previous relevant training						
Education						
Knowledge and skills						
Appearance (where relevant)						
General rating						

Figure 6.3 Candidate's interview performance form

If you prepare a separate form in respect of each candidate, you can record any new information that came to light during the interview, and jot something down that will enable you to remember which candidate is which – some distinctive feature or something they were wearing. When you have interviewed 10 candidates in a row, it is difficult to recall who said what. Remember you are going to have a discussion with your interviewing colleagues afterwards, and you will want to make a sensible and meaningful contribution.

Using the application form

Some interviewers recommend basing the interview structure on the contents of the application form, so that the form acts as a kind of checklist. This is not always a good idea: the completed application form contains factual information, but it may also include information that the applicant wished to present to you. The structure of the interview, however, should be planned by those who are going to conduct it. In this respect, it is useful to scrutinise each application at the planning stage.

The aims of the interview

The main aim of the interview is to select the best person for the job, which is achieved through predicting the in-job performance of each candidate. To aid this objective, the interviewer elicits information that supplements the information that was gathered from tests, other assessment methods and references (if they are available at that stage), and of course, the factual information on the application form.

Types of interview

Interviews may be held as one-to-one, two-to-one or panel interviews. Where there are several interviewers, the person who takes the lead should be a good interpersonal communicator, have a sound knowledge of the job for which the selection is being made, and be capable of controlling the track of the interview and of establishing and maintaining a healthy rapport with the interviewee throughout.

Initial exchanges

At the outset, you will know more about the candidate than he or she knows about you or the company, and it is a good idea to redress this imbalance right away. Your manner when you are doing this should help to put the candidate at ease. A nervous interviewee will give you less information about him or herself than will one who is relaxed. From that point on, the interviewee should do most of the talking. Between 70:30 and 80:20 per cent is the recommended balance; the longer you talk, the more you will deprive the candidate of the opportunity to tell you things about him or herself.

Questioning techniques

How you ask a question is every bit as important as what you ask. Questions should be framed in a way that invites the candidate to reply in full. Questions may be closed, open or standard-revealing. A closed question is one that invites a short but informative answer: question: 'How old are you?' answer: '25'. Some writers advise against the use of closed questions, but they can be useful, especially at the beginning of an interview when trying to establish a rapport, the answers usually being easy and non-contentious. Open questions are those that begin with 'Why' or 'What do you think of …?' Such questions should not be too long or convoluted, and you should ensure that there is only one question in there. If you ask more than one question in a single statement, you will only get an answer to the last one. Here is an example of the difference between open and closed questions:

Open version: **'Why do you enjoy working in business development?'**

Closed version: **'So you enjoy working in business development?'**

Comment: the answer to the open version allows the candidate to explain the outcomes of the work and why they are enjoyable, while the answer to the closed version is 'Yes.'

The more relevant information you have about the candidates, the more able you will be to make a good-quality selection decision.

Standard-revealing questions

These are questions which, because of the way they are phrased, contain the answer. By asking such questions, one risks revealing the required standard. For example, a question to a potential shop floor worker might be, 'Could you process 100 of these a day?' When you mention a figure, the interviewee will take that as the standard and will, of course, say 'Yes.' The question should have been, 'How many of these could you process in a day?'

The job for which you are interviewing might be one that demands a special quality, which could be difficult to tease out at an interview. If we take leadership as an example, how do you assess an individual's leadership skills at an interview? If an assessment centre has been used as part of the selection process, the candidate will have been through an appropriate test; otherwise, you have to study the levels and responsibilities held previously and question the person about them. If the questions are phrased appropriately the answers could reveal incidents in which the candidate was involved that required good leadership.

Questioning and equal opportunities

When questioning candidates always bear in mind that their domestic situation and personal circumstances have no bearing on the case for employment. If the recruitment process has been handled according to good practice, the shortlisted candidates will only have proceeded with their applications if they are sure they could meet the demands of the job. One approach is to ensure that all questions relate directly to the job, its technicalities, duties, responsibilities and the performance required.

Closing the interview

When you have got all the information you need, the interview is almost at its end. It is then that you should give interviewees the opportunity to make any points or ask questions. Candidates may have studied the job requirements and come to the interview hoping to put across several points which they feel are in their favour. During the course of the interview, they will have taken any opportunities that arose to express these points, but there may be something they wish to say that they feel would complete their case for being appointed.

Making the decision

Selection decisions are seldom made by just one person sitting alone, and while HR people do contribute with information and legal guidance, they should make such decisions only if the position is in the HR department.

The objective is to select the best person for the job, and the decision has to be made fairly and legally. To achieve this, you have to be sure that all of the candidates received exactly the same treatment, that the selection process (including any selection tests) was structured in the same way for everyone, and that they all received an equal opportunity to make a case.

The whole process has to be fair, and seen to be fair. A structured decision-making process that focuses upon how each of the candidates rated throughout the selection process, in which evidence from tests and interviews is seriously considered, has the hallmarks of a fair system. Notes can be compared and agreements reached about the performance of each individual. One suggestion is to develop a *candidate ranking form* (see Figure 6.4) on the basis of the person specification, on which each candidate may be graded according to his or her performance in the interview and on any tests that were carried out.

In Figure 6.4, the left-hand column indicates the seven most important criteria for selection. The criteria are taken from the person specification and entered on the form in their order of

Candidate name:			Interviewed for (job title):		
Criteria	Assessment				
	1	2	3	4	5
1 Most important	Low				High
2					
3					
4					
5					
6					
7 Least important					

Figure 6.4 Candidate ranking form

importance. During the interview, prearranged questions that relate to the criteria are asked and the interviewee is scored according to his or her responses. Obviously, the best performers would be candidates who scored well in the top right-hand area: that is to say, people who scored highly against the most important criteria.

Having borne in mind the demands of fairness, legality and the provision of equal opportunities, it is up to the decision-makers to select the candidate they think is the best person for the job. This is a difficult decision to make, not least because the very idea of selecting just one person makes the whole process discriminatory.

Making an offer of employment

An offer of employment is usually made 'subject to satisfactory references'. The candidate's permission to take up references should be obtained, especially since one will be from the current employer (if any). If there is more than one possible choice, it is wise to wait until the offer has been accepted in writing, before communicating the final decision to the rest of the candidates.

Making internal appointments

Internal appointments should be handled sensitively, especially in terms of equal opportunities. Minority groups often feel that they would not be considered for promotion and that making an application might even put their current position in jeopardy, depending of course on the culture of the organisation. The straightforward way through this situation is to encourage minorities to apply. This is not a plug for positive discrimination – quite the reverse, since the objective is still to appoint the best person for the job. The point here is that to some selectors, the concept of equal opportunity seems less relevant when internal appointments are being made.

Self-test questions

1. What are the similarities and differences between traditional and modern approaches to selection?
2. Why is there an emphasis on the importance of selecting new employees?
3. What are the principal purposes of selection?
4. What factors have influenced changes in selection systems?
5. Why is it good practice to structure a selection interview?
6. What are the main disadvantages of carrying out unstructured interviews?
7. What do you think has caused the increase in the use of selection tests?
8. How would you define an assessment centre?
9. What is the difference between job simulation and work sampling?
10. Why are minority group members sometimes reluctant to respond to internal job advertisements?

Induction and retention

CHAPTER 7

Learning objectives

After studying this chapter you should understand:

- the purposes of induction and the variety of approaches that are used in today's organisations

- the typical causes of the induction crisis and the steps that may be taken to prevent it

- the importance of retaining key employees

- the measures that may be put into action to achieve effective retention and be able to contribute to the retention plan.

Introduction

The purpose of this chapter is to discuss, first, the systematic induction of new employees into the organisation after they have been appointed in their positions. Second, retention is explained and discussed. Retention plans are designed to encourage people, especially key employees, to remain with the organisation.

In most books on HR, induction is found in a chapter on 'recruitment and selection' or 'employee development', and retention is found in a chapter on 'human resource planning'. The approach in this chapter, however, relates to the *planning* of induction and retention, and to the *activities* involved, which are not triggered until *after* the new member of staff has started work. Hence this topic follows the chapters on HR planning and recruitment and selection. Staff induction and retention are related in the sense that if a person is going to leave the organisation, he/she will probably do so within the first year of employment. The likelihood of this is reduced if the induction of the new employee is handled appropriately.

Induction

Some writers say that induction commences before the person's first day at work and that in fact it generally starts as part of the recruitment and selection process (Foot and Hook 1999, p134). Alternatively, it may start with the person's impression of the organisation from the recruitment advertisement. If the person then applies for the job and the correspondence starts to flow, he/she then internalises an impression of the style of the organisation and the kind of employer it might be. Also, an applicant will begin to notice elements of the organisation's external publicity, and all of these events can be regarded as the initial stages of the induction process.

Definition: induction

Induction is a process through which new employees, prefer-ably on joining, are introduced to the organisation in the broad context; its culture, rules and procedures; then in the local context where they meet their new work colleagues.

The purpose of induction

The primary purpose of induction is to make the new employee effective in the job and able to meet the required performance standards as soon as possible after joining. Linda Maund defines induction as:

> **The period of time when a new entrant to an organisation makes initial contact with the organisation until s/he has reached the desired standard of performance.**
>
> **(Maund 2001, p182)**

An individual's best performance will not emerge, however, until he/she has attained a sense of direction and identity in the place and settled into his or her job. Correctly handled, the induction process will help the individual to become effective more quickly.

The importance of induction

Attitudes towards induction differ widely from one organisation to another. While some regard it as relatively unimportant, ('You'll soon get the hang of things around here'), others are prepared to invest resources in ensuring that the new employee's first experience of the organisation is informative, pleasant and useful. How the organisation handles the process, therefore, is determined by the level of resources that are allocated to it and the level of expertise available to carry it out.

It has to be borne in mind that when people first come into the organisation to work, they will be keen to gather as much information about the place as possible; they go through the process of *socialisation* (see below). This is a critically important stage, since in the absence of a formal system of induction, the new employee will learn about the organisation by default. His/her work colleagues will present their own interpretations of 'the way things are around here', which do not always match the facts or the culture that the organisation is trying to achieve.

Indications that your induction system is successful and effective include:

- new employees taking little time to become effective in their jobs
- an increase in the rate at which employees adapt to their surroundings
- good interpersonal relations between new and longer serving employees
- a reduction in staff turnover, thus saving on finance and disruption
- a satisfactory staff retention rate and stability index.

Definition: socialisation

Socialisation is the process through which individuals become familiar with their environment and learn about the kind of behaviour that is expected of them. It is experienced in our early developmental years, and what we learn then stays with us for the rest of our lives. When we enter an organisation, we go through it all again. This time it is a kind of micro-socialisation, which involves learning a culture which is different from that of the outside world and different from that of any other organisation.

The induction crisis

As the new employee begins to get to know the job and the organisation, there may be second thoughts about the decision to join, and it is at this stage that he or she may decide to leave. The strength of these feelings depends on the degree to which the job and the organisation match up to the new employee's expectations. Additionally, the decision to stay or leave may be determined by other factors, such as pay, working time and the possibility of finding another job.

If the strength of the crisis is not enough to justify leaving, the person may decide to 'put up with it for now', and hope that things will improve. In this case a period of *accommodation* (see below) may follow, in which he/she begins to adjust. During this period, his/her perceptions may modify and expectations are rationalised. Inside the first year there may be further minor crises, but if the person stays for more than a year, then he/she will usually stay for more than two.

Definition: accommodation

In the context of a new experience, accommodation is the process in which individuals alter their perception of a situation so that the original perception is replaced by the new one. People do this when they discover that things are not what they thought they would be. For example, if a job does not in fact match up to the job description and to what others have told him or her about it, the person taking the job has to re-establish his or her perception of it. Naturally, this will also change the person's attitude towards it.

Influential factors

If the individual has replaced a previous job holder, the expectations of others are influenced by the behaviour of the previous incumbent, with whom they were familiar, compared with the behaviour of the new person. This can influence the strength of a crisis, since his or her co-workers may not approve of the different behavioural style of the new employee, and this will be communicated verbally and non-verbally.

Alternatively, it might be that there is a discrepancy between what the individual was told about the job and the actual job situation. Clearly, if this happens, there may be something amiss with the job description and the person specification. If, however, those documents are correct, it may be that the selectors misunderstood the nature of the job. If this becomes a feature of the induction of several new employees, then the recruitment and selection processes need to be reviewed and possibly modified.

Approaches to induction

The differences in senior managers' attitudes to induction determine the level of resources that they are prepared to invest in it. This varies from zero to substantial, and the quality and effectiveness of systems vary accordingly. Well-run organisations have several induction systems which are relevant to each type and level of employee in terms of the jobs they do and their level of seniority. Some systems, therefore, are more complex and longer in duration than others. These are some examples:

- *In writing*, in which the new employee is presented with an *induction pack*. This may include a copy of the annual report and accounts, a copy of the corporate structure, a brief history of the organisation and something about its plans for the future, a map of the site indicating the locations of the car parks, the staff canteen and any other facilities, the 'company handbook' containing the terms and conditions of employment and the disciplinary and grievance procedures.
- *Walk'n' talk*, in which the new employee is shown around the site and is given explanations about each work activity on the way. Towards the end of the tour the department in which he/she will work is visited and a more detailed explanation of what happens is given. This is a good time to take the opportunity to introduce the new employee to the staff.
- *Induction training*. This is the most successful and effective form of induction, and a large number of organisations have adopted it. The approach takes the form of a number of training sessions, each of which deals with a particular subject and is usually delivered by a person who specialises in that subject. The duration of the training sessions varies, and sometimes they are staggered across a number of days or even weeks, depending on the amount and complexity of the information to be delivered.

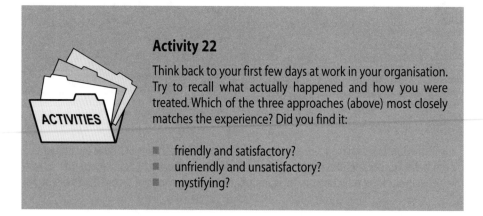

Activity 22

Think back to your first few days at work in your organisation. Try to recall what actually happened and how you were treated. Which of the three approaches (above) most closely matches the experience? Did you find it:

- friendly and satisfactory?
- unfriendly and unsatisfactory?
- mystifying?

ACTIVITIES

Stages of induction

People may be inducted at two main levels, corporate and departmental. First, they will be keen to learn about the organisation as a whole, and second, they will want to see their place of work, meet their new work colleagues and learn something about the job itself.

Initial briefing

The HR practitioner, who is usually the person who receives new employees, will explain the main points, which include the kind of information that was in the pack referred to above, although using a so-called 'induction pack' and nothing else is not a very effective method. At this stage, the opportunity should be taken to present a favourable picture of the organisation, especially in terms of its employment policies. A detailed briefing about the organisation is not normally offered at this stage.

Many new employees are a little nervous when they first enter the organisation, and it could be a waste of time to fill them in on every last detail. They will probably suffer from overload, and therefore not remember half of what you tell them.

After the initial briefing:

> **new employees should be taken to their place of work and introduced to their manager or team leader for the departmental induction programme. Alternatively, they may go straight to a training school and join the department later.**
>
> **(Armstrong 1999)**

Induction training

Induction is best handled through training. It is possible to overload people with information, and if you send them home at the end of their first day carrying an armful of documents, they 'may get down to reading them one day' and some of the information is critical. On the other hand, if the information is put across in a training environment, clearly and in a controlled way, the person will absorb and internalise it more easily, and it is more likely to 'stick'.

Formal training course

New key specialists and managers are usually inducted on a one-to-one basis and do not normally undergo an 'induction training course' as such. The training school, however, will accommodate several new employees who are due to work in different departments at roughly equal levels. In most cases the course will be led by an experienced HR practitioner, although some of the sessions will include inputs from managers and specialists from relevant departments.

Methods and media

If the amount of information to be delivered justifies it, the course may consist of a number of discrete sessions livened up with a variety of media, such as seminars, PowerPoint, videos and other visual aids. In this way, each subject can be given its own position in the programme and the main points can be explained and discussed.

Purpose

The purpose is to provide the inductee with a thorough understanding of the organisation, its mission, history, products, current situation and its plans for the future. A complete corporate picture will include details of the organisation's main policies, its status in the industry, photographs and thumbnail biographies of the members of the board and other senior managers, along with charts indicating the organisational, management and workforce structures.

Inducting minority groups

Care needs to be taken over inducting employees who are new to this country. While there are some very knowledgeable and skilled people arriving here, the English language is not always the best part of their repertoire. Furthermore, the culture in which they were originally socialised will have little meaning here. In many cases, they have a mountain to climb. They have to settle into the job, learn a new language, be socialised into the local community and the organisational culture; and all of this learning takes place concurrently and in strange surroundings.

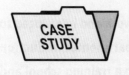

Case study 7: Positive action

Michael Wynne is the HR manager of Classic Kitchens Ltd (CKL), a medium-sized manufacturing company based in north-west England; the company employs 2500 people. CKL regards itself as a manufacturer of top-quality products and every effort is made to impress potential purchasers with the classic image.

Michael has noticed that in recent years many of the new employees from minority groups, especially ethnic minorities, have failed to be selected for promotion, despite the fact that it was clear they possessed the knowledge and practical skills required for the higher positions.. Michael is very concerned since research within the company has revealed that the proportion of immigrant workers in middle and senior positions falls short of a match with non-minority groups.

Liz Forsythe, who leads the HR planning function, has also noticed the trend ,and she can see that if it continues, it is going to be very difficult to satisfy the HR demand for managers and supervisors in forthcoming years. She knows that the skills that are required do exist within the current workforce, and cannot understand why such a large number of promotion candidates have failed. Liz and Michael discussed the situation and decided to commission a study to find out where the problem lies.

The resulting report pinpointed the promotion selection policy as a problem area. For the past two years, CKL has been using psychometric tests as part of the selection process, and James Willis, the consultant who carried out the study and produced the report, pointed out that CKL had been discriminating against new immigrants by placing them at a disadvantage. James went on to explain that new immigrants do not know how conduct themselves at, for example, assessment centres, nor do they know how to take tests.

Question: What can CKL do to ensure a supply of the right people with the required knowledge and skills? (see below).

What organisations can do

According to the Commission for Racial Equality (CRE), organisations can help in the following ways:

- review recruitment, selection, promotion and training procedures regularly
- draw up clear and justifiable job criteria which are demonstrably objective and job-related
- offer pre-employment training, where appropriate, to prepare potential job applicants for selection tests and interviews
- consider positive action training (see below) to help ethnic minority employees to apply for jobs in areas where they are under-represented.

Legal point 4: positive action

This is a concept that should not be confused with *positive discrimination*, which means favouring members of a particular group at the point of selection for a job. Positive discrimination is unlawful in the UK. *Positive action* means that it is lawful to take measures designed to encourage members of under-represented groups to apply for a job, for example. In all cases, however, selection must be made on merit alone.

Positive action training

Where particular racial groups have been under-represented in particular work at any time in the past 12 months, the Race Relations Act 1976 (RRA76) allows positive action measures to be taken in order to:

- *encourage applications* from an under-represented group for vacancies in particular work
- *provide training* in order to help to fit members of an under-represented group for the particular work.

Pause for thought

Clearly, the principles and actions recommended by the CRE apply not only to tests and interviews used for promotion but also to the initial selection process.

Duration of induction programmes

Induction programmes vary in their complexity and duration. There are programmes that last no more than a day and yet are very effective. Others may last several days, or even weeks, although a new employee would benefit from no more than one day during his or her first week. There is no set pattern or universal blueprint for an induction programme; the content and process of it is determined by the varying needs of new employees and the complexities of different organisations.

Terms and conditions of employment

The induction training environment is an ideal place in which to provide new employees with a copy of the particulars of the terms and conditions of employment. It is advisable to make this a discrete event, rather than issue it along with a sheaf of other documents such as an induction pack, because often new employees just accept the pack and put it to one side as 'something they'll get down to reading another time'.

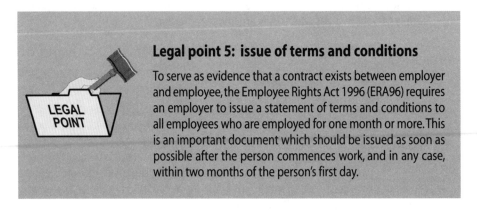

Legal point 5: issue of terms and conditions

To serve as evidence that a contract exists between employer and employee, the Employee Rights Act 1996 (ERA96) requires an employer to issue a statement of terms and conditions to all employees who are employed for one month or more. This is an important document which should be issued as soon as possible after the person commences work, and in any case, within two months of the person's first day.

LEGAL POINT

The company handbook

All organisations have rules of behaviour which are written down in the forms of procedures and regulations. In most organisations these are presented in the *company handbook*. A copy of the company handbook and any other documents that are relevant to the organisation's regulations should be given to all new employees as part of their induction. The rules relate to general behaviour in the workplace, and copies of the disciplinary and grievance procedures are usually included in the handbook. The contents of the handbook may also include details of:

- the payment systems, including the frequency of payment and the deductions that are made, eg tax, NHS contributions
- sickness absence procedure
- promotion policy
- discrimination and equal opportunities policy
- health and safety policy
- education and training policy
- provisions for employees' well-being
- available benefits and facilities
- trade union and joint consultation arrangements.

Activity 23

Does your employer issue a handbook? If so, read through it and see how its contents compare with the above list. What could happen in the organisation that would make you turn to the handbook for information?

ACTIVITIES

Departmental induction

When all of the main points have been explained and any questions answered in the companywide context, the new employees are moved on to *departmental induction*, which is more directly concerned with the new employee's role in his/her immediate work area. Departmental induction is concerned with the technicalities and other details of the job itself; in fact the new employee's expectations are founded upon the job description and person specification. It is, however, a less formal approach than corporate induction since the idea is to settle the new employee into the place and make him/her feel welcome.

A new entrant will be primarily interested in the departmental environment, including the locations of the refreshment facilities, doors etc, the person for whom he/she will be working (the immediate boss and the departmental manager), new work colleagues, the atmosphere in the place and the location of his/her work station. It is normal to show the person around the place and introduce everyone. So far as the job is concerned the important information will come from the departmental manager and the person's section/team leader. It is important for the departmental manager to be present during this stage; he/she needs to be seen as an active colleague, rather than an 'ivory tower' boss.

Once the new employee becomes accustomed to the place, the job can be explained in terms of how it contributes to the department's objectives. The should be done in a way that arouses the person's interest, not only in the job itself, but also in the department and the organisation as a whole. The level of involvement and enthusiasm of whoever is providing the information will be communicated verbally and non-verbally to the newcomer, and this should have a motivating effect. The information should include details of the expected performance standards and career prospects.

Induction interviews

Induction interviews should be given to all employees taking up jobs for the first time, whether from inside or outside the organisation (Tyson and York 1996). When people start a new job they may feel insecure and anxious about an unknown future.

In the training school and at departmental level, they may have seen or heard something about which they feel uncertain or simply do not understand, and an interview will provide them with the opportunity to have their questions answered. The interviews are a kind of 'wash up' session after experiencing the corporate and departmental components, during which they will have taken in a considerable amount of new information.

The interviews are carried out by the HR practitioner and the line manager or team leader.

Tyson and York go on to say that the main purposes of the interview are to provide reassurance and to develop positive attitudes, confidence and motivation. Induction interviews should cover the following points:

- the job description and person specification so that job holders fully understand what is required of them
- how the job relates to the work and purposes of the group and the organisation as a whole
- all the attendant circumstances of the job, eg pay, conditions, welfare, etc
- the performance appraisal system and what part the job holder will be required to play
- an assessment of any training and development needs that require immediate action
- general plans for training and development
- career prospects.
  (adapted from Tyson and York 1996)

Buddy system

When the new person actually starts to work on the job itself, the section or team leader should introduce him/her to a 'buddy', someone to whom the individual can relate and who will act as a kind of guide. Alan Fowler suggests that:

> **there is much to be said for these initial guides to be people who have not been long with the organization. As relative newcomers, they are likely to remember all the small points that were a source of worry to them when they started work, and so help new employees to settle in quickly.**
>
> **(Fowler 1966)**

Retention and why people work

According to Alan Price, 'people work because in most cases they have to. Few of us have the private resources needed to maintain a satisfactory lifestyle without an income from employment' (Price 1997). On the other hand, people who are not in a desperate financial state will pick and choose what they do for a living.

Socialisation

Other theorists will say that people are drawn into work because as they develop socially, they experience a psychosocial transition from infancy, through adolescence into adulthood. When they are on this path they observe the pattern of human activity that accompanies each stage. After early infancy, they go to school and college. In adolescence, they either start work or go to university hoping to improve their prospects of 'getting a good job', or to study the subject that they believe is their vocational calling. Finally, they take up employment.

This is the pattern of the western world, and if people deviate from the accepted path by not wishing to work, they risk being stigmatised as layabouts. Some people, therefore, go to work because it is expected of them and because employment carries status in that if an employer is prepared to pay for their knowledge and skills, they are a worthwhile person.

Money

According to Goldthorpe (1968), however, most manual workers are motivated to work by money and other tangible rewards. In other words, they see it as the means by which they are able to sustain, and possibly improve, a particular lifestyle, which means that they value the ability to spend money more highly than any psychological involvement in the work they actually do.

Clearly, there are many factors that have to be taken into account when trying to understand why people make particular employment choices. For example, those who have a 'vocational calling' will occupy positions in the church, nursing and perhaps overseas aid, despite the comparatively low rewards for doing so. Alternatively, there are vocational callings that are well rewarded, such as medical or legal practice.

So what is work?

According to Arendt (1958), the distinction between work and labour is that the latter is an effort to satisfy the immediate needs of the body whereas work produces items of lasting use and is a source of satisfaction itself. For some people, however, work is something to be avoided; for others it is the main source of pleasure in their lives. Those to whom it is a source of pleasure are usually good at something, and that 'something' may well be what you are looking for in terms of knowledge and skills.

Pause for thought

Why would you go to work? If you are on a degree or professional course, why did you choose that particular subject? Are you drawn to it as an occupation you think you are likely to enjoy? Or do you have a vocational calling?

Retaining staff

In the light of what is said above, it is clear that success in bringing in and retaining the right people is determined not only by ensuring that they are indeed the 'right' people in terms of knowledge and skills, but additionally by their attitudes to work. The time, money and other resources spent on recruiting, selecting and inducting the right people is only a worthwhile investment if they remain with the organisation in the medium to long term. An appropriate psychological test should provide indications of the individual's attitude to work.

Retention became an important issue when organisations recognised that human resources, and in particular key specialists, are vital to the success of the business, and that they are also hard to find and sometimes hard to keep. Manfred Kets de Fries (cited in Williams 2000, p28) states that 'today's high performers are like frogs in a wheelbarrow: they can jump out at any time'. The message from this is clear: organisations that wish to retain their core staff should take positive steps to ensure that they do.

According to Linda Maund:

> **Many organisations are of the opinion that, once employed, individuals will remain with them unquestioningly believing that a wage or salary secures their loyalty and long service. However, the strategy involved in recruiting new employees should be progressed into plans for their retention, and failure to do so is likely to result in demotivated staff and a high labour turnover.**
>
> **(Maund 2001, p192)**

Retention plan

An increasing number of organisations have heeded this message (or have been bitten by experience!), and organisations that succeed in keeping their key staff have a retention plan which is based upon the results of the staff turnover analysis. Retention measures can include some or all of the following (Bevan 1997, IDS 2000):

- *Pay and benefits*: competitive rates of pay, deferred compensation (eg share options, generous pension scheme), retention bonuses, flexible benefits, benefits package that improves with service.
- *Recruitment and selection*: set appropriate standards, match people to posts, provide an accurate picture of the job.
- *Training and development*: good induction processes, provision of development opportunities to meet the needs of the individual and the organisation, structured career paths.
- *Job design*: provision of interesting work, as much autonomy and teamworking as possible, opportunities for flexible working to meet the needs of the individual.
- *Management*: ensure managers and supervisors have the skills to manage effectively.

Buckingham (2000) argues that employees are more likely to remain with an organisation if they believe that their manager shows interest and concern for them, if they know what is expected of them, if they are given a role that fits their capabilities, and if they receive regular positive feedback and recognition. 'Put simply, people leave managers, not companies' (p45). However, he also suggests that 'most organisations currently devote far fewer resources to this level of management than they do to high-fliers' (p46) (cited in Beardwell *et al* 2004, p176).

Retention and HRM

While positive retention planning has become an integral part of HR strategy, the activities that are implied by typical retention plans in organisations that have adopted the principles and practices of HRM are aimed largely at key staff. Peripheral workers on the other hand are not treated so generously. The underlying rationale here appears to be that 'There is a talent war going on out there and if we're lucky enough to get the high-fliers, then we should make every effort to keep them. We can pick up the rest whenever we need them.'

This is a pragmatic and practical view, and few would argue with the fact that all organisations need highly talented staff at the core, but it does create a visible class system between and among employees. A complete retention plan should include arrangements for ensuring the retention of peripheral staff, since a high turnover in any section of the organisation is costly and counter-productive. It is costly in terms of finding replacements for peripheral staff – which could become a serious problem if peripheral staff are made to feel inferior – and it is counter-productive since continuity is vital if productivity is to be maintained. Additionally, care needs to be taken to ensure that equality, fairness and compliance with the law are maintained when benefits and facilities are on the retention agenda.

Summary

Induction

The purpose of induction is to make the new employee effective in the job as soon as possible. New employees are in a learning situation as soon as they join: they need to attain a sense of identity in the place and a perception of their role. They need to understand the organisational and departmental cultures and the expectations that others have of them. Some employees experience an 'induction crisis', which occurs shortly after joining, and happens as a result of the job failing to match up to expectations. An induction crisis may make someone decide to leave. An effective induction system is handled through training, and contains corporate and departmental induction processes. Indications of a successful induction programme are:

- new employees quickly becoming effective in their jobs
- an increase in the rate at which employees adapt to their surroundings
- good interpersonal relations between new and longer serving employees
- a reduction in staff turnover
- a satisfactory staff retention rate.

Retention

Retention became an important issue when organisations realised that the success of the organisation depended on its ability to attract and retain people who were capable of making contributions that would give it a competitive advantage. In order to achieve this, organisations formulate a *retention plan*, the components of which are designed to encourage such people to remain with the organisation.

People are more likely to remain with the organisation if:

- they believe that their manager shows interest and concern for them
- they know what is expected of them
- they are given a role that fits their capabilities
- they receive regular positive feedback and recognition; 'people leave managers, not companies'.

Retention plans seem to be aimed largely at keeping key staff, and peripheral staff are not treated so generously. There is, however, a business case for the retention plan to include peripheral staff. If it is evident that there is a visible distinction between core and peripheral staff, we should not be surprised to see the leaving rate increase among peripheral staff.

Self-test questions

1. What are the main purposes of induction?
2. When does induction begin?
3. What do socialisation and accommodation mean in the context of induction?
4. What is meant by the 'induction crisis'?
5. How would you advise an organisation that wishes to reduce the prospect of induction crises?
6. What are the main purposes of the induction interview?
7. What are the main elements that should make up an effective induction programme? Write up a brief description of each.
8. What are the two main levels at which new employees are inducted?
9. Why may new immigrants perform poorly when undertaking psychometric tests?
10. What is the difference between 'positive action' and 'positive discrimination'?
11. What would you expect to find in a company handbook?
12. How are induction and retention related?
13. If a key employee began to experience an induction crisis, what steps would you take first, to encourage the person to remain with the organisation and second, to ensure that induction crises do not appear frequently?
14. What arrangements would you make to identify an individual's attitude to work, and why would you do this?
15. Why do people work?
16. What has made staff retention an important issue in recent years?
17. What are the factors that provide the basis for a retention plan?
18. What measures would you expect to find in a retention plan?
19. What grounds does Buckingham have for saying that 'people leave managers, not companies'?
20. Why should a retention plan include arrangements for ensuring the retention of peripheral staff?

People and performance

Learning

Learning objectives

After studying this chapter you should:

- understand the strategic importance of learning

- understand who benefits from learning

- be able to define learning

- understand the principles of learning

- understand the different ways in which people learn

- be able to identify your own learning style

- start thinking about planning your career.

Introduction

The purposes of this chapter are first, to discuss the strategic importance of learning; second, to examine ways in which the organisation and the individual may benefit from learning; and third, to define and explain learning. This is followed by a discussion of the principles of learning and an examination of some early and more recent theories. Finally, we consider learning styles and explain how you can identify your own way of learning.

The strategic importance of learning

Nobody would argue with the view that the need for organisations to stay ahead of the game in the midst of fierce global competition has brought the importance of learning and development to the forefront of strategic thinking. Several authorities have commented on this. For example, the president of the Chartered Institute of Personnel and Development (CIPD) in the 2000 annual report said, 'People are our only source of differentiation and sustainable competitive advantage' (Beattie 2002). The director general of the CIPD maintains that: 'Staff management and development will become the primary weapon available to managers to generate success' (Rana 2000b).

The government has also demonstrated its belief in the importance of learning and development with a series of initiatives. In 2001 training and enterprise councils (TECs) were superseded by learning and skills councils (LSCs), which exist to make England better skilled and more competitive. 'We have a single goal: to improve the skills of England's young people and adults to make sure we have a workforce that is of world-class standards' (www.lsc.gov.uk). All of this underlines the importance of learning, and there are clear implications for the individual employee. (*Note*: we return to government involvement in Chapter 9.)

Human capital and knowledge management

If everybody did exactly what was in their job descriptions and nothing more, you would never get anything done.

Key concept 8: human capital

Human capital includes the pre-specified sets of knowledge and competences that are required for particular jobs, but it also includes the higher performance standards that people achieve through learning. It includes the flexibility of individual employees that turns them into valuable assets when, through learning, they find themselves able to make high-performance contributions to the organisation.

The intangible nature of the employee's willingness to be flexible and put in a high performance makes knowledge a difficult commodity to identify precisely, and therefore to manage. The employee's willingness is intangible because it is a product of the individual's attitude to the work, and to the nature of the job and the organisation. It is this extra human quality that gives the organisation its competitive advantage.

Knowledge adds value to the organisation, and several academics have attempted to turn learning into a principal organisational discipline to be regarded as an essential ingredient for success. Such exhortations, however, have not met with universal acceptance, which may be because of senior managerial attitudes to the steps that have to be taken in the organisation in order to push learning up the agenda.

Mayo (1998), for example, defines knowledge management as a set of processes:

- managing the generation of new knowledge through learning
- capturing knowledge and experience
- sharing, collaborating and communicating
- organising information for easy access
- using and building on what is known.

Commenting on the concept of the *learning organisation* (see Chapter 9), Len Holden suggests that 'like most large scale initiatives, implementation of such systems requires a massive change of attitudes in most organisations that is not always easy to achieve' (Holden 2004).

The principles of learning

This purpose of this section is to define, explain and discuss learning. While the theoretical ideas underlying learning were proposed with educational institutions in mind, the ultimate aim here is for you to develop an understanding of the situations, methods and media that cause learning to take place in organisations.

Definition: learning

Learning takes place when an individual has understood and internalised new information and/or has developed a new skill as a result of an experience. Evidence that learning has taken place may be inferred from a change in the individual's behaviour. Learning is an active process which may occur socially, systematically or experientially.

Self-learning

'All development is self development' (Drucker 1977). In this context, Drucker was saying that people can teach, train and coach you, but nobody can learn for you. Learning is a 'do-it-yourself' activity. It is important here because it forms the basis for education, training and development, and now that 'jobs for life' no longer exist, learning, including self-learning, sustains the individual's employability. Information technology facilitates self-learning as never before, since it has broadened and deepened the available range of methods and media through which learning may take place (see Chapter 9).

At work today, the development of *competence* (see Glossary) is a critical factor; your employability depends on it. You need to be aware that traditional ways of working are dying out while new ways are continually evolving, and these demand more than just competence: they require new knowledge and skills, creativity, flexibility and commitment on your part. From the above definition we can see that learning may take place socially, systematically or experientially.

Social learning

Learning takes place during socialisation (see Chapter 7). It is part of our natural development. We learn to conform to societal, group and family norms by observing and copying the behaviour of others and through a system of reward and punishment. If, for example, in the early stages of development, we behave in a way that invokes the disapproval of parents or teachers, they express that disapproval with more or less strength, depending on how seriously they regard the behaviour. On the other hand, they will reward behaviour that is in accordance with their expectations. As time goes by we develop patterns of behaviour based around the societal norms that we have learned, many of which we have internalised as habits, so that much of what we do is done without conscious thought.

Systematic learning

This is the learning that is experienced through formal education, or through training and instruction in the organisation or externally in a local college or university. Whereas social learning occurs naturally and teaches us the norms of our society, *systematic* or *organised learning* occurs when something specific is to be learned and is developed within you with instruction and guidance from others, usually through the processes of formal education, a training course, or coaching and counselling sessions.

The factors of learning

For education, training and development to be successful, learning must take place. Superficially, this seems obvious, but the circumstances in which learning is acquired have been the focus of academic interest for at least 100 years. Clearly, those responsible for teaching and training must be skilled in developing others and the learner has to know *how* to learn. Research has shown that in an organised learning situation, such as a training course, the *amount* of learning that takes place is determined by three factors:

- the personal characteristics of the learner, such as the motivation to learn and the intellectual ability to understand what is being said and done
- the effectiveness of the trainer in terms of his or her knowledge and competence as a trainer, and the nature of the methods and media through which he/she delivers the training
- the physical situation in which the training takes place.

Activity 24

Think about how you dress, how you speak and how you behave generally when you are out with your friends. Compare that with how you behave at work, in the classroom or at home with your family. What is it that determines the nature of your behaviour? *How do you know* how to behave in those very different situations? You were not born with such social skills and therefore you must have learned them.

Personal characteristics

The motivation to learn plays a significant role. If the learner lacks interest in the subject and is therefore unwilling or reluctant to learn about it, learning will not take place. The learner also has to be *able* to learn. The learner, for example, may be highly motivated but if his/her intelligence is such that he/she is unable fully to grasp the ideas or achieve the necessary performance standards, the likelihood is that *sufficient* learning will not take place.

The trainer

To be effective, trainers have to possess several particular qualities. First, and rather obviously, they must be well versed in the subject matter of the training. Second, they must have the ability to transfer their knowledge and skills to others to the extent that those others become competent enough to meet, and preferably exceed, the required standards.

Third, the trainer must have credibility. If, for example, I announced that I was going to deliver a talk on the finer points of rugby union, I would be lucky if just two or three people turned up for the event. Conversely, if I announced that I had managed to get Jonny Wilkinson to deliver such a talk, he would have a full house. Someone who is known to be an authority on a subject has credibility, especially if his/her expertise is apparent in the content and the style with which the material is delivered. Credibility may also be earned by a trainer through the obvious authority with which he/she delivers the material and generally conducts the training session.

Key concept 9: two separate skills

The fact that someone is regarded as an expert in that he/she possesses particular knowledge and skills does not carry with it the guarantee that he/she has the ability to develop those qualities within others. That is a separate skill.

The learning situation

This refers to the physical environment in which the learning takes place, the ambience of the location and the shape and size of the training room. All of these factors have to be conducive to learning and appropriate and suitable in the light of the subject to be learned. Considerable time and ingenuity have been invested in the study and creation of effective learning situations. As we shall see later in this chapter, there is a variety of situations in which learning typically takes place.

Experiential learning

In a sense, what I have described as social learning is *experiential learning*. As a baby gradually becomes aware of the environment into which he/she has been born, he/she begins to attempt to make sense of it all.

Deep down we are all learners. No one has to teach an infant to learn. In fact, no one has to teach an infant anything. They are intrinsically inquisitive, masterful learners.

(Senge 1990, p4)

Pause for thought

In the light of all that you have just read about learning, what are the implications for you? If, for example, we are all natural learners from birth, is it possible that your non-work learning could turn out to be useful in the workplace? If you reflect on this, you might conclude that what you learn from carrying out tasks such as maintaining your home and your car, and what you learn from others, becomes interchangeable currency in all theatres of life.

When the term 'experiential learning' is used in a professional context, it generally refers to learning from organisational situations. Sometimes such situations occur unexpectedly, as for example when there is an emergency and you have to find a way of dealing with it. By its nature, it may be something that you have never previously encountered, so you have to analyse the situation, diagnose the problem and find and implement a solution. When this happens to, say, a busy manager, he/she will handle it and then move on straightaway to the next task.

If the emergency was indeed something the manager had never previously encountered, two questions might be relevant. First, where and when did the person gather the knowledge and skills that enabled him/her to cope with the situation? Second, should the manager reflect upon what he/she learned from the experience, instead of dashing off to the next task? Maybe the pressure to move on did not allow for reflection, in which case the opportunity should be taken at the next convenient time. Otherwise, whatever learning was gathered might be forgotten.

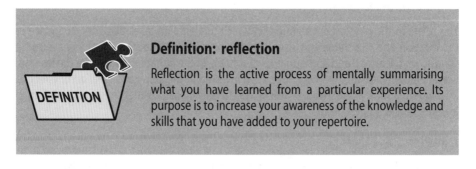

Definition: reflection

Reflection is the active process of mentally summarising what you have learned from a particular experience. Its purpose is to increase your awareness of the knowledge and skills that you have added to your repertoire.

Planned experience

This may occur as part of a staff development programme in which employees are placed in situations from which they learn. A manager, for example, might assign a task to an employee, after which the employee reports back on what was learned from the experience. In most cases, however, when a manager delegates a task he/she does so simply because it needs to be done. To a good manager, one of the most important aspects of allocating work is selecting the employee who is to do it.

For example, there are times when a task has to be completed quickly in order to meet a customer's delivery deadline. At such times, the manager will select an employee who is fully competent to do the job, with all the required knowledge and skills. There are also times when things are not so urgent, however, which is when the manager might select an employee who would have to learn something in order to complete the task successfully. This might be referred to as *developmental delegation*; it provides the employee with vital experience and concurrently gets a necessary job done.

Early theories of learning

In this section, we examine the theories of learning that were proposed in the early part of the twentieth century. The early theorists were mostly interested in learning as a psychological process, while the later theorists took the psychological aspects into account, but tended to focus upon the practicality and effectiveness of deliberately created learning situations.

When you study the early theories of learning, therefore, you are trying to develop an understanding of the three main psychological divisions of learning theory, which include *classical conditioning, operant conditioning* and *cognitive learning*.

Classical conditioning

The first theory of classical conditioning was propounded by the Russian physiologist Ivan Pavlov, who published his theory of 'conditioned reflexes' in 1927, although he carried out most of the research much earlier than that. He was interested in internal reactions to external stimuli, and he used dogs as the subjects of his experiments. He fed the dogs at the same time every day and as he gave them the food, he rang a bell. One day he rang the bell but did not feed the dogs, and he discovered that they were salivating, obviously not at the sight or the smell of food, but at the anticipation of it. They were reacting automatically to the sound of the bell, an indication that they associated it with the food. It is important to note that in 'classical' conditioning, the subject of the experiment always has a passive role.

Operant conditioning

The American psychologist E.L. Thorndike, a contemporary of Pavlov, was the founder of operant conditioning (sometimes referred to as *instrumental conditioning*). The subjects of his experiments were cats. Operant conditioning differs from classical conditioning in that the subject's response occurs before the reward is given.

In Thorndike's experiments (1913), a hungry animal was placed in a cage from which it needed to escape in order to get food. The animal therefore had to learn how to escape, usually, by pulling on a wire or pressing a lever. This differs from Pavlov's experiments in that the animal played an active role. Thorndike maintained that when the required response is followed by the reward, the behaviour is more likely to occur again, provided the circumstances are similar; he called this the 'law of effect'.

Today, the researcher mainly associated with operant conditioning is the American B.F. Skinner, whose work (1953) is really an extension of the work of Thorndike. Experiments involving animals typified the work of both researchers, although Skinner, after researching mainly with rats and pigeons, went on to research into human learning, to produce what he called *stimulus–response psychology*, which is generally known for short as S–R psychology.

Behaviourism

The works of Pavlov, Thorndike and Skinner classify them as *behaviourists*. This is an approach to the study of human behaviour that was first proposed by John B. Watson in 1913, and it is an approach that is not universally accepted by psychologists. Behaviourists work within limited parameters, and their approach to the study of animal and human behaviour excludes factors that many psychologists regard as basic requirements (Watson and Rayner 1920).

Cognitive learning

Cognitive theorists are mainly interested in changes in individuals' knowledge, since they regard this as more important than changes in what the learner does. Cognitive learning includes all of the elements of human consciousness that the behaviourists ignore: imagination, creativity, problem-solving, human intuition and perception. The cognitive approach has two components: *insight learning* and *latent learning*.

Insight learning. Having an understanding of what is being learned is an important feature of cognitive learning. To take a problem-solving exercise as an example, experience of working with children has shown that when a person is given a problem to solve, he/she sometimes studies it, analyses and thinks about it and then, after a period of time, during which an onlooker might think that the person was stumped, the solution is suddenly produced. Wolfgang Koehler (1959) carried out experiments with chimpanzees after which he claimed that such insight was not exclusively human behaviour.

Latent learning. According to cognitive theorists, learning may also be latent. This means that something can be added to someone's knowledge and then used only as and when needed. An interesting feature of latent learning is that the learner does not always appreciate that he/she has gathered something new and added it to his/her knowledge. Trainees, for example, sometimes come away from a course complaining that they have learned nothing. It is not until a later date, perhaps at work, that they find that they can solve particular problems or carry out tasks of which they were incapable prior to the training about which they had complained.

Modern theories of learning

Most of the modern theories of learning have their roots in the theories explained above. Indeed, the psychological aspects of some of the older theories still exercise a degree of influence over current practice. Modern theorists, however, are not so keen on developing hard and fast rules of learning. They are more inclined to empower individuals over the means through which they are developed.

Kolb's learning cycle

The *experiential learning cycle*, developed by David Kolb in 1979, is probably the most well-known model in modern theory (Kolb 1985). If we study what happens in learning situations today, it is not difficult to challenge Kolb's perception of the approaches of teachers and trainers to developing people. He claimed that students and trainees in the classrooms were being processed under the *authority* of the teacher or trainer, while the learner played a passive role. This situation, he said, detaches the learner from reality. The implication here is that the learner is taught something, but does not actually have to demonstrate the ability to do it or that he/she knows it. It is 'separated' learning and doing, as if they were different activities. In fact this has not been the case, at least not in the UK, for several decades.

Kolb contrasted this 'teaching at people' type of learning with problem-solving, in which the responsibility for producing solutions rests with the learner. In other words, he distinguished between 'teacher-centred' and 'student-centred' learning. Kolb regarded the classroom situation as a necessary function, his main criticism being that insufficient attention was being paid to other forms of learning such as problem-solving. When developing his experiential learning cycle (Figure 8.1) he incorporated the features of both the classroom and problem-solving situations.

Kolb explained this cyclical process with the following analysis:

1. Concrete experience is the first point in the figure (8.1) in which the learner practises a skill for the first time, such as using a machine.
2. This is followed by a process of familiarisation, in which the learner makes observations and reflects on the experience.

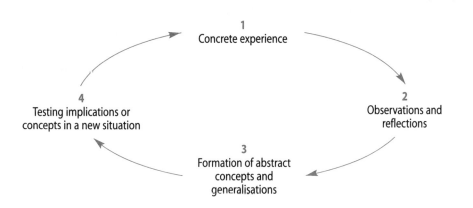

Figure 8.1 The Kolb experiential learning cycle

3. From there, he/she begins to make sense of the structure of the machine. In other words, he/she formulates abstract concepts and generalisations, and begins to realise how the machine functions – what it is for.
4. The learner then returns to the machine. This produces a new situation because it includes prior learning, which is then tested in the new situation, which includes using the machine, bringing the learner back to the first point in the cycle, in which the use of the machine provides a new experience.

Learning improves as the cycle continues. Kolb emphasises that this whole process is driven by the individual learner, thus empowering the individual to strive towards his/her own internally motivated needs and goals.

Gagne's hierarchy of learning

One important question to be answered is the relationship between simple and complex forms of learning. In his attempt to explain this relationship, Gagne (1977) reasoned that there are eight hierarchically ordered forms of learning, ranging from 'primitive' to 'complex' learning. Although different from each other, many of these forms of learning are interdependent. From the hierarchy (Table 8.1, overleaf) we can see that each form of learning is progressively a little more complex than its predecessor. The third, 'chaining', for example, having been built upon the first and second, is more complex than signal learning and S-R learning.

From Table 8.1, you should be able to see relationships between Gagne's classification and some of the early learning theories. The classification allows us to identify the processes whereby skills of all levels are acquired, and hence suggests how to facilitate learning and prevent failure to learn at the various levels (Collin 2004).

Transfer of learning

Where learning results from specific training, *learning transfer* is the most important aspect of training programmes. Psychologist Murray Porteous (1997) says that:

if the training does not transfer from the setting of the training

programme to the workplace, then the training is useless, and if it does not transfer from one task to another, it is less useful than it would be if it did.

Table 8.1 Hierarchy of learning

Type of learning	Description
1 Signal learning	Involving the response to something that is taken as a signal. This is typified by the bell in Pavlov's studies with dogs
2 Stimulus–response learning	Based on operant conditioning in which a learned response as opposed to an instinctive response is made. Also the response is made in pursuit of the satisfaction of some need or goal
3 Chaining (based on 1 and 2)	Involving the connection of a number of previously learned sets of stimuli and their associated responses. For example, when we do two things at once, such as guiding cloth underneath the needle of a sewing machine while using the treadle
4 Verbal association	Learning and using a language, involving connections between words and the ability to speak them in a meaningful sequence
5 Discrimination learning (based on 3 and 4)	Involves responding differently to stimuli which are related to but different from each other. This is more sophisticated than simply associating a single stimulus with a response, since it calls upon the learner to separate the meanings of stimuli
6 Concept learning	This includes 'discrimination' and 'rule learning'. It is a form of learning in which we make a common response to concrete or abstract stimuli which are of the same category, but different in their physical characteristics. This higher form of learning requires internal information processing to classify and reorganise concepts.
7 Rule learning (based on 6)	Acquiring a chain of several concepts; eg 'if X then Y'
8 Problem-solving (based on 7)	This involves the use of 'insight' in developing new rules from previously learned rules, giving the ability to solve problems, especially in new situations involving human beings.

Source: Gagne (1977).

Staying with Porteous, the following steps (OPRAM) have been shown to increase the probability of transfer taking place.

- *Overlearning of skills*. Skills should be practised past the point of proficiency, ie do not stop when 'you have got it'.
- *Principles* should be emphasised until they are well understood. It is much better to know why something is done or works, not just how to do it.
- *Realistic simulation*. Make the training situation as similar to the work situation as possible. If possible, deal with real situations, real customers, etc.
- *Adaptive*. The training programme should contain aspects where something does not always fit or work out right as it should. This forces the trainee to adapt the material to the context or situation. By seeking their own solutions outside of the common procedures, trainees learn far more and the transfer is enhanced.
- *Monitoring*. Newly trained staff should be subject to an in-depth and frequent follow-up programme until the effects of training are well established. It is quite common, especially when there is any form of outside pressure, for the trainee to relapse into trusted old but inefficient methods. It is also even more common to assume that once someone has done the training course, he/she is qualified to (say) operate a machine. In many cases, real learning only begins after the training and when the individual is exposed to the vagaries of reality (Porteous 1997).

Learning styles

Learning is a psychological event and since individuals are all different from each other, they all learn differently. In other words, everyone has his/her own *learning style*. Some learn best from experience, while others prefer to study or hear about the subject and reflect upon what they have learned. Yet others are dependent on being shown or taught, requiring detailed coaching and real-time feedback, while others again prefer not to be coached but to be given time to learn alone.

In the light of this, a good trainer will construct the course to reflect the learning styles of the trainees. Additionally, trainees benefit, first, from understanding their own learning style, and second, from knowing how to learn. With these factors in mind, several researchers have produced 'models' and 'inventories' designed to assist students, and in particular management trainees, to identify their own learning styles.

Alan Mumford states that the 'stimulus to my own thinking beyond "people learn differently" was provided when I first encountered the work of David Kolb. ... [H]e would not, I think, claim his concept of the learning cycle was wholly new.' With Peter Honey, he took Kolb's original concepts and developed a questionnaire and improved processes for making use of the results (Mumford 1993) (see Figure 8.2 overleaf).

The implication here is that an individual can be classified as having a particular learning style. He/she might, for example, be an *activist, reflector, theorist* or a *pragmatist*. Several learning styles inventories (questionnaires) have been produced, most of which were based on Kolb's (1985) experiential learning theory.

Strengths and weaknesses

Now see if you recognise your own characteristics in the lists overleaf.

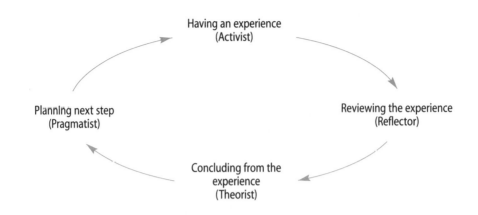

Figure 8.2 Honey and Mumford's learning cycle

Activity 25: what is your learning style?

Think of a skill you have learned recently. Perhaps it was how to operate a new mobile telephone, use new software, play a musical instrument or fix a broken window. Now consider how you went about learning the skill. The following questionnaire is based on Honey and Mumford's learning cycle and is designed to allow you to identify your own learning style; no one style is better or worse than another. As you complete the questionnaire, give a high rating to those words you think most closely characterise the way you learn, and a low rating to those words you think are least characteristic of the way you learn.

You may find it difficult to choose the words that best describe your learning style because there are no right or wrong answers. Different characteristics described in the inventory are equally good. The aim of the inventory is to discover your own personal learning style and not to evaluate your learning ability.

Procedure

There are nine sets (the columns) of four words (the rows) listed below. Working on a row at a time from left to right, rank each set of four words 1–4, assigning 4 to the word which you think best and most closely characterises the way you think you learn, 3 to the next best, 2 to the third best and 1 to the word you think least characterises the way you learn.

Important: be sure to assign a different number to each of the four words in a row. Do not rate any two words equally in a row. Taking the top row for example:

discriminating [2] tentative [1] involved [3] practical [4]

A		B		C		D	
1 discriminating	[]	tentative	[]	involved	[]	practical	[]
2 receptive	[]	relevant	[]	analytical	[]	impartial	[]
3 feeling	[]	watching	[]	thinking	[]	doing	[]
4 accepting	[]	risk-taker	[]	evaluative	[]	aware	[]
5 intuitive	[]	productive	[]	logical	[]	questioning	[]
6 abstract	[]	open observer	[]	concrete	[]	active	[]
7 present-oriented	[]	reflecting	[]	future oriented	[]	pragmatic	[]
8 experience	[]	secret observer	[]	conceptualiser	[]	experimenter	[]
9 intense	[]	reserved	[]	rational	[]	responsible	[]

Scoring

Add the columns using only the scores for the row number shown below in brackets, then plot the scores for each of the columns A,B,C and D on the learning styles axes:

[A 234578]   [B 367891]   [C 234589]   [D 136789]

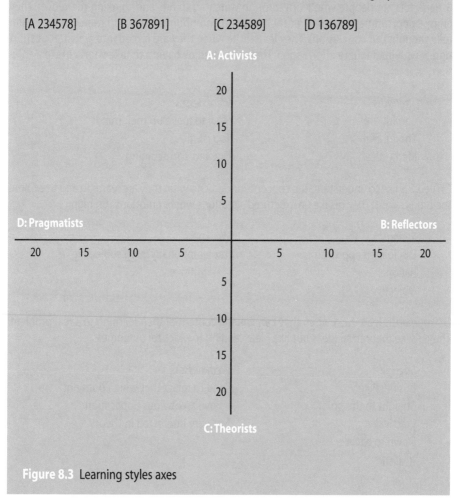

Figure 8.3 Learning styles axes

Conclusions

You will find that you have scored unequally on all four axes. In other words there are elements of all four styles in all of us. The axes bearing your highest score represents your predominant learning style.

A: *Activists* value the opportunity to take an active part in their learning. They like high-profile activities, such as giving talks.

Strengths	Weaknesses
Keen to try out new ideas	Act without thinking
Flexible	Take unnecessary risks
Open-minded	Get bored with implementation

B: *Reflectors* are people who learn through watching things and thinking them over. They enjoy opportunities to mull over their ideas in an unhurried way and then produce carefully thought out conclusions. They learn little when they are forced into activities at short notice with inadequate information. They do not enjoy having to take short cuts to a solution.

Strengths	Weaknesses
Careful	Slow to make up their minds
Thoughtful	Too cautious
Methodical	Not very forthcoming

C: *Theorists* like to understand the concepts underlying what they are learning and to explore the implications. They dislike unstructured situations where emotions run high.

Strengths	Weaknesses
Disciplined approach	Intolerant of anything subjective
Rational	or intuitive
Objective	

D: *Pragmatists* learn best when they can link the content of their learning to a real problem. They dislike theoretical ideas but like ideas leading to practical outcomes.

Strengths	Weaknesses
Businesslike	Tend to reject that which does not
Straight to the point	have an obvious application
Practical	Not very interested in theory
Down to earth	
Realistic	

Choosing a career

While learning and development are critically important at work, they are also predominant in your mind when you are at the stage of choosing a career for yourself. Many students have made this choice before entering university, and obviously, it is a choice that has helped them to decide on the nature of the course they will take. Others, however, use the university course as a 'dip your toe in' exercise; to learn about particular subjects which in turn, will help them to decide.

Personality and career choice

Above, I alluded to the importance of learning and development, but research also shows that career choice is related to personality type. Holland (1985), for example, developed a theory of career choice rooted in personality. He maintains that people in each personality type (see Table 8.2) are drawn towards a small set of jobs. They are drawn in this way because they are seeking work that is compatible with their likes and dislikes. Holland's theory is based on six different personality types.

There is also research evidence that suggests that when people choose a career that suits their personality, they are more likely to be satisfied with their choice and less likely to change professions (Feldman and Arnold 1985). It is worth noting at this point that there are obvious implications here for personality testing as part of the recruitment process and for employee development and retention.

Theories such as Holland's, however, while compelling, do not take account of the fact that people change over time, they become wary of getting into a rut or career trap, and as a result, even after many years, might decide on a career change.

ACTIVITIES

Activity 26

Study Table 8.2 and try to find a set of personality characteristics that most closely matches your own. How does it relate to your career plan?

CASE STUDY

Case study 8: Learning and career planning

Anna Grey has just successfully completed the second year of a degree in general business studies. So far, she has studied many aspects of organisational behaviour, change and globalisation, and the influence of HRM. The business subjects she has taken include HR, finance, marketing, and business planning.

Table 8.2 Personality types and career choice

Personality type	Occupational choice
Realistic	
Outdoor type who enjoys, and is usually good at physical activities requiring strength and/or coordination.	Farming
	Sport-related
	Carpentry
	Architecture
Investigative	
Tends to get involved in observing, organising and understanding data. Good at abstract thought.	Mathematics
	Engineering
	Dentistry
Social	
Enjoys the company of others more than being engaged in intellectual or physical activity. Tends to be warm and caring and enjoys the process of informing, training and enlightening others	Religion
	Social work
	Diplomatic service
	Teaching
Conventional	
Likes rules, regulations, structure and order, and is prepared to subordinate personal needs to situations where personal or organisational power and status exist. Usually well organised but is not very imaginative.	Accounting
	Finance
	Military
	Clerical work
Artistic	
Dislikes ordered and repetitive situations. Prefers to express feelings and ideas, and be imaginative. Enjoys drama, music and art.	Advertising
	Interior design
	Entertainment business
Enterprising	
Enjoys activity rather than observation and reflection. Likes to use verbal communication skills to persuade others and gain power and status.	Publishing
	Employee relations
	Sales management

At present she is unsure about the kind of career that she would enjoy and in which she would be successful. Above all, she wants to avoid making a wrong choice, but having had no business experience at all, how could she make the right choice? She found that the uncertainty was stressful and decided to seek advice from the university's career advisory service. The service was run by Gerry Macmillan, an experienced adviser of many years' standing.

Gerry told her that the first thing she had to do was to assess herself in terms of her strengths and weaknesses, preferences and prejudices, likes and dislikes. He also recommended that she wrote up a summary of her knowledge, skills and competences: not just the work-related aspects, but things that she had learned through hobbies, in social and domestic situations and things she had learned from friends.

Anna winced at the thought of the amount of time it would take her to do all this, but Gerry mentioned that the advisory service runs a 'self-awareness' course which is specifically designed for people experiencing the quandary in which she finds herself. He explained that when you 'know yourself', are aware of your strengths and weaknesses, and so on, you will know what you have to offer a potential employer. He said that the course 'will help you to reflect upon your past experiences in a systematic way, the learning you have achieved within the university and outside of it, so that you can write up a complete and correct analysis of your past experiences'.

When Anna took the self-awareness course she was very surprised by what she discovered about herself; the volume of data was much greater than she had anticipated. Subsequently she was able to identify several areas of business which attracted her, and after looking into them more deeply, she realised that she would have to draw up a personal development plan, since there were gaps in her understanding which might be of concern to a potential employer.

Gerry was able to organise some work experience for her and that really opened her eyes to what she should expect as a full-time employee. She got on well with the people in the company, the managers noticed how keen she was to learn and to advance herself, and when she had finished her degree, she was offered a job for a probationary period.

Self-test questions

1. What factors have highlighted the importance of learning in the past 15 years?
2. Who are the beneficiaries of training and how might they reap such benefits?
3. How would you define learning?
4. What are the factors of learning?
5. How would you define competence?
6. What is meant by the term experiential learning? Describe a situation in which this might take place.
7. What was the basis for Kolb's criticism of traditional teaching methods?
8. Why is the transfer of learning important?
9. People sometimes find that they have made the wrong choice of career. How might the risk of this have been reduced?
10. If you have read all of this chapter, you should have a fairly sound understanding of learning. How would this understanding help you to design a training course?

Human resource development | CHAPTER 9

Introduction

The first aim of this chapter is to explain and discuss the current status of human resource development (HRD), particularly in terms of its importance to individuals, organisations and the country. Second, we examine and discuss the factors that comprise HRD, including training, development and experience. Third, we explain the practical aspects of HRD.

The strategic importance of HRD

Recognition of the importance of HRD in recent years has been heavily influenced by the intensification of overseas competition and the relative success of economies such as Japan, Germany and Sweden where investment in employee development is emphasised (Holden 2004).

In this book, space limitations prevent a lengthy discussion of the history, but if the long road to the current perceptions of HRD interests you, the 'further reading' given at the end of the book will provide you with a excellent start. Suffice to say here that after the inception of HRM in the early 1980s, UK employers gradually began to recognise the factors that contributed to the success of their major global competitors. Prominent among these factors was HRD.

Other major contributing factors include first, the organisational changes brought about by the implementation of HRM practices – through which knowledge and competence of the human resource is regarded as a valuable means of achieving a competitive advantage – and second, technology, particularly IT and the Internet, which allowed organisations to reach out to a worldwide audience.

Definition: human resource development

Human resource development (HRD) is a strategic approach to investing in human capital. It draws on other human resource processes, including resourcing and performance assessment to identify actual and potential talent. HRD provides a framework for self-development, training programmes and career progression to meet an organisation's future skill requirements (Price 1997).

Training and development

Armstrong (1999) defines training as:

> **the planned and systematic modification of behaviour through learning events, programmes and instruction which enable individuals to achieve the level of knowledge, skill and competence required to carry out their work effectively.**

In short, this means that training is the means by which employees acquire the competences they need in order to carry out their work to the required standard.

Whereas training is needed in the shorter term, to carry out tasks that are needed now, the term 'development' refers to the broader landscape. It relates to the future, to the longer-term development of people throughout their careers, providing them with the kind of confidence, maturity and stability that enables them to adopt greater responsibility. Training produces competence while development produces continuous *psychological growth*. It could be said, therefore, that training is for *now*, while development is for *the future*.

The relationship with recruitment

Ewart Keep argues that the relationship between training and recruitment is a close one. If the organisation wishes to improve the knowledge and competence of its workforce it may choose to train its existing employees or it may decide to employ new staff who already possess the knowledge and competence it needs. In that respect, recruitment is important here, and the fact that the organisation may choose either to train or recruit sometimes makes it impossible to discuss either activity in isolation (Keep 1989).

Clearly, the choice that this argument puts forward is limited to a requirement for particular items of knowledge and competence, since new employees who have been selected on this basis will still need to be trained for the purposes of induction and their general role in the organisation.

The HRM view

Several academic writers are concerned with the generally perceived relationship between training and development. David Goss (1996), for example, says that the terms 'training' and 'development' are frequently treated either as synonyms or as representing mutually exclusive activities. From an HRM perspective, they are better understood as being linked, such that training is seen as both a part of and a precondition for development. He attributes this to the hierarchical divisions in organisations, and says that training has evolved as something that is provided for non-managerial workers, whereas development has been treated as the preserve of management (hence the still common pairing: 'management development').

Goss (1996) makes the further point that this approach is incompatible with the central principles of HRM, which maintains that all employees are valued assets and should therefore have their competences developed.

Hendry (1995), on the other hand, says that 'increasingly, we are *getting away from* the divisive notion that managers are "developed" while the shopfloor are merely "trained" and that the principles of adult learning apply to each'. Training therefore applies to everyone, as one of several components of HRD.

One of the concerns of these writers is that if development is reserved for managers, then how can members of the workforce be regarded as valued assets? Surely they too need to be developed to their maximum potential – especially where flexible and multiskilled workers are concerned – since, like managers, they cannot easily be replaced. Furthermore, the assumption that managers are 'developed' and workers are 'trained' implies that training is the exclusive preserve of non-managerial staff, whereas obviously, managers also need to be trained since their work involves the exercise of particular competences, such as leadership, performance assessment, work organisation and decision-making.

The beneficiaries of HRD

'Who should pay for training and why?' It is now more than 30 years since that question appeared on a national examination paper of what was then the Institute of Personnel Management (IPM, now the CIPD). The candidates who achieved the highest grades cited the stakeholders as first, the *individual*, second, the *organisation*, and third, the *state*. An answer that states how all three parties would benefit from training and therefore should invest in it would still receive a good grade today.

The individual

Individual employees benefit from training and development in several ways. First, if they understand how their tasks should be carried out, they are more motivated to do them well and thereby experience satisfaction from what they do. If they know they are good at what they do, they feel valued and respected. Training makes people competent, gives them confidence and feelings of security, and they feel that that their presence in the organisation is worthwhile.

Second, people who seek a career and plan their own future development will regard training sessions as important opportunities to extend their repertoire of knowledge and competence. This enhances their employability and their promotion prospects. Many employees, with the support of their employers, have created their own personal development plans (PDP) in which the identification of their developmental needs forms an integral part of the performance management system.

Pause for thought: continuing professional development (CPD)

Do you have a personal development plan? The CIPD defines CPD as a personal commitment to keeping your professional knowledge up to date and improving your capabilities throughout your working life. It is about knowing where you are today, where you want to be in the future, and making sure you get there. We return to CPD later in the chapter.

The organisation

The definition of HRD (above) says that it is a strategic approach to investing in human capital. The organisation benefits when the knowledge and competence of its employees, combined with their commitment and involvement, are specifically geared to the achievement of objectives, and thereby the realisation of strategy. Those who lead today's organisations have grown to understand the strength of the relationship between human performance and organisational success, which is why they now see HRD as a critical factor in the organisation's future.

The state

The state benefits when organisations perform well in the home market and compete effectively with their overseas industrial counterparts. A knowledgeable and skilled workforce contributes enormously to the economy of the nation, creating wealth from which the whole of society benefits.

Advancing technology removes the requirement for traditional jobs and creates jobs that demand new knowledge and skills. An organisation that keeps pace with change by anticipating technological advances and preparing its workforce in good time will suffer least from the effects of the skills gap. For as long as technology continues to advance, organisations that fail to prepare their workforce will always experience the effects of the skills gap.

Vocational education and training (VET)

Until recently, the background to government initiatives in this respect recorded only moderate success. National vocational qualifications (NVQs) emphasise the 'competency approach' to training, which implies the importance of outcomes defined by what people can actually do that they could not do before taking the course. Additionally, the General National Vocational Qualification (GNVQ) is the vocational equivalent of an academic A level. Successive government bodies have provided the framework for NVQs and GNVQs, and in 2003 they were merged with the school curriculum authority to form the Qualifications and Curriculum Authority (QCA).

National employer training programme

The main approach of the government is to prepare people for work, and the framework provides for educational courses that develop competences needed by employers. Recent developments, however, include the government white paper: *Skills: getting on in business, getting on at work*, which builds on the first national skills strategy that was published in 2003. The purpose of the white paper is to ensure that the right skills are available to employers for the success of their businesses. It also helps individuals to gain the skills they need to be employable and personally fulfilled.

The white paper sets out proposals and reforms designed to:

- Put employers' needs centre stage in the design and delivery of training. Employers' needs will be met through the delivery of a new National Employer Training Programme (NETP).
- Support individuals in gaining the skills and qualifications they need to achieve the quality of life they want. Skills for adult learners will be promoted by a clear, attractive ladder of progression which challenges and encourages people to achieve at every level. It will be designed to stimulate people's aspirations to progress and fulfil their potential. From 2006/7 there will be a national entitlement to free tuition for a first full level 2 qualification, and new extensive support for learning and level 3 (www.dfes.gov.uk/skillsstrategy).

Investors in People

Undoubtedly, the most successful initiative has been Investors in People (IiP). IiP is a private company that was introduced in 1991. It was developed from the combined work of the National Skills Task Force (NSTF), the Confederation of British Industry (CBI), the then Department of Employment, the Trades Union Congress (TUC) and the IPD (now the CIPD). Recognising the powerful relationship between employee performance and business success, IiP provides a national framework that specifies 'the principles which tie training and development activity directly to business objectives'. IiP has been taken up by over 37,000 organisations across the UK and no doubt that figure will increase. Generally they report that achieving the required standards for recognition as an Investor in People is extremely beneficial.

Investors in People – the revised standard

To achieve IiP recognition, the employer has to adhere to the prescribed standard, although the standard recognises that organisations will meet the principles in their own way. The standard was first published in 1993 and in 2004, after consulting employers, stakeholders, business advisers and IiP ambassadors, IiP revised the standard. The central ethos of the standard remains the same – improving organisation performance through people development – but following intense consultation with a wide variety of employers and organisations, particular key changes have been made.

IiP recognises that organisations use different means to achieve success through their people and does not, therefore, prescribe any one method for doing this. Instead, it provides a framework to help organisations to find the most suitable means for achieving success through their people. The main outcome of the review of the standard is the provision of a simplified structure to provide a better fit with how organisations operate. The focus is on helping employers to 'Plan, Do, Review' their business strategy. You can obtain a copy of the standard if you visit the TSO online bookshop.

Project proposal

Your organisation, or an organisation with which you are familiar, would like to be recognised as an IIP organisation. Get a copy of the new IIP standard and prepare a programme that should lead to this achievement.

Systematic training

In corporate terms, the ultimate purpose of training is to improve the performance of employees, and thereby the whole organisation. Individuals, however, may regard training as one of the means by which they can improve themselves in order to enhance their career prospects. Viewed in this way, training may be driven by the organisation and its employees.

Training policy

Since the advent of HRM in the 1980s, the importance of developing staff has grown markedly. Training was once regarded as a comparative luxury. Senior managers seldom regarded it as one of the organisation's top priorities and therefore were reluctant to allocate significant resources to it. That attitude has now changed and modern organisations realise that it is in their best interests to formulate a clear and cost-efficient statement of intent to provide resources for a training programme that is accessible to all areas of the enterprise.

It is the responsibility of the HR manager to develop such a policy and have it accepted at the top level. Additionally, he/she should have a training needs analysis (TNA) carried out, the findings of which will determine the specification of the training programme. The HR manager may achieve this by setting up a training committee, with a membership drawn from all areas of the organisation. To be an effective player on such a stage, HR practitioners must equip themselves with the knowledge and skills that enable them to provide training at operational level.

Developing a training course

Since the professional expertise in training resides in the HR department, the responsibility for its provision lies in the department, and in particular with the HR specialist – who may have the title 'training and development manager' or 'HRD manager' – assisted by HR practitioners (alternatively referred to as 'HR advisers').

Developing a training course involves the practitioner in a well-known sequence of activities. The activities form a cyclical process that is generally referred to as the *systematic training cycle* (STC) (see Figure 9.1, overleaf).

The components of the STC

From Figure 9.1, you will see that the STC, sometimes referred to as the *systematic approach to training* (SAT), is made up of six interdependent and interrelated components. It has been used successfully in industry and the public sector for many years and is regarded as a sound basis for cost-effective training.

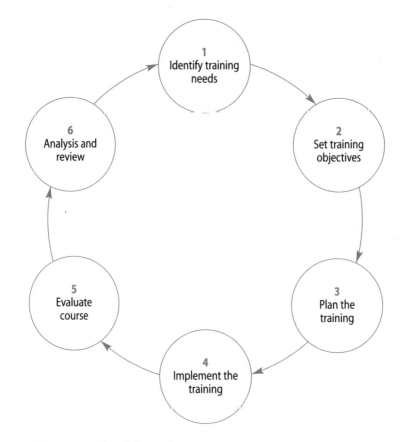

Figure 9.1 The systematic training cycle

According to Tyson and York (1996), the interdependence of the components is crucial:

> **the malfunction or neglect of any one of them inevitably affects the others and the total system. Thus, if job analysis has not defined the criteria for effective performance, training needs cannot be identified by performance appraisal. If needs have not been properly identified, it is not possible to design and provide needs-related training to assess ultimate effectiveness in terms of subsequent work performance.**

The following pages include an examination and discussion of each of the components, after which you should have a good understanding of how the total system works.

Stage 1: Identify training needs

The most objective and effective approach to this task starts at job level. In Chapter 4, you will have seen that *job analysis* forms the basis for the production of job descriptions and specifications. The knowledge and competences that a job holder needs in order to meet the required standards, and the standards themselves, are clarified in a completed job analysis. The next stage is to identify the *competence gap*. This is a term used to express the difference between what the job holder is able to do and what he/she actually should be able to do. In behavioural terms this can be expressed as what the job holder is *expected* to do and what he/she *actually does do*. Where there is a gap between actual and required performance, it may be filled by training (see Figure 9.2).

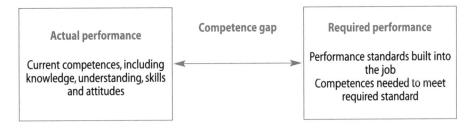

Figure 9.2 The competence gap

Conversely, the employee may possess the ability, and the gap between actual and required performance may be caused by lack of motivation to perform (see Chapter 10).

How training needs are identified

There are several ways in which training needs may be identified:

- Managers identify training needs in their day-to-day monitoring of staff performance and when they carry out formal performance appraisal sessions. From Figure 9.2 you will see that performance is more than just 'can do' the job. For example the manager identifies a training need when an employee's standard of performance needs to be raised.
- Individuals may notice their own lack of knowledge of techniques or systems, or they may identify gaps in their skills when asked to carry out particular tasks.
- Training needs may also identified during the selection process. The 'best person for the job' hardly ever possesses every single item of knowledge, skills and competence that the job demands.

Training needs analysis

The technique for identifying training needs at individual, group and corporate levels is known as a *training needs analysis* (TNA). This may be carried out through a formal training survey which is conducted across the whole organisation. Typically, this is needed when a company-wide change is taking place, such as when new technology is being introduced, when restructuring becomes necessary or when a programme of *organisation development* (see Glossary) is being run. In such cases, new competences need to be learned and tasks and responsibilities are redistributed. A company-wide training survey is a massive undertaking, and its effectiveness will be maximised if it is started well in advance of the anticipated change.

Stage 2: Set training objectives

The next stage is to set the training objectives. In general, the objective of training is to develop in people the knowledge and understanding, skills and competence that they need in order to meet required performance standards. The training objectives, therefore, should be set out in behavioural terms, specifying what the trainee should know and be able to do as a result of the training. As an example, if you look at the box at the beginning of every chapter in this book, you will see how the learning objectives are set out.

> ## Memory aid
>
> The acronym SMART is often used as a mnemonic to aid those who regularly set objectives for others. SMART means that objectives should be: **S**pecific, **M**easurable, **A**ttainable, **R**ealistic and **T**ime-related.

Specific means making a clear statement about the knowledge or skill that the trainee should be able to do and actually demonstrate at the end of the course. This includes the level of operation such as, 'After the training, the trainee should be able to use the machine safely and efficiently to produce the product at the specified quality.'

Measurable means that the standard of the trainee's performance after the training can be measured in terms of, for example, quality and number of items in a specified period of time.

Attainable means that it should be possible for the trainee to achieve the objectives in the light of the situation, the practicability, and the intelligence and motivation of the trainee.

Realistic means that the objectives should be obviously useful and clearly related to the type of work that the trainee carries out.

Time-related means that the trainee should be able to develop understanding, attain concepts and demonstrate skills within a pre-specified period of time.

Stage 3: Plan the training

Bearing in mind the nature of the subject matter in which the employee needs to be trained, decisions have to be made about how and where it is to be carried out. There are several choices. Most training, however, falls into one of two categories:

- *On-the-job training* which, as the term implies, takes place while the trainee is actually working. This can include:
  - e-learning (electronic learning), using the Internet or the organisation's own intranet
  - coaching, in which the trainee is taken through the steps of, say, machine operation;
  - use of instruction manuals.
- *Off-the-job training* which may be external training, when, for example, an individual or a small group is sent out to a local college or training centre, or to a higher education institution to undertake a professional qualification. Off-the-job training may also be in-house training, for example when the trainee undertakes a short course, or carries out an assignment, supervised by the manager.

What is said above puts the spotlight on the importance of the training venue, and the main options are listed in the box.

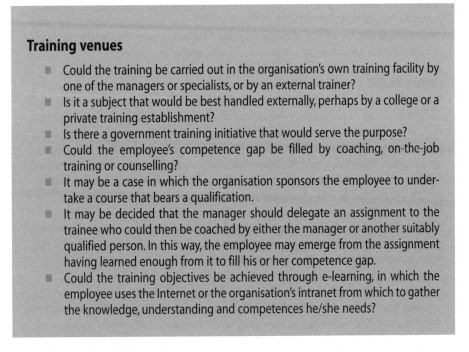

Training venues

- Could the training be carried out in the organisation's own training facility by one of the managers or specialists, or by an external trainer?
- Is it a subject that would be best handled externally, perhaps by a college or a private training establishment?
- Is there a government training initiative that would serve the purpose?
- Could the employee's competence gap be filled by coaching, on-the-job training or counselling?
- It may be a case in which the organisation sponsors the employee to undertake a course that bears a qualification.
- It may be decided that the manager should delegate an assignment to the trainee who could then be coached by either the manager or another suitably qualified person. In this way, the employee may emerge from the assignment having learned enough from it to fill his or her competence gap.
- Could the training objectives be achieved through e-learning, in which the employee uses the Internet or the organisation's intranet from which to gather the knowledge, understanding and competences he/she needs?

The advantages and disadvantages of all these options have to be weighed carefully, since training can involve considerable cost and commitment on all sides. While cost is an important factor, the nature of the training objectives is the key to the answer. The factors of learning that are outlined in Chapter 8 should also be considered. They may provide a good starting point for making this decision.

Stage 4: Implement the training

If it is decided that external training would be the most appropriate way forward, the HR practitioner becomes involved in administering the event: for example, securing the trainee's entry to the course, ensuring that the fee is paid and monitoring the trainee's progress. The trainee's manager, however, should be involved in a different way, as the following case study shows.

Case study 9: Taking an interest

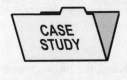

CASE STUDY

Jeremy had worked for Harvey Plastics as a product designer for three years. He was excellent at his job and popular with his work colleagues. During a performance appraisal interview with his departmental manager, Julie Brown, she told him that she was pleased with his overall performance, and started to talk to him about his career.

> During the conversation, she mentioned that there was a vacant position as a team leader in the department, and said she would like to put his name forward as a candidate for the job. Jeremy pointed out that he had not had any supervisory experience, but Julie replied that she had noticed that his colleagues had become accustomed to approaching him for advice. She also said that if he were to get the job, the company would sponsor him on a team leadership course at the local college.
>
> Jeremy applied and was selected for the position, which would become vacant owing to the present incumbent's retirement in eight weeks. The HR department provided Julie with a copy of the course curriculum and she and Jeremy met to discuss it. It was a 12-week course and Jeremy would have to attend on two evenings a week, so he would be well into the course by the time he took up the new position. The selection process had included a psychometric test and Julie had a copy of the test report. While they were discussing the course content Julie pointed out several areas to which she wanted Jeremy to pay particular attention.
>
> After Jeremy started the course, they had further meetings during which they discussed the items she had highlighted for his attention, asking him what he had learned from them and how he thought they were relevant to his new position.
>
> Julie requested an interim report from the course leader at the college, and this showed that Jeremy was making excellent progress. He was performing well in the seminars and often emerged as the leader when they were carrying out group work. Finally, Julie said that if he wanted to discuss any part of the course with her, she would always make the time to see him.

It has to be pointed out that not all managers take such an interest in the development of their staff. This is evidenced by the fact that at enrolment in colleges for part-time and short courses, you will usually find that it was the student's, rather than their employer's, idea to take the course.

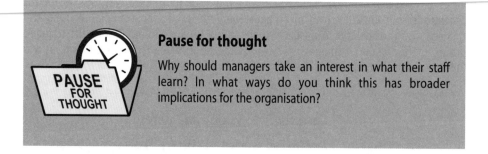

Pause for thought

Why should managers take an interest in what their staff learn? In what ways do you think this has broader implications for the organisation?

Running an in-house course

If it is thought that in-house training would be the best way forward, the HR practitioner becomes involved in organising and administering the course. This includes setting the date and organising the venue for the training, and ensuring that the prospective trainees and their managers receive sufficient notice of the times and dates of the training events.

Where the subject matter is HR-related, such as training managers in a new system of appraisal or in selection interviewing, the HR practitioner is expected to be able to deliver it. Otherwise, a trainer who is an expert in the subject should deliver the course, especially if it is a technical subject. For this purpose, it may be possible to enlist the services of a manager or specialist from within the organisation.

Training consultants

Some HR departments have a register of external specialists who come in to deliver the training. When this happens, the HR practitioner will have made the consultant aware of the training objectives and the consultant will have developed an appropriate course which he/she will bring to the training area. It is necessary to be certain, however, that the course meets the needs of the trainees precisely, and this may involve meetings with the consultant.

It is important at such meetings not to allow the consultant to dominate the proceedings. With the appropriate managers, the HR practitioner will have set the training objectives, and it is only by these that the training must be driven. While the views of an experienced consultant might be valuable, he/she cannot know the organisation and its training requirements as well as its staff do, so do not allow the training to be driven by excerpts from the consultant's repertoire.

Cost-effectiveness

Earlier I alluded to the cost of training, and while we almost instinctively relate cost to college fees, engaging external trainers, travel expenses and so forth, it can still be costly to run an in-house course. Cost-effectiveness may also be related to the number of trainees on the course at any one time, since many organisations calculate the cost per capita.

There is a balance to be achieved here in the sense that while the number of trainees has to justify the cost of the course, it also has an influence on the ambience of the event. Too few trainees may not provide a suitable mix or allow for syndicate work, while too many may make it difficult for the trainer to deal with questions. A large number may also influence your decisions about the methods and media to be used (see below) and the duration of the course. If, for example, you decide to use syndicate work, you have to consider the amount of time it is fair to allocate to delegates when they return from their discussions to present their findings.

Course development

Let us now assume that the subject matter of the training is HR-related and that you are going to organise and deliver the training. First, the course objectives have to be studied carefully and you have to decide how they are going to be achieved. Second, therefore, you decide what the course should contain and what methods and media would be most likely to achieve the objectives.

Methods and media

Perhaps at this stage we should distinguish between what is meant by 'method' and what is meant by 'media'. In our context, and for our purposes, we can say that a method is a technique that has been selected as the most appropriate means of developing knowledge and competence in other people, while media are the means through which the knowledge and competence are communicated. You might, for example, decide that group work is the best method for running a problem-solving session, and that PowerPoint is the best medium for putting across the related information. There is a wide range of methods, and those that are most frequently used are listed in Table 9.1.

Table 9.1 Training methods	
Method	**Usage**
Lecture	Presenting information, particularly to a large number of people
Seminar	Ideal to discuss a topic or concept. The trainer may introduce the subject and run a group discussion on it. Trainees can present their views on which the trainer may comment.
Case study	These may describe hypothetical situations, while others are based on reality. They are a useful way of exposing trainees to organisational situations that are relevant to what the trainer wishes to communicate.
Role play	This is a case study in which the trainees adopt the roles of the characters in the situation. Usually, it is a problem-solving situation related to the subject of the course. Ideal for exercising interpersonal skills. Where necessary, the trainer intervenes to offer guidance.
Syndicate work	Normally a problem-solving session in which the trainees are given a problem based on an organisational situation. The course members are divided into small groups and asked to occupy syndicate rooms (where they are available) and try to find a solution to the problem. When they return to the main training area, they present their findings to the group.
Exercises	These are suitable for trainees to learn and practice skills for the first time. The 'Learning styles' activity in Chapter 7 is a typical example of this.

Training media

Information technology has extended the range of training media, especially in the area of visual aids. These include PowerPoint and DVDs. Other visual aids include overhead projector (OHP), whiteboard, flip chart, videos and films. Written material such as handouts is also a form of medium. Finally, your voice as a medium must not be overlooked, since it is a means by which you are conveying information.

There are occasions when the media you use are determined simply by what is available in the training facility, and sometimes therefore you just have to make do. Having said that, each of the media that are mentioned above lend themselves to particular subject matter. Meanwhile, Table 9.2 lists the most commonly used media and the purposes for which they are suitable.

Table 9.2 Commonly used visual training aids

Medium	Usage
PowerPoint	Everything is prepared on the computer. The package, usually includes instructions for use. It is usual to run off copies of the PowerPoint frames to hand out to the trainees as *aides memoire*. With this medium you can use colour and animation.
OHP	Suitable for presenting material in a piecemeal fashion, explaining and discussing as you go.
Whiteboard and flip chart	Handy for summarising syndicates findings, trainees' answers to your questions and for laying out the main points of a talk.
DVD, video and film	There is an infinite selection of these. Some are made specifically for training purposes in which actors adopt roles in case studies and problem solving situations. Others are well-known feature films in which there are leadership and motivation issues.

Preparing the course

Thorough preparation is the key to delivering a successful course, and there are several factors to be considered. You need to:

- assess the training venue and see what media hardware is available and in good working order
- create the course structure
- decide what methods and media you are going to use
- draft your presentation notes
- develop the visual aids
- select the DVDs/videos/ films (if any) you intend to use
- see what you can find out about the trainees.

Assessing the venue

It is important to take the time to visit the training facility. You need to know:

- The size and layout of the place. Will it accommodate your trainees comfortably? From which point in the room will you deliver the course?
- What visual and other training aids are available and are they all in working order?
- How many syndicate rooms are there (if any)?
- How does the place 'feel' in terms of its ambience? In other words, is it conducive to a pleasant and successful experience for the trainees?
- What are the catering facilities like?

Creating the course structure

Having decided on the duration of the course, you now have to decide how much of the time to allocate to each of its elements. Here, your priorities are governed partly by the importance of the elements in relation to each other, and partly by their detail and complexity, the latter implying that the trainees will need time to understand and internalise them. You also have to create a logical sequence in which they are to be delivered, allowing for reasonable breaks between each session.

Methods and media

These are listed in Tables 9.1 and 9.2, and bearing in mind the course objectives and the nature of the material you need to deliver, you have to select the methods and media which you regard as the most suitable in terms of purpose and clarity. Some subjects seem naturally to lend themselves to particular methods and media.

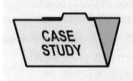

Case study 10: Testing your learning

Alison Haines, HR adviser at Harvey Plastics, had been involved in planning the company's new approach to performance appraisal, and was now designing a one-day course to train managers in how to implement the system. To explain the details of the course, she decided to deliver an illustrated talk using PowerPoint, to be followed by a question and answer session (Q&A) to clear up any points the managers raised. She knew that in addition to the knowledge input the talk would provide, the managers would want to give the system a run, so she decided that after the Q&A session, there would be a brief refreshment break at which the managers could chat to each other about the system. This would be followed by a role play exercise in which the managers would conduct one to one interviews with each other on the basis of fictional performance records. Obviously, the roles would be 'appraiser' and 'appraisee'. She injected a little humour into the fictional performance records to ensure that the session was enjoyable as well as instructive.

Drafting your course notes

Work out what you are going to say and how you are going to say it. Go through each element of the course carefully, draft a separate set of notes for each element and place them in a file in the order of delivery. On the right of each page, leave a margin that is wide enough to take 'reminder' notes such as when an OHP foil should be shown or when the trainees may need a slight pause while they absorb a particular point or concept. You need to get to know your notes so well that you hardly ever have to refer to them; just take them in as your security blanket!

Developing visual aids

Some visual aids come ready-made, such as videos and films. Others, such as OHP foils and PowerPoint presentations, you have to make yourself.

OHP foils

Handwritten or hand-drawn foils will make the presentation look amateurish, so if you can, use a computer. If, however, you must prepare them by hand, always slip ruled paper under the foil in order to get straight lines. Use block capital letters with a colour-fast OHP pen.

Foils prepared on a computer can look very attractive. The print is clear, and colour and appropriate images can be introduced to brighten things up. They will also help to hold the attention of your audience. Never transfer a page of typescript to an OHP foil: it looks amateur-ish and in any case, the type is far to small for the trainees to read. The basis of a good OHP foil is clear script in letters large enough for the people at the back of the room to read. Provide enough information for the reader to take in quickly, just four or five bullet-pointed lines on each foil.

Prepare notes to cover the contents of the OHP foil, but do not distribute them until the end of the session. If you do, your audience will be reading them while you are speaking. Tell the audience in advance that you will be handing out notes, otherwise they might try to make notes while they are listening to you.

Flip chart

This is quite a versatile tool. One of its main advantages is its portability. You may have to run a session in an area which is not customised for training, and if it is off-site, the flip chart will fit into the back of your car. Alternatively, syndicate groups can make their presentations on a flip chart, having prepared them during the syndicate session. In this way, different people's conclusions and recommendations may be compared, contrasted and discussed in a subsequent plenary session.

Running a training session

In advance of actually running a session, a good trainer will go through his/her notes thor-oughly and learn them so well that he/she seldom needs to refer to them. If you have never done it before, practise your delivery as if you are in the real situation.

To run a session effectively, you have to be skilled in the use of visual aids. You may be able to develop the skills if you are on an HR course. Many universities offer a short course in the use of media and training aids generally.

Establishing rapport

Before introducing the subject matter, you need to develop a friendly but businesslike atmosphere that is conducive to learning. If I have a class of students or trainees whom I have never previously met, I always write my name on the whiteboard and tell them something about myself. I ensure that trainees have their forenames on cards in front of them, not only so that I will know who they are, but in case they have never met each other.

Icebreakers

At this early stage, you can run a brief interactive session. The idea is to get the trainees talking to each other. I have used the following as an icebreaker and can assure you it can be very entertaining.

Example 9: Icebreaker

Ask each of the trainees to tell the group about him or herself: where he/she works and the job he/she does, where he/she lives, any hobbies and interests he/she has, and his/her likes and dislikes. These introductions need to be brief. If the session lasts about 20 minutes it will be time well spent. Don't forget to include yourself!

Introduction

It is vital for you to arouse the immediate interest of your audience with a good introduction of the subject. Without going into too much detail, tell them what you have planned for the session and the order in which each part of the course will be delivered. Then, just in case it was not understood by everyone, summarise it so that you are sure everyone knows what to expect.

Main sections

At this stage you start to deliver the first section of the course. Speak fairly slowly at first (without boring the audience) to make sure you are getting your points across. Use simple, everyday language and speak clearly. Never use jargon and avoid specialised terms except when it is absolutely necessary. Round off one idea or concept, pause, and then introduce the next.

There is a limit to the amount of information you should express verbally; good visual support material is essential. Focus your attention on concepts rather than detail; you can always provide detail on handouts at the end of the session. If you have included citations on your OHP foils or PowerPoint frames, leave them up there long enough for the trainees to jot down; otherwise include them on your handouts.

Pause for thought

If you are on a course, observe your lecturer; see how he or she delivers the material and at the end of the session, think about the planning that must have gone into it.

Handling questions

Keep a close eye on the clock! If you overrun you may not have time to answer questions. It is wise to lay the ground rules for questions from the beginning of the session. There are several ways of handling this. First, are you willing to take questions at any time? Second, would you prefer to take them at the end when you can see how much time you have left? (As your experience of training grows you will become adept at timing the sessions.) Third, you may decide to ask for questions at sectional points when, for example, you have just finished explaining a concept. There are advantages and disadvantages to all of these options.

Advantages

1. *Interruptions*. You may decide to turn these to your advantage. They may allow you to focus upon particular points of interest and engage your audience by encouraging them to participate with their thoughts and to change the pace and direction of your delivery. It is not unusual to be interrupted by someone who wishes to have a point clarified. This can be useful, since the understanding of what follows may depend on this.
2. *Taking questions at the end*. If you decide to do this you can be sure of a free run throughout your delivery, which would allow you to focus exclusively on what you are doing, while avoiding any digressive discussions.
3. *Inviting intermittent questions*. Again, this is an opportunity to engage the audience and give them a sense of participation. Also, it provides you with on-the-spot feedback: first, on how you are being received and second, to check the trainees' understanding.

Disadvantages

1. *Interruptions.* If you take questions 'on the hoof' you risk disrupting your timing of the session, or worse still, it might cause you to have to cut the duration of the session. Interruptions can interfere with the smooth flow of your talk, giving your audience a 'stop–start' impression, but more importantly, interruptions can cause you to lose track of where you are in the delivery sequence.
2. *Taking questions at the end.* If you decide to do this you could leave your audience stranded and feeling isolated, especially if you have not planned sufficient time for this part of your talk.
3. *Inviting intermittent questions.* Normally this is fine, but it could strike up a time-consuming discussion that runs out of control. If this happens, you have to cut it short and offer to continue the discussion at the end of the session.

Stage 5: Evaluate the course

Running and participating in a training session – perhaps a one or two-day course – should prove to be an interesting and exciting event for the trainer and the trainees. It is a socially interactive process after which the participants should feel confident that they have all learned from the experience. Additionally, it should also be effective in terms of achieving the training objectives; and it should be cost-effective.

Pause for thought

For developmental and financial reasons, evaluation is a vitally important process and yet most organisations pay little attention to it. They have ineffective systems of evaluation, or they ignore the need completely. Do you think that training without evaluation is a risky investment? Why?

Training evaluation is commonly seen as a feedback loop, starting with course objectives and ending by collecting end-of-course reactions which are then generally filed away and not acted on (Easterby-Smith and Mackness 1992).

Assessing cost-effectiveness

Earlier, I alluded to training needs analysis as the process through which corporate needs are identified, but for ease of understanding, I have placed most of the emphasis on meeting individual training needs. In both contexts, corporate and individual, training is an investment in terms of time and resources, and when it has been carried out, the question to be asked is, 'Did it pay off?' In other words, has the performance of the individual(s) and the organisation improved in accordance with expectations?

Assessing individuals

An experienced trainer can roughly assess the effectiveness of the training while he/she is delivering it. When, for example, exercises and group work are carried out, the trainees' answers to the questions provide at least an inkling. One of the most popular methods is to distribute a questionnaire immediately after the session. Often referred to as a 'happiness sheet', the trainees are asked to respond to questions about the effectiveness of the trainer, what they have learned, how strongly their new knowledge/skill relates to their work, and so forth. There are, however, several more informative and objective methods.

- *Examinations*, tests, assignments and projects typify assessment at the end of formal award-bearing educational courses.
- *Interviewing* the trainees to elicit their reactions to the course.
- *Performance appraisal*. This is a main section in Chapter 10. Suffice to say here that the trainee might have been sent on to the course when the need was identified during the appraisal process, or the trainee might have put in a request to attend the course as part of his/her personal development plan.

Tyson and York (1996) say that there are two stages when as assessment of the individual needs to be made: first, on completion of training to determine whether training objectives have been achieved, and second, after a lapse of time following the completion of training to asses the effects on work performance.

Training for performance

You should infer from the foregoing that the results of a formal training evaluation will tell you about the effectiveness of the course in terms of the degree to which the training objectives have been achieved. We saw in Chapter 8 that learning changes people's behaviour. In this context the behaviour in which we are interested is the employee's performance, and truly, it is performance that speaks loudest. In the final analysis, the training objectives are to develop new knowledge and skills in people so they can put in an extra or improved performance.

Stage 6: Analysis and review

It is rare for a training session that is being run for the first time to achieve every single aspect of every objective, and even more rare for it to fail completely. Analysis and review is the final stage of the systematic training cycle. The task is to review how the course was received and to examine its effectiveness. An analysis of the results of evaluation will reveal areas that need to be improved. Evaluation, analysis and review are components of a continuous process, so after a course has been run a second time, it is reviewed again and re-evaluated in order to achieve improvements.

Self-test questions

1. What were the main factors that focused managers' attention on HRD?
2. How would you define HRD?
3. Who benefits from HRD and why?
4. If you were asked why you have a personal development plan what would you tell the questioner?
5. What is the National Employer Training Programme?
6. What are the components of the systematic training cycle?
7. How would a job analysis help you to identify training needs?
8. What is meant by the acronym SMART and how would you explain each of the elements?
9. How would you distinguish between training methods and training media?
10. Why is it important to evaluate, review and modify training courses?

Performance management

Introduction

The aim of this chapter is to explain performance management and discuss it as a management function. To clarify your understanding of this, there are separate definitions and descriptions of *performance management, performance* and *performance appraisal*. The main body of the chapter explains and discusses the principles and processes of performance management and the traditional and modern approaches to assessing performance.

Background

Organisations have always been interested in employee performance but the term 'performance management' is relatively new. It has its foundations in the HRM belief that organisational success is determined by the performance of its employees. Systems of appraisal are still used to monitor performance in retrospect, whereas performance management is a carefully planned attempt to ensure a high future performance. This involves running programmes of employee development and encouraging employees to have their own personal development plans.

Performance management is an organisation-wide concept. That is to say, if an organisation realises its overall corporate strategy, then it must have performed according to plan, been successful in the pursuit of its goals and achieved its objectives through the efforts of the managers, teams and individuals. Viewed in this way, performance management can be seen as a concern of everyone in the organisation.

Definitions

Academics' perceptions of performance management vary. For example, it is:

a strategic and integrated approach to delivering sustained success to organisations by improving the performance of the people who work in them and by developing the capabilities of teams and individual contributors.

(Armstrong and Baron 1998)

On the other hand:

Performance management (or more accurately forms of performance-related pay) has formed a key activity for managers and management in the quest to increase the benefits gained by the application of labour power.

(Pointon and Ryan 2004)

Definition: performance management

Performance management is a systematic and strategic approach to ensuring that employees' performance, as individuals and team members, enables the organisation to achieve a competitive advantage by producing the level and quality of products and services that lead to customer satisfaction and, thereby, the achievement of objectives and the ultimate realisation of strategy.

Performance management through development

The main purpose of performance management is to improve the performance of all employees across the whole organisation; *employee development,* therefore, is a key issue. To improve performance it is necessary for the organisation to have a set of effective development programmes that are accessible to everyone. Improved performance is also achieved through encouraging individual employees to create their own personal development plans (PDP) so that they can build on their repertoire of competences and monitor their own performance.

To make this work, managers have to develop a personal communication style that informs and involves employees to the extent that they understand what is required of them in terms of standards and competence, and elicits their co-operation, commitment and involvement. Managers need the co-operation of employees in order to achieve the objectives of teams and departments, and it would be unreasonable for them to expect employees' co-operation unless they are told precisely the nature of what is required.

Managers should also listen to and think about what employees have to say, and where desirable and feasible, act upon their ideas.

Example 10: Achieving co-operation

Just before the battle of El Alamein in the Second World War, Field Marshal Montgomery wanted to talk informally to his troops. He wanted to tell them about his plan for the battle and why he thought it was the best way forward. Instead of lining them up in formal ranks, he asked them to gather around him and he addressed them from the top of a bren carrier. He wanted their co-operation: after all, they too had an interest in achieving a victory. That was indicative of the style with which he led them into one of the most significant turning points in the war. It succeeded.

Principles of performance management

These were summarised in 1996 by the IRS as follows:

- It translates corporate goals into individual, team, department and divisional goals.
- It helps to clarify corporate goals.
- It is a continuous and evolutionary process in which performance improves over time.
- It relies on consensus and co-operation, rather than control or coercion.
- It encourages self-management of individual performance.
- It requires a management style that is open and honest and encourages two-way communication between supervisors and subordinates.
- It requires continuous feedback.
- Feedback loops enable the experiences and knowledge gained on the job by individuals to modify corporate objectives.
- It measures and assesses all performance against jointly agreed goals.
- It should apply to all staff; and it is not primarily concerned with linking performance to financial reward.

Pause for thought

Think about what you have just read. Do you think you now know what performance management is? Could you paraphrase one of the definitions?

What is performance?

Before taking this discussion any further, it is as well to clarify what is meant by the word 'performance'. It is one of those words that one would think hardly needs to be defined since we all somehow think we know what it means. In organisational terms it seems to be difficult to define without mentioning *measurement*, which of course, introduces the subject of *performance appraisal*. For example: 'Performance is a multi-dimensional construct, the measurement of which varies, depending on a variety of factors' (Bates and Holton 1995).

Performance as behaviour

In fact, performance is behaviour and it is not anything else, because when you perform – you are doing something – you are behaving. It may be the cause of an outcome, but it is not the outcome itself. In the organisational context, therefore, performance is about doing the job. Actors perform, and as in the workplace, some perform better than others, and some perform brilliantly in one role and not so brilliantly in another.

Key concept 10: determining performance

The level and the quality of an employee's performance are governed by two factors: first, by his or her ability to carry out the work and second, the motivation to do so: Performance = Ability x Motivation (P = A x M).

You can, therefore, talk about the level and the quality of performance, and clearly an individual can only do a job if he/she possesses the necessary knowledge and skills. However, the fact that a person possesses knowledge and skills does not guarantee that he/she will use them to the organisation's advantage; people have to be motivated. People only ever do what they are motivated to do.

Example 11: The influence of motivation

Two people are doing exactly similar work and both are equally competent, yet one of them is putting in a better performance than the other. Since you know that neither one is better than the other at doing the job, you have to ask yourself what could be the cause of the difference in performance? The only possible answer is a difference in their motivation. Perhaps the poorer performer is unwell or distracted by a personal problem, in which case he/she is motivated to focus on that, rather than on the job. Alternatively, he/she might not like doing the job.

Factors influencing performance

Those who are responsible for managing performance focus on the two factors: ability and motivation. A sound and reliable recruitment and selection system will ensure a supply of competent and/or trainable people, while an employee development programme that is job-related should go a long way towards the provision of the ability factor. The *motivation* to perform, however, is influenced by many factors, some of which are organisational, while others are related to the individual's attitudes and other personality factors.

Organisational factors relate to the work environment such as the state of the employee relationship, the leadership and communication style of the managers and the general organisational culture (see Table 10.1).

Table 10.1 Organisational factors influencing motivation

Factor	Effect
Training and development	Raises morale and brings about feelings of competence, visible changes in the employee's behaviour and tangible benefits in terms of performance improvement. An important outcome of training is that it increases the versatility of the employee; multi-skilling and sharing complex tasks imbues confidence and mutual respect.
Employee relations	Sound and fair policies and procedures sustain an individual's motivation to work. Since the 1980s, an appreciation of the mutual interest that managers and employees have in the survival and enrichment of the organisation has a motivating effect.
Reward	This plays a vital role in work motivation. Reward in the financial sense is seen by employees as a return on the investment of their time, skills and efforts. If, therefore, they see reward as fair and reasonable, they will continue to be motivated to work.
Leadership style	Many employees still see themselves as 'working for', rather than 'working with' their managers. The style with which managers communicate with their staff, therefore, has a significant effect on the effort that the employee is prepared to put in *for the manager!*

Table 10.1 shows the main organisational factors that influence motivation, and as one would expect, the same factors also influence morale. Morale, however, is a *group* phenomenon whereas motivation is an *individual* phenomenon. Culture, for example, which is an organisational factor, may be benign or hostile and may raise or lower the morale of the employees as a group, whereas *personality factors* may relate to the individual's attitude to work, the job itself and the organisation.

All individuals are different from each other in terms of their attitudes towards things, their likes and dislikes and so forth. When you make an offer of a job to someone, you usually do so on the grounds that he/she closely matches the requirements of the job as written up in the person specification. When he/she comes into work, however, it is not just the qualities you want that turn up: it is the whole person, complete with hang-ups, preferences, prejudices, personal values, needs and expectations. Remember, however, that appropriate psychological testing will indicate these factors before the person is employed.

Attitudes to work

As an academic subject, attitudes to work are complex and usually appear in texts on occupational psychology and organisational behaviour. We have to recognise the distinctions between different individuals' attitudes to work and the following, which is included for explanatory purposes, describes just two broad 'worker types'.

Security seekers. To these employees work is not the top priority in their lives, they simply use it as a means to some other end. If the job meets their needs in terms of, *inter alia*, income, the length of the working week, holiday entitlement, pension scheme and the distance between work and home, they would be prepared to accept it. If they were to lose the job, they would seek alternative employment in the same area with roughly the same terms and conditions. They value the friendships and family ties that they have in their community and are not prepared to uproot and move away for the sake of taking up a particular job.

Pause for thought

Writing in *Employee Benefits* (3 July 2002 p3), Cary Cooper, then head of organisational psychology and health at the University of Manchester, suggests that 'not all employees are brimming over with motivation,' but Cooper believes that this is not necessarily a problem: 'as long as they are doing a good job, and that's all they want to do. … [W]hy not just accept it? 'Why do they have to be high flyers? Not everybody can be a high performing employee. … [Y]ou need some people who can do the job and get it done properly.'

Question: What might be the implications for the organisation if all managers thought this way?

High flyers. These are people to whom work is the number one priority. Most often, they are professional or managerial people who are career-conscious, promotion-seeking and earnestly striving to do well. Alternatively, they may be specialists in fields that demand high levels of technical knowledge and skills. Such people enjoy what they do and are deeply committed to the purpose and/or the technology that their work involves. They would readily move to another country, even to the other side of the world, if that was where their work took them.

These, of course, are very broad distinctions between individuals; 'worker types' may be classified in much greater detail (Porteous 1997, p19).

Motivation

While there is no universal definition of motivation, it is generally accepted to be 'the willingness to apply one's efforts towards the achievement of a goal that satisfies an individual

Pause for thought

Read the section on motivation and then consider what job factors you think would be most likely to arouse the motivation to work in (1): *security seekers* and (2) *high flyers*.

need.' It is a natural human response to a stimulus. The response involves action designed to satisfy a need or attain a particular goal.

Work motivation is 'the willingness to apply one's efforts towards the achievement of the organisation's goals, while concurrently an individual need is satisfied'.

The main interest of managers is to achieve their objectives by maximising their resources, including the human resource. Their goal, therefore, is to elicit a performance from their staff that will lead to the achievement of their objectives.

To reach that goal managers often look for clues in motivation theories, on the grounds that 'a motivated workforce is a high-performing workforce'. While there is little research evidence to support this statement, logic tells us that it is safe to assume that there is some substance in it, since there is no such thing as an 'unmotivated' person and it is motivation that triggers behaviour.

Motivation is a constant factor in human behaviour and it cannot be switched off. Even if you were to drop off to sleep, a psychologist would rightly assume that is what you were motivated to do. The manager's aim, therefore, should be to change employees' motivations from what they are to what he/she wishes them to be.

Scientific management

It is more than 100 years since academic interest in the human side of industry was stimulated by Frederick Winslow Taylor, a US steel engineer, when he worked in Chicago as a management consultant at the Bethlehem Steel Corporation (BSC). It was there that he carried out the work for which he is most well known. While he did not propose a formal theory of motivation, he did devise a practical way of improving the productivity of manual workers, using money as the incentive.

Taylor developed a set of principles that formed the core of a system that was later referred to as *scientific management* (Taylor 1911, 1947). His central principles were:

1. Apply scientific methods to management by using work measurement as a basis for accurate planning and production control.
2. Establish the best work methods: give each worker a clearly defined task.
3. Select, train and instruct subordinates scientifically.
4. Pay people fairly: high pay for successful completion of work.
5. Obtain co-operation between management and men and divide responsibility between them.

Taylor studied the jobs of tough manual labourers, who spent the day loading pig iron on to railway tenders. He studied the capabilities of the human body and the length of time it took to carry out particular tasks. In other words, he invented what we now call *work study*. He then tied the pay of the workers to their performance. Today this is referred to as *payment by results*, or PBR schemes, which are now far more sophisticated (see Chapter 12).

Taylor's development of scientific management is one of the most well-known studies in the history of management thought. He was concerned that industry was afflicted with problems that were rooted mainly in a severe lack of knowledge. 'Management,' he declared, 'is ignorant of what men can produce ... and they make no effort to find out or even define what a day's work is.' The workers took it for granted that there would be delays, 'down time' and other problems because they did not realise that there might be a better way of doing things; nor did they know how to improve their performance because they had not been shown.

Taylor's aim was to remove the guesswork from management and replace it with facts. He showed the men how to use their physiques to the best effect in order to increase their productivity, and he motivated them to do this by tying their pay to their performance.

Pause for thought

Reflect on your organisation, or one with which you are familiar. How many of Taylor's five principles are evident in the way that work is carried out?

It was Taylor's belief that people worked in order to obtain financial rewards rather than because they were interested in what they were doing. His main objective was to increase productivity, and it seemed logical to him to simply show the workers how they might increase their rewards: 'The more you produce, the more you will earn.' The notion that the labourers with whom he dealt would benefit psychologically from job satisfaction and involvement probably did not occur to him.

Theories of motivation

Two main approaches to motivation were proposed in the twentieth century. The first is based on *content* or *arousal theories,* in which people are said to have needs which may (to some degree) be satisfied by the factors that make up the job. Second are *process theories*, in which our experience has taught us that certain behaviours produces particular outcomes and we do what we do in the expectation of achieving desired outcomes. In this way, motivation is generated through a mental process, rather than as a response to particular job factors.

Content theories of motivation

By far the most well known of these theorists was Abraham Maslow (1954, 1972). He proposed a *theory of growth motivation*, in which he classified five human needs and said that we behave in ways that are designed to have those needs met in a particular order of priorities. The classification, which is referred to as a *hierarchy of needs*, is as follows:

1. *Physiological.* These are the basic biological needs that lead to our survival. Human beings are born with primitive emotions that are aroused when the body needs something and we respond by behaving in ways that are designed to reduce the emotions, thus:

Emotion	Motivated behaviour
Thirst	Drinking
Hunger	Eating
Fear	Escaping or confronting
Fatigue	Resting/sleeping
Sex	Ensure survival of species

2. *Safety and security.* The need for a danger-free, non-threatening and secure environment.
3. *Belongingness.* The need to feel part of humanity; attached to other individuals and groups.
4. *Love and esteem.* The need to know where we stand with our relationships with others; how we are seen in terms of respect, especially by those whom we ourselves value.
5. *Self-actualisation.* The need to be self-fulfilled by developing our capacities and expressing them through our behaviour.

Maslow maintained that we progress through the hierarchy so that when we are sure that our physiological needs are or will be met, we will move up and turn our attention to safety and security. Next we turn to love and esteem needs and so on until we reach self-actualisation. He further classified the first, second and third levels as *lower-order needs* and the fourth and fifth as *higher-order needs*.

Other motivation analysts have proposed content theories similar to that of Maslow: for example Clayton P Alderfer, whose research and publications took place between the 1940s and 1980s.

ERG theory

Alderfer (1972) proposed three categories of need which were a kind of contraction of Maslow's classification. Essentially, what he did was to draw a parallel between Maslow's five categories and three categories of his own, which he referred to as *existence, relatedness* and *growth*.

Existence needs are concerned with physiological, safety and security needs and cover all needs of a material nature that are necessary for human survival. *Relatedness* needs mean those for love, esteem and belongingness, while *growth* needs are represented by achievement, recognition and the realisation of potential: what Maslow called self-actualisation.

Motivation–hygiene theory: F.W. Herzberg *et al*

Herzberg (Herzberg *et al* 1957) was principally interested in job satisfaction. He wanted to know which job factors created feelings of satisfaction within employees and which created dissatisfaction. The subjects of his research were asked to recall things that had happened at work that produced feelings of satisfaction and dissatisfaction. Herzberg labelled the factors that produced satisfaction as *motivators* and those that produced dissatisfaction *hygiene factors*. The most frequently occurring *motivators* were:

- achievement
- recognition
- the work itself
- responsibility
- advancement.

The most frequently occurring *hygiene* factors were:

- company policy and administration
- supervision – the technical aspects
- salary
- interpersonal relations – supervision
- working conditions.

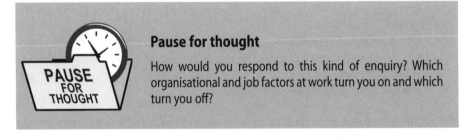

Pause for thought

How would you respond to this kind of enquiry? Which organisational and job factors at work turn you on and which turn you off?

Extrinsic job factors

A distinction needs to be drawn between the individual's perceptions of the working environment on the one hand and the nature of the job itself on the other. The work environment is seen as the context in which the job is set; not only the physical environment but also in terms of what motivation analysts call *extrinsic* job factors. That is to say that these factors are outside what one might refer to as the job–person unit. Extrinsic job factors might be listed as:

Company policy	Health and safety
Managerial style	Working time
Culture	Holiday entitlement
Peer relationships	Pension scheme

Note that none of the above factors is a central feature of the job itself.

Intrinsic job factors

Within the job–person unit are what the content theorists call the *intrinsic* job factors. These include the tasks that the job holder has to carry out, but they also include what might be regarded as personal features (see Table 10.2).

This is not to say that the employee feels as if he/she is working in a psychological cocoon, although sometimes it may seem to be so, especially where the job requires high concentration. Depending on how the job has been designed, the intrinsic job factors might affect the job holder personally, and whether or not the job holder feels the need to modify such factors may be determined by the appropriateness of his/her knowledge and skills.

Table 10.2 The job–person unit

Intrinsic job factor	Meaning
Authority	The right amount for what I do and for the position of the job in the organisation/department
Responsibility	For my own productivity and quality of my work
Autonomy	Freedom to be a 'self-starter'; to make decisions about how the job might be carried out
Variety	The opportunity to exercise a variety of skills, removing boredom from the job
Recognition	For the quality of my work and general performance standard

Alternatively, it may be determined by personality factors in terms of how he/she is affected by actually doing the job.

Pause for thought

Depending on such factors as the work system, it might be possible to design a job to fit the person, but should we do this? Or should we, through training and counselling, try to alter the individual's attitude towards the job?

Job characteristics model

Hackman and Oldham (1976, 1980) carried out research that was based on the idea that differences between and among individuals determine how employees respond to the nature and design of their work. Hackman and Oldham identified five core job characteristics:

1. *Skill variety.* This refers to the number of different skills that are required in order to carry out the tasks efficiently and effectively. It is preferred to the dullness and boredom of carrying out just one or two repetitive tasks that can be completed in a brief work cycle.
2. *Task identity.* This is the degree to which the individual performs a complete task, rather than just a small part of it. For example, the way the work used to be designed for assembly line car workers meant that they did not always know to which part of the car they were contributing.
3. *Task significance.* In what way, if at all, does what they do affect the lives of others, in terms, perhaps, of well-being, pleasure or service?
4. *Autonomy.* This is the degree to which individuals have freedom to exercise choice and discretion in their work. For example, are they allowed to order their own materials?
5. *Feedback.* To what extent are performance indicators built into the job?

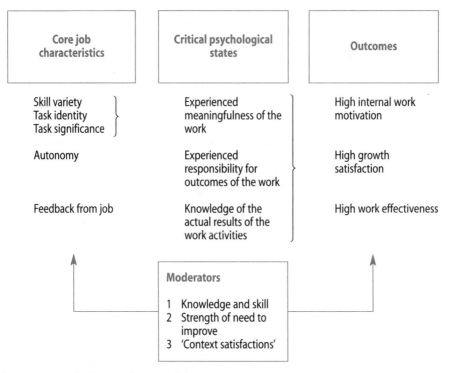

Figure 10.1 Job characteristics model

Source: Hackman and Oldham (1980).

Other content theories

Theory X and Theory Y

McGregor (1960) claimed that managers who wish to motivate their staff have a dimensional view of how they might be motivated. At the *Theory X* end of the dimension is the individual who has an inherent dislike of work, is indolent and will avoid it whenever possible. Continuous prodding, coercion and even threats are needed in order to get this kind of person to work. Managers who are authoritarian by nature tend to treat people in that way.

Employees at the *Theory Y* end of the dimension do not need to be cajoled or coerced because they have the opposite view of work. They are 'self-starters' to whom work comes as naturally as relaxation and play.

Theory X and Theory Y are terms that are still used in industry today, but they are used not to describe particular types of employee, rather to describe particular types of manager because of their characteristic approach towards the control of workers. In other words, it is said that there are 'Theory X managers' and 'Theory Y managers'. So far as the employees are concerned it is probably true to say that their attitude to work is normally distributed across the whole dimension, with the most work-shy at the Theory X end and the least work-shy at the Theory Y end.

Criticisms of need-based/content theories

There are several criticisms of these theories. In the case of Maslow, for example, the structured progression through the lower-order to higher-order needs seems not to occur for many people. Research has shown (Rauschenberger *et al* 1980) that a significant number are happy to accept the satisfactions provided by the lower-order needs. People need to fulfil themselves, yes, but in many cases, that fulfilment is achieved by pursuing interests outside the workplace. More general criticisms of the various theorists are:

- Needs did not group together in the ways predicted
- There was no clear relationship between needs and behaviour, so that, for example, the same behaviour could reflect different needs, and different behaviours the same needs.
- Needs were generally described with insufficient precision.
- The whole notion of a need as a biological phenomenon is problematic in that it ignores the capacity of people to construct their own perceptions of needs. (Wahba and Bridwell 1976; Salancik and Pfeffer 1977)

Process theories of motivation

Expectancy theory

This theory was first proposed by Vroom (1964), and is based on the idea that as we develop we come to understand that our behaviour has consequences. Sometimes we enjoy the outcomes of our behaviour and sometimes we are hurt or saddened by them, and we learn to avoid behaving in particular ways and try to repeat the behaviours that produce pleasure.

Expectancy theory is alternatively referred to as *instrumentality theory* or *VIE theory*, *V* meaning valence, *I* meaning instrumentality and *E* meaning expectancy. In this, individuals select their behaviour from a number of possible alternatives, depending on the degree to which they value the anticipated outcome. In other words, people ask themselves:

- *Expectancy*: am I capable of doing what I plan to do; what will be in it for me?
- *Instrumentality*: would performing the action lead to the desired outcome?
- *Valence*: to what extent do I value the outcome I am expecting?

Porter and Lawler's expectancy theory

While the content theorists attempted to demonstrate that job satisfaction leads to improved performance, Porter and Lawler's (1968) further development of Vroom's ideas indicates that it is in fact performance that produces satisfaction (see Figure 10.2, overleaf). Porter and Lawler point out that effort alone is not enough to produce a good performance; the individual has to be equipped with the right knowledge and skills and have the kind of personality that is attracted by the second-level outcomes. They say that while there is a relationship between motivation, satisfaction and performance, all three are discrete variables, and that the *levels* of motivation, satisfaction and performance are determined by the individual's perception of the outcomes.

In both the Vroom and the Porter and Lawler models, rewards may be intrinsic or extrinsic, and different behaviours produce different outcomes. Depending on their personality characteristics and their ultimate aims, individuals variously prefer intrinsic and extrinsic rewards. One individual might behave in a particular way because he/she is aiming for an extrinsic, need-related reward, while another individual will behave differently because his/her aim is for an intrinsic need-related reward.

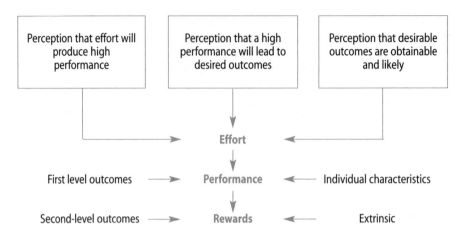

Figure 10.2 Expectancy theory: a model of behaviour

Source: Porter and Lawler (1968).

Equity–inequity theory

This process theory (Adams 1961) is based on the concept of fairness, or more accurately, a *fair exchange*. We know that people expect certain outcomes from their behaviour, but what is their perception of those outcomes in terms of value? In the work situation, for example, how does the value of the worker's input compare with the value of the related outcome: for example, 'a fair day's work for a fair day's pay'? This is a question of *perceived* value. Individuals have a perception of both values, intrinsically and extrinsically, and might ask themselves: is the reward worth the effort I put in?

Adams' central theme is that it is the quest for perceived equity that motivates the work effort:

- Where reward values are perceived to exceed input values, the work effort will increase because of feelings of guilt or inadequacy.
- Where the input values are perceived to exceed the reward values, the work effort will decrease in an attempt to redress the balance.

It is likely, however, that the individual's perception of fairness, or a *fair exchange*, in the above respects will influence his/her *behaviour* rather than exclusively the work effort. An alternative to feelings of guilt or inadequacy, for example, could be fear, especially where the perceived value of the reward is considerably greater than the value of the worker's input. The worker may decide to look busy, as if he/she is overloaded with work, without actually putting in any extra effort. Where the value of the work is perceived to be greater than the reward, rather than decrease the work effort, the individual might review his/her perception of the values on the basis that: 'after all, the rewards seem to be acceptable to those doing work that is similar to mine'. Alternatively, the individual might decide to seek employment where the perceived value of the rewards matches that of his/her input.

Summary of motivation theories

Content theorists stress the importance of environmental and in-job factors and say that employees are more or less motivated by the presence or absence of desired factors. Process

Case study 11: Relative values

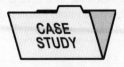

Gerry Reed, a labourer, was working on one of two office blocks that were being erected by different contracting firms on opposite sides of a road in a new out-of-town business park. One day, Gerry had just started to have his lunch when he looked across the road and saw that his cousin Pete, also a builder's labourer and a near neighbour, was working on the building opposite, so Gerry went across to see him and they had their lunch together. After exchanging the normal greetings, the conversation turned to pay, and Gerry discovered that Pete was earning £1.50p an hour more than he, for doing similar work.

During the rest of the building programme, Gerry and Pete saw each other across the road and they smiled and waved to each other, but did not engage in conversation; nor did Gerry walk across to have lunch with Pete. Instead, Gerry preferred to stay on his site and have lunch with his workmates, all of whom were on the same pay as he was.

Question: Considering the ideas within the content and process theories discussed above, which theoretical ideas do you think most closely match Gerry's behaviour? What other actions do these theories suggest Gerry might take?

theorists, on the other hand, say that people *choose* to behave in particular ways because they expect to achieve desired outcomes. It is a *mental process* that motivates us towards a particular course of behaviour, and we speculate or predict the outcomes before we act. It is important for managers and HR practitioners to have a sound understanding of what motivates people to work. Motivation leads to performance, and the degree to which a knowledgeable and skilled individual will apply his/her best efforts to a task is determined by the degree to which he/she is motivated.

Despite the criticisms of content theories, there is no doubt that most employees are motivated by such extrinsic rewards as money, friendly relationships with workplace peers and a managerial attitude that offers recognition, respect and consideration. It is also true that when people are faced with a number of alternative courses of action that might lead to the achievement of their desired outcomes, they go through the mental process of choosing the most appropriate behaviour.

Additionally, it is important to bear in mind the element of individual differences. People have their own unique attitudes to work, the job and the organisation, and they are not all turned on by the same motivators or possible types of outcome.

Performance assessment systems

First, this section discusses and critically reviews the traditional approaches to managing individual performance which are still widely used in the UK. Following that we shall move on to discuss modern approaches.

Performance management activities are designed to assess and improve employees' performance. How the activities are carried out has undergone considerable review since the 1980s, when HRM drew attention to the importance of performance as a means of achieving a competitive advantage. Some organisations, however, have either ignored or only partially adopted the principles and practices of HRM, and in UK industry today there is a variety of assessment systems.

Reward and potential

Many organisations use systems that include mechanisms for calculating, on the basis of the person's performance, the amount of pay he/she should receive in future and the individual's suitability for promotion. Systems of this nature often involve the use of complex calculating mechanisms designed to culminate in 'grading' the appraisee. How he/she is treated thereafter in terms of pay and promotion prospects depends upon the level of the grading given. Clearly, such systems should be fair and assessment should be based on valid evidence.

Three types of appraisal

It has been suggested that performance, pay and promotion are the three main purposes of appraisal, and that each should have its own separate system (Randell et al 1984). If you put pay on the agenda at an appraisal interview, then it is likely that pay, rather than performance, will predominate in the appraisee's mind.

So far as promotion is concerned, if an appraisal interview is conducted properly, the informational outcome will not be relevant to any decision about promotion. That is to say, that an individual performs well in one job might only indicate a similar performance in another job (the one to which he/she might be promoted) if the knowledge and skill requirements are the same: and in the case of promotion, they usually are not. In any case, the process used to identify and select employees with the potential to adopt greater responsibility is quite different from that used for performance appraisal. When considering someone for promotion, you are trying to predict in-job performance, just as you would in employment selection.

The results of performance appraisal may be used for a variety of purposes. In addition to those mentioned above, they may be any of the following:

- to reinforce performance standards
- to agree future standards
- to motivate the appraisee
- to identify training needs
- to address any problems the appraisee has encountered
- to assist in progressing the individual's personal development plan.

Establishing assessment criteria

Regardless of the approach that is used, the criteria against which assessments are to be made have to be clear to the person carrying out the appraisal and to the appraisee. The key factors that are identified through job analysis are used as criteria, and the performance requirement in terms of standards is set when the job is first described.

Traditional systems

There are several approaches within the traditional models of performance appraisal, but the one that is familiar to most managers and employees involves the manager in an annual interview with each individual employee in order to carry out a review of his/her performance. The stages involved in this model are as follows:

1. About two weeks prior to the interview, the employee is given a *self-assessment form* which is designed to give the employee a measured way of assessing of the key points in the job. The underlying idea is that the questions on the form will focus the employee's attention on to the various features of the job, and cause him/her to try to make an objective assessment of his/her own performance.
2. The manager also has a form which he/she too completes in advance of the interview. It is important that the manager assesses the employee in the light of valid and verifiable information.
3. The two then get together to reach agreement over the degree to which the employee has met the required standards.

How the system works

The main features that emerged from the job analysis are listed and rating scales are set against each one. The factors on the list include such job-related features as the knowledge and skill requirements, and perhaps several personal qualities such as initiative, intelligence, social skills, etc, depending on the nature of the job and its requirements. Employees are then rated on the degree to which they possess these factors. Rating scales may be designed in several ways (see Table 10.3).

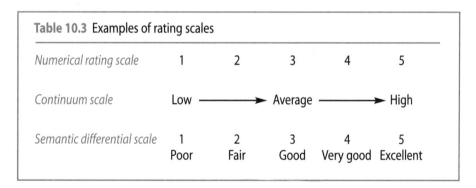

Table 10.3 Examples of rating scales

Numerical rating scale	1	2	3	4	5
Continuum scale	Low ⟶		Average ⟶		High
Semantic differential scale	1 Poor	2 Fair	3 Good	4 Very good	5 Excellent

Behaviourally anchored rating scales (BARS)

This is more recent than any of the other traditional models and it differs from them in that it attempts to measure performance in terms of behaviour. This is what the individual actually does, rather than the person's capabilities or other qualities, although personal qualities such as initiative are deduced from what the individual actually achieves. Scales for this model are devised after discussion, observation of behaviour and analysis, usually by managers, HR practitioners and sometimes external consultants. Job analysis is critical to this process, since the first objective is to identify the key categories of performance in each job or *job family*.

When the categories have been identified and verified, examples of *poor, average* and *good* performance are provided by the managers and HR practitioners. The number of categories, or anchors, assigned to each job varies, depending on the structure and complexity of the job. Each category is given a numerical value on a semantic differential scale, ranging perhaps from 1–7 on a 'least efficient' through to the 'most efficient' performance, or actual job-related behaviour.

Criticisms of appraisal systems

While BARS was hailed as a significant advance in performance appraisal, subsequent experience of actually applying the model showed that the preparatory work – identifying performance categories and developing scales, and so on – was costly and time-consuming. All appraisal systems have to be reviewed from time to time, such as when organisational changes create the need to redefine jobs, and it was found that reviewing the BARS system was a tedious process.

It also has to be borne in mind that all appraisal systems are susceptible to subjectivity on the part of the manager and the employee. The BARS approach reduces the effect of this through a consensus, since several people establish the performance criteria. Unfortunately, however, there is one dominant factor which might at worst undermine the whole system, and at best will only affect the outcome of one appraisal. That is what might be called the *relationship effect,* which in basic terms means how the manager and the employee get on with each other.

On the question of subjectivity, Ian Roberts (2001) says that 'The inherent subjectivity of the assessment process may lead to claims of favouritism, bias and arbitrariness.' During a study by Geary (1992, p46), one of the employees asserted: 'Your appraisal depends on your supervisor. If you are liked or socialise with him you're more likely to get a good review!'

A further problem is indifference or lack of interest, in which the process becomes a kind of form-filling exercise: an annual ritual in which the manager and the employee meet primarily to complete the forms which end up gathering dust in a cabinet in the 'personnel office'.

More recent approaches

Since the 1980s the attitudes of organisations to people management have changed. In organisations that have adopted the principles and practices of HRM, with its lean and flattened structures, the manager and the employee have a close working relationship. The old-fashioned 'boss–subordinate' relationship has been replaced by what is more like a working partnership.

Performance agreement/contract

In the situation described above, it is easier for the manager and the employee to reach agreement over the performance requirements and the job's key result areas. This can be turned into a *performance agreement*, or *contract*. The agreement, therefore, is based on the assumption that the employee is clearly aware of what is expected in terms of performance and of how his/her performance will be assessed.

360-degree feedback

This is a comparatively recent development that has grown in popularity. Alternatively referred to as *multisource assessment*, the idea, as defined by Ward (1995) is that it is 'The systematic collection and feedback of performance data on an individual or group derived from a number of stakeholders on their performance.'

What happens is that the people with whom the individual has day-to-day contact provide measures of his/her performance by completing a questionnaire which includes a rating scale (see Table 10.3) designed to measures competences. Their data is fed into the process to be collated (see Figure 10.3).

Ward's reference to stakeholders (above) may include, for example, the person's immediate boss, peers such as team colleagues and individuals, internal and external customers and suppliers, other work colleagues and subordinates. Clearly, in advance of the formal assessment, the manager and the employee already possess much of the criteria-related information that will be used, but it is equally clear that the manager will not always be present when the employee encounters the stakeholders in the course of the job.

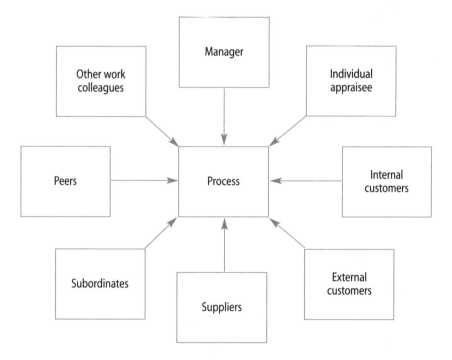

Figure 10.3 A model of 360-degree feedback

In Figure 10.3, you can see that all of the stakeholders feed their assessment data into the process. I have placed a relatively large number of participants in Figure 10.3 so that you can appreciate the range of possibilities.

Use of the outcomes

360-degree feedback is a versatile model serving the purposes of the organisation and the individual. For example, research has shown that organisations use it primarily for appraisal, but also for career management and resourcing purposes (Handy *et al* 1996). The outcomes are also used for decisions on promotion and pay, although there is evidence of strong disagreement.

Employee development

Developmental needs may have been identified during the process of assessing past performance, but development/training may also be discussed by the manager and employee when, for example, they are setting and agreeing future objectives.

Managers have been heard to complain that the model is costly and time-consuming, but the research referred to above does demonstrate considerable benefits. Armstrong (1999) says that the problems also include:

- people not giving frank or honest feedback
- people being put under stress in receiving or giving feedback
- over-reliance on technology
- too much bureaucracy.

The performance review

While in modern terms, managers and employees work closely, a tradition has been established in which the normal practice is to hold an annual review of each employee's performance. Traditionally, the purposes are to:

- review the employee's performance over the past appraisal period
- identify training/counselling needs when discussing shortfalls in performance and future development
- motivate the individual and set and agree future objectives and performance standards
- agree arrangements for future development and in particular, discuss and exchange ideas about the employee's personal development plan.

Importance

The manager should attribute due importance to the event, and be seen to do so. To the employees, the interview is very important; they are usually well prepared when the day comes and they make a special effort with their appearance.

PAUSE FOR THOUGHT

Pause for thought

How would you feel if, after taking so much trouble, you entered the interview room to find that the manager was short of time, hell-bent on getting the forms filled in and – the most crushing factor – appears to be thinking about something else when you are talking? It happens!

Preparation

Particular attention should be paid to the venue. It should be held where both parties can be certain they will not be disturbed (for example, in a quiet room where there is no telephone or other distraction). The review itself should be planned well in advance, and an appropriate amount of time reserved for it. All of the relevant documentation and information should be studied, and any static information already entered on the forms. This heads off the need for copious notes to be made during the interview so that both parties can pay full attention to each other.

Outcomes to aim for

At the end of the interview, the employee should leave the room:

- believing that the manager is aware of his/her total job situation
- knowing exactly what lies ahead in terms of the standards and objectives to be achieved and that they are attainable
- understanding that arrangements will be made to fill in any gaps in knowledge or skills
- with a general feeling that the perceptions, decisions and agreed action were fair and reasonable
- motivated to perform well.

Interviewing style

The interview has been defined as a conversation with a purpose. The purpose here is to exchange views and information about the employee's performance. Clearly, the manager is running the interview, but he/she should allow the employee equal participation. Wright and Taylor (1984) identified five interviewing styles, and said that the extent of participation on one side or the other is determined by which style the manager chooses to adopt. The styles are as follows:

1. *Tell*. The 'tell' style produces the most one-sided interview. Typically, it is used by the authoritarian manager who does not feel the need to discuss matters in order to gain information. The manager does not listen and the interview therefore occupies very little time. This is a very old-fashioned approach in which it is assumed by the manager that the employee's views are of no consequence.
2. *Tell and sell*. Quite similar to the tell style except that the manager's attitude is persuasive rather than authoritarian. Using phrases such as 'You know I am right', the manager dominates the interview and the employee is left feeling that what he/she might have had to say matters little.
3. *Tell and listen*. Here, the manager opens the conversation with his/her own review of the employee's performance, emphasising the high-performing areas and pointing out those in which there is room for improvement and perhaps development. The manager then invites the employee to respond to what he/she has said. While with this style the manager retains full control, the employee is given the opportunity to express his or her views.
4. *Ask and tell*. First, the manager questions the employee about his/her performance and the employee provides an explanation. The manager then takes over again, telling the employee what steps to take next and spelling out his/her decisions about the employee's future development.
5. *Joint problem-solving*. This is a style in which the manager and the employee participate equally in the whole process, from reviewing the past to making plans for the future. The emphasis is on the future, and the manager adopts a supportive, counselling approach, rather than simply sitting there and telling. The employee is positively encouraged to think through the possible solutions to any problems and the manager offers guidance on a personal development plan.

These descriptions of styles say more about the manager than about the employee. The problem-solving approach is clearly the most productive. Some employees, however, whose performance is far from satisfactory, have to be given instruction in very straightforward terms about how they must improve.

Pause for thought

It has been said that 'performance appraisal looks like a good idea on paper but seldom works well in practice'. Do you think there is any truth in this statement? If you do think so, why?

Personal development plan (PDP)

Armstrong (1999) includes personal development planning (PDP) as an essential component of performance management, and the CIPD encourages its members to develop themselves and take responsibility for their own continuing professional development (CPD).

Definition

Personal development planning is a dynamic process. The plan itself is a draft describing how you propose to learn and develop yourself and your achievements to date. You need the active cooperation of your line manager or an HR practitioner to guide you through the process, although you are responsible for your own further development.

Getting started

Gannon (1995) suggests three main stages of planning:

1. Analyse current situation and developmental needs.
2. Set goals under such headings as improving performance in the current job, improving or acquiring skills, extending relevant knowledge, developing specified areas of competence, moving across or upwards in the organisation and preparing for changes in the current role.
3. Prepare action plan.

Who benefits from PDP?

There are two main considerations in PDP. First, the organisation needs you to develop yourself in order to enhance your performance. Second, there are your own needs in terms of career development. You develop transferable competences, increase your repertoire of knowledge and skills, and thereby enhance your flexibility and employability. These considerations are not mutually exclusive, since you may centre your planning around your current job. You can achieve these aims concurrently by:

- identifying your developmental needs and setting learning objectives
- costing and timescaling your plan (most employers will underwrite this)
- using a wide range of developmental methods

- making yourself aware of your own learning style and using it to advantage
- identifying suitable sources of relevant information and practical support
- maintaining a comprehensive record of your current and future development.

A PDP is made up of your past, present and future learning. First, this involves reflecting upon your past and current experiences and writing down what you have learned from them. Second, clarify your current position by reviewing and recording the competences you now possess. Third, you can then identify the point at which your future planning commences.

Learning activities

You cannot go through a day without learning something:

- all of your experiences of listening to what others have to say
- observing what they do and how they do it
- solving problems at work and at home or in your local community
- helping others to develop by coaching them
- reading good-quality material and watching TV documentaries.

Traditionally, many people initially turn to training courses in order to develop themselves and undoubtedly, if you are motivated to learn and careful about your choice of course in terms of its relevance to your needs, your knowledge and competences will increase. There are, however, several additional learning sources and in the following we list just a few:

- *E-learning (electronic learning)*. Information technology makes it possible for you to learn sitting at the computer.
- *Project and assignment work*. This is learning from experience. Usually it involves problem-solving and training. You have to learn in order to complete the work satisfactorily.
- *Learning from others*. See how other people go about their work. You need to find those people who are generally regarded as being good at what they do. Talk to them and find out why they do things in the way they do.
- *Studying job descriptions and role definitions*. Choose more senior-level jobs or jobs that you aspire to. Study them in order to identify the knowledge and competences that are required to do the work.

Self-appraisal

As you make progress, write down the details of your development and review your situation intermittently. This involves studying and updating your plan, noting your recent learning and deciding on the best way forward. A good time to do this is immediately after your appraisal interview at work, when you have all of your boss's comments to hand along with the suggestions he/she has made for your future development.

Suggested project

In your organisation, or one with which you are familiar, analyse the performance appraisal system with a view to updating and improving it. Prepare yourself to answer questions on why your proposed changes would improve the system.

Self-test questions

1. How would you define performance management?
2. What is performance?
3. What factors influence performance?
4. How would you differentiate between *intrinsic* and *extrinsic* job factors?
5. Do you think McGregor's X–Y theory describes managers' or employees' attitudes?
6. Why is it important to assess employees' performance?
7. How might the organisation use the outcomes of 360-degree feedback?
8. Which interviewing style do think would be the most productive?
9. How would you define personal development planning?
10. Who benefits from personal development planning and in what ways?

The employment relationship

Learning objectives

After studying this chapter you should:

- be able to define the employment relationship and understand its legal framework

- understand the contract of employment and the main statutory provisions that contribute to the regulation of the employment relationship

- understand the psychological contract

- understand the collective bargaining process

- understand employees' contractual and statutory rights

- be able to explain the processes of the internal justice system

- be able to contribute effectively in handling disputes, grievance and matters of discipline.

Introduction

The aim of this chapter is to provide an understanding of the employment relationship and the elements that shape its formal and informal structure. This includes the contractual and statutory rights and obligations of the employer and the employee; the importance of the psychological contract within the employee relationship; and the rules and procedures that are put in place in order to manage the employment relationship collectively and at individual level.

The employment relationship

In simple terms, this means exactly what it says: that there is a relationship between the employer and the employee. There are formal and informal aspects to the relationship and both parties have rights, obligations and expectations. The formal side is regulated through the provisions of the *contract of employment,* and in the UK, legislation sets common standards for the conduct of the relationship. The relevant legislation is explained and discussed later in this chapter. In very broad terms it can be said that the informal side of the relationship is governed by what is known as the *psychological contract,* which is also discussed later.

Differences between contracts

All employees have a contract of employment. While it is based on what both parties have agreed to be a *fair exchange* (the employee's time and skill in exchange for a salary or wage), it is

Definition: the employee relationship

The formal employment relationship that exists between the organisation and the employee is regulated by and defined within the *contract of employment*. The parties engaged in the relationship include the organisation as a corporate entity, the managers and the employee and their representatives.

different from a commercial contract such as, for example, the sale and purchase of a car or house. Such contracts have completion dates and terms and conditions that are an integral part of the agreement. The employment contract, on the other hand, is continuous in that both parties intend that it should go on until one side or the other wishes to terminate the relationship.

The components of a contract

A contract contains four main elements:

- an offer
- an acceptance
- consideration
- the intention to form a legal relationship.

Example 12: Buying a car

Have you ever bought a second-hand car? What happened? The car was for sale, you liked it and started to negotiate a price. Eventually, you made an *offer* for it. Your offer may have been a sum that was less than the original asking price but the person selling the car *accepted* your offer. He/she accepted it in *consideration* of your offer as the agreed purchase price. A contract is drawn up and you both sign it. You hand over the money and the seller hands over the car. The car is now yours; end of *legal relationship*; end of contract.

Unlike the type of contract described in the above example, in which the terms and conditions were agreed on a once-and-for-all basis, the terms and conditions related to the employment contract are subject to continuous renegotiation and change.

Terms and conditions of the employment contract

These fall into three categories:

1. *Express terms and conditions.* This is the list of the terms and conditions that govern and specify the details of the contract, which is given to the employee in writing usually shortly after joining the organisation.

2. *Implied terms and conditions.* These are integral parts of the contract, although they are not usually given in writing. It is assumed, for example, that the employer will be fair and reasonable and provide a healthy work environment.
3. *Statutory terms and conditions.* The employer should abide by the provisions of employment legislation which, for example, lays down standards for health and safety, working time, data protection and discrimination.

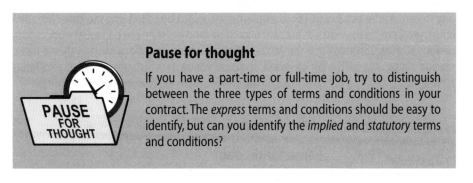

Pause for thought

If you have a part-time or full-time job, try to distinguish between the three types of terms and conditions in your contract. The *express* terms and conditions should be easy to identify, but can you identify the *implied* and *statutory* terms and conditions?

Different types of employment contract

As you are probably aware, there are people who work in or for the organisation who do not have a permanent and continuous employment contract such as that discussed above. There are a variety of ways in which agreement may be reached when, for example, an employer needs to access particular skills and the people who possess those skills are willing to trade them. The skills may be needed for a fixed period of time, in which perhaps one specific project needs to be carried out. Alternatively, there may be tasks that need to be carried out intermittently but on a regular basis. To cover various knowledge and skill needs, organisations offer several types of contract.

Temporary contract

This type of contract may have a specified termination date, or alternatively, the contract may not include a predetermined finishing date on the mutual understanding that the job is not permanent. In either case, the worker may not make a claim for unfair dismissal, nor is he/she entitled to redundancy payment. A temporary contract may be made permanent, in which case the person is offered an open-ended, continuous contract and officially becomes an employee of the organisation with all of the rights of a permanent employee. The term 'temporary' is not to be confused with the position of, say, a temporary secretary or temporary administrator in an office. This type of worker is employed and paid by an agency, with which the organisation has a commercial contract to supply temporary staff.

Fixed-term contract

This kind of contract always has a clearly specified duration, spelling out the start and finishing dates. People are engaged on a fixed-term contract when they have come into the organisation to carry out a specific project, or for example, to stand in for a permanent employee who is away on maternity/paternity leave, absent because of a long-term illness or on an external secondment. Even though the term is fixed and cannot be changed, the worker enjoys some of the rights of a permanent employee, such as equal pay and pension provision. Additionally, the employer is not allowed to require or request the worker to waive his/her right to protection against unfair dismissal or redundancy (Employment Relations Act 1999).

Zero hours contract

With this kind of contract the worker is not guaranteed any paid work at all. The worker must be available, however, to be called upon when there is a need. While it may not appeal to many workers, a retired teacher or nurse may find it attractive since it provides an opportunity to earn a little extra cash. For example, he/she might be called upon to cover for a sick employee. Zero hours contracts are also offered to shop assistants to do casual work at busy periods such as Christmas and the January sales. Other organisations, such as theme parks, seaside shops and stalls offer so-called 'seasonal' contracts which are, in effect, zero hours contracts.

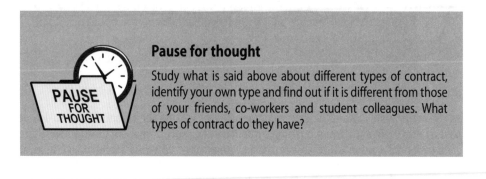

Pause for thought

Study what is said above about different types of contract, identify your own type and find out if it is different from those of your friends, co-workers and student colleagues. What types of contract do they have?

Termination of contract

Ultimately the employment contract comes to an end, and there is a variety of circumstances in which this might happen. It might be because the mutual satisfaction no longer holds (Torrington and Hall 1998), in which case the employer and the employee agree to part company. The most common reasons fall into two categories: first, the employer may terminate the contract and second, the employee may terminate it.

Termination by the employer

Employees' conduct when working on behalf of the organisation is governed by rules and regulations, procedures and other requirements:

- *Disciplinary dismissal.* Employees who persistently break the rules or fail to meet requirements risk being dismissed, subject to the outcome of a disciplinary hearing and depending on the severity and frequency of the offence. The dismissed employee may have grounds for appeal to an employment tribunal for unfair dismissal.
- *Lack of capability.* It is legitimate for the organisation to dismiss an employee on the grounds that the person has shown him/herself to be grossly unsuitable for the job; this may relate to attitude or aptitude. Admittedly the organisation will have had the opportunity to test an individual's knowledge, competence and personality prior to engagement, but the law recognises that errors can occur.
- *Redundancy.* This occurs when the organisation no longer requires a job, or set of jobs, to be carried out. With this kind of severance, the employee has a statutory

entitlement to compensation. The employee may have grounds for an appeal to an employment tribunal for *unfair selection for redundancy*.

- *Retirement.* This is triggered by the organisation when the employee has reached the firm's 'retirement age'. What this means is that the organisation can require the employee to leave on the grounds of age, but in some cases, especially where the employee possesses a rare skill, the organisation may prefer the person to remain in its employ. On the other hand, the employee may insist on leaving if he/she so wishes. Yet again, the organisation may offer the retiring employee a part-time contract, or opportunity to act in a consultant capacity.

Termination by the employee

There is a wide range of reasons that an employee may decide to terminate the relationship. Largely, they are either personal or career-related and several typical examples of each are listed below:

Personal reasons:
- to take care of a sick relative
- to move to another area or country
- to escape from a hostile culture or unfriendly co-workers.

Career-related reasons:
- resigning to take up a post with another employer
- to undertake a full-time course
- the desire for a career change.

Key concept 11: exit interviews

Exit interviews may be used with several purposes in mind. The data that is gathered from them is useful to those who manage the employment relationship and to HR planners. The purposes of exit interviewing are explained and discussed in Chapter 4.

Flexible working

Employment contracts that are different from the continuous, open-ended type, such as *temporary, fixed-term* and *zero hours* contracts, have been used in industry in one form or another since the nineteenth century but now, more than ever before, they are an increasingly common feature of employment. Today, businesses can only afford to employ people whose productivity, versatility, general performance and willingness to be flexible matches the needs of the organisation. This subject is discussed in greater depth later in the book. Suffice to say here that the growth in the use of these types of contract has resulted from the need for organisations to compete effectively. To achieve a competitive advantage, the organisation, and its employees, need to be flexible in the way they respond to the demands made upon them. So far as employees are concerned, this is referred to as *labour flexibility*.

Key concept 12: flexitime

An organisation that operates flexitime abandons the rigid nine-to-five day, in which employees normally work seven hours, allowing an hour for lunch. Flexitime extends working hours across a longer working day, perhaps from 8 am to 7 pm (starting and finishing times vary from one organisation to another). With this arrangement, employees still work the same number of hours but are allowed to vary them between the starting and finishing times. Usually, there is a time zone in the day when the presence of all employees is required (see Table 11.1).

Table 11.1 A simple example of flexitime in a seven-hour day

0800 – 1400	Employees may choose hours of work
1400 – 1700	All employees must be present
1700 – 1900	Employees may choose hours of work

Attendance records are kept and in many cases the time range extends across a five-day working week, rather than daily, in which case the employee must register an average of 35 hours a week; similarly, times may be ranged across a month.

Labour flexibility

What we have referred to as *labour flexibility* serves several purposes. First, it reduces costs; second, it increases the likelihood that a competitive advantage will be achieved; and third, it puts the organisation in a position to continuously adjust the size and competences of the workforce in order to respond rapidly to customer demands. There are four main types of labour flexibility:

1. *Functional flexibility*. This involves the rotational deployment of staff and adding to their range of tasks/jobs. Since the workforce is smaller, it has to be more productive (see paragraph above entitled 'flexible working') and managers have to rethink staff development, since employees need to be multiskilled in order to cope effectively with a wider range of tasks.
2. *Numerical flexibility*. This involves varying the size of the workforce in order to control productivity in accordance with demand. Market demands fluctuate not only quantitatively, but also in terms of product type, design and specification. In the case of the multifunctional specifications of mobile telephones, for example, not only does their specification make them more versatile, they have also become a 'must-have' fashion item. Other products are similarly affected, and organisations have to maximise on the skills of their highly trained staff.
3. *Temporal flexibility*. This type of flexibility maximises on the use of plant and

machinery by keeping the organisation at work for perhaps 16 or even 24 hours a day. This involves some staff in shift working while others, such as those with part-time and zero hours contracts, may be brought in at any time. Temporal flexibility places pressure upon the organisation's infrastructure and on such peripheral activities as cleaning, catering and security, but efficient handling of these services ensures that the benefits outweigh the costs.

4. *Financial flexibility*. This is designed to reduce employment costs by linking pay to performance. Care has to be taken, however, to ensure that pay does not fall below 'going rates' (see Chapter 12).

Patterns of attendance

Underlying labour flexibility is the need to meet business requirements, but there are examples in which it also meets the needs of individual employees. According to Foot and Hook (1999, p156), meeting the needs of business can be synonymous with meeting employees' needs if a company wishes to retain valuable staff. Some employees find that varying patterns of attendance at work can be useful and convenient to them, depending on their domestic circumstances. Several different modes of working have increased in recent years, and these are explained and discussed below.

Teleworking and telecottaging

Developments in information technology and telecommunications have made it possible for employees to work for an organisation without being on the employer's premises, except perhaps for the occasional visit. Particular categories of employee can use their IT expertise at home or in a telecottage.

DEFINITION

Definition: telecottage

This is a centre containing equipment that is shared by people who work at a distance from their employer or are self-employed. In some cases, the owner of the telecottage manages it. The prefix *tele* comes from the Greek word for distance. *Tele*vision and *tele*phone, for example are means of communication from a distance.

Distance working

A survey by Huws (1996) describes two categories of distance working:

- This category is similar to teleworking, but it includes multilocational working, which means working in a variety of places, including overseas and the employer's own premises.
- This is also similar to what is said above, for example it includes telecottaging, but it also includes call centres, which today of course may be anywhere in the world (IDS 1996).

Advantages and disadvantages

To return to the question of the needs of both the individual and the organisation, distance working or teleworking have advantages and disadvantages.

Advantages to the individual

This kind of working may appeal to people who are disabled to the extent that they have difficulty in getting around. It may also appeal to carers who look after aged or infirm relatives. Such people may favour the financial benefits of work more than the state's provision of allowances. There are additional factors such as first, the interest of the job itself; second, the nature of the employer's business; and third, the psychological benefit of feeling valued for the input of knowledge and skills.

Additional advantages include:

- *Hours of work.* Some people are at their best in the mornings (these are the *larks*), while others are more alert later in the day and even into the night (these are the *owls*). Mostly, there is freedom to work when it best suits the employee.
- *Costs.* The cost and stress involved in travelling are reduced, although there may be hidden costs owing to the use of facilities at home or in the telecottage.

Disadvantages to the individual

Some people enjoy solitude while others find that working alone brings unwanted social isolation. Some writers claim that training and briefing sessions are the answer to this problem, but such events tend to occupy only a fraction of the employee's total time. It is a difficult problem to resolve, since the arrangement of extra events as a solution may be intrusive to the extent that the employee's performance is reduced.

Individuals differ in the degree to which they are attracted to distance working, and therefore some are drawn positively to the idea, while others would never consider it. Problems are experienced by carers and by the disabled, who do not normally have the luxury of being able to choose where and when they work.

ACTIVITIES

Activity 27

Think about the problems experienced by those who are engaged in distance working of one kind or another; especially those who, given the choice, would work within an organisation. Can you identify a solution to, say, social isolation?

Advantages to the organisation

By employing teleworkers, organisations save on costs since they do not have to provide facilities such as office accommodation and furniture, although they do usually provide the home work station, including a computer and stationery, etc.

Disadvantages to the organisation

It is not always possible to contact teleworking employees when you need to, which can be troublesome if the need to make contact is urgent.

The psychological contract

This is a contract that is based upon the employee's subjective expectations of, and beliefs about, the relationship between him/herself and the organisation. It is tacit, not negotiated, and includes subjective assumptions made by both sides.

A major feature of psychological contracts is the concept of mutuality – that there is a common and agreed understanding of promises and obligations the respective parties have made to each other about work, pay, loyalty, commitment, flexibility, security and career advancement.

(Pointon and Ryan 2004, p520)

With the exception of pay, all of these promises and obligations are items you would not find in the formal employment contract, but they are important determinants of behaviour.

It was Edgar Schein who first identified the concept and used the term 'psychological contract'. He said that 'the notion of a psychological contract implies that there is an unwritten set of expectations operating at all times between every member of an organisation and the various managers and others in that organisation' (Schein 1965). Even before that, respected academics (Vroom 1964; Katz and Kahn 1978) used the terms 'behavioural expectations'.

It is within the reciprocal spirit of the psychological contract that people are motivated to work, gain satisfaction from what they do, develop feelings of job security, belongingness and commitment, and enjoy a culture of trust and mutual respect. All of this implies that the *exchange* aspect of the psychological contract is manifest in the form of mutual expectancies and need satisfactions.

Breaching the psychological contract

The psychological contract needs to be handled with care. As with any other kind of contract, it is capable of – and even susceptible to – being breached. Where it is breached by the organisation it seriously affects employee morale. Goodwill is one of the mainstays of a positive relationship between employer and employee. It leads to mutually advantageous informal employee behaviour, such as carrying out tasks that are not on the list of duties. Such behaviour should be fostered, since if everyone did exactly what was on their job descriptions and nothing else, you would never get everything done. Goodwill can take a long time to establish, yet it can be destroyed with a single thoughtless act.

Pause for thought

Do you feel as if you have a psychological contract with your employer? What do you expect from your employer that is not in your employment contract? What do you think your employer expects from you? Additionally, what about your tutors and the university? Is there a psychological contract there?

Employees' statutory rights

While employees have rights under the terms of the employment contract they have with the organisation, they also have rights that are created by legislation in the form of Acts of Parliament, such as those for equal pay, data protection and discrimination. A large proportion of this legislation has its roots in European Union directives.

The UK legislation covering employee rights is the Employment Rights Act 1996 (ERA96). Before this Act, employees' rights were provided by employment protection legislation, most of which was enacted in the 1970s and 1980s. The ERA96 consolidates the provisions of the earlier legislation and includes additions. It should be borne in mind that the legislation relating to employee rights lays down minimum standards and that many organisations enhance those standards, for example with a view to retaining valued staff. Alternatively, agreement over enhancing certain rights may be reach through collective bargaining. In this book, space limitations prevent the coverage of all statutory rights; those explained below are the main rights.

Statement of terms and conditions

One of the most important rights of an employee is to receive a statement of the terms and conditions of employment within two months of joining the organisation. The details that the Act requires to be included in the statement are:

- the names of the parties to the contract
- date of commencement of period of continuous employment
- hours of work
- location of the workplace and an indication if there could be a requirement to work elsewhere
- details of pay: the rates of pay, how it is calculated and frequency of payment, eg weekly, monthly
- job title or a brief description of the duties and responsibilities
- holiday entitlements
- arrangements about sick pay and sick leave
- details of the pension scheme
- entitlement to receive notice of termination of employment and obligation to give notice
- date of termination if it is a fixed-term contract
- any terms of a collective agreement that affects working conditions.

Company handbook

Most medium-sized and large organisations issue a copy of the company handbook to all employees on joining. Most of the items listed above are included in the handbook, as are copies of the disciplinary and grievance procedures.

Changing terms and conditions of employment

Employers may change terms and conditions of employment but employees have certain rights if the changes are made. For example, a sudden reduction in pay rates that is made without consultation and an agreement represents a serious breach of the contract. Similarly, the contract would be breached if unilateral changes were made to other terms and conditions of employment, such as holiday entitlements and company pension contributions.

Termination of employment

This refers to the amount of notice of termination given by both the employer and the employee.

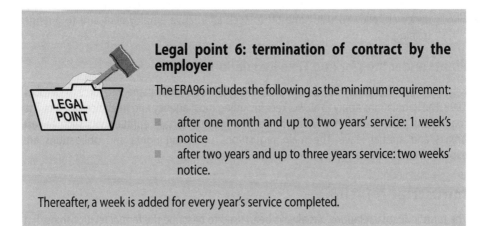

Legal point 6: termination of contract by the employer

The ERA96 includes the following as the minimum requirement:

- after one month and up to two years' service: 1 week's notice
- after two years and up to three years service: two weeks' notice.

Thereafter, a week is added for every year's service completed.

Maternity rights

All pregnant employees are entitled to a period of 26 weeks' maternity leave regardless of length of service. If, however, the employee has completed 26 weeks of continuous service by the beginning of the 14th week prior to the expected date of birth, she is entitled to an additional 26-week leave, giving her 52 weeks in total. To qualify for maternity leave she must provide the employer with four main items of information before the end of the 15th week prior to the expected day of birth:

1. She must tell her employer that she is pregnant.
2. She must advise the expected week of childbirth. She must also provide a medical certificate that confirms this if the employer requests it.
3. She must advise the employer of the date she intends to start her maternity leave. Normally, this can be any date that is no earlier than the beginning of the 11th week before the expected week of childbirth up to the birth itself.
4. She must write to the employer within 28 days of her notification stating her proposed return date. Subsequently, she may change that date if she gives her employer 28 days notice of the change.

During the 26 weeks' leave she is entitled to benefit from all of her normal terms and conditions of employment except for pay. At the end of it she has the right to return to her original job. If the job no longer exists the employer must offer her a suitable alternative, but if this is not possible, she may be entitled to redundancy pay.

Other rights to time off

There is a long list of rights to time off, some of which are given below as examples:

- Employees with at least one year's service are entitled to 13 weeks' unpaid parental leave in respect of each child born or adopted.

- Time off for public duties. Employees who hold certain public positions are entitled to reasonable time off – which is paid – to perform the duties associated with them.
- An employee who is an official of an independent trade union must be allowed reasonable time off with pay to carry out those duties.
- Employees with more than two years' service who have been given notice of redundancy are allowed paid time off to seek alternative employment and to arrange training.

Rights under the Working Time Regulations, 1998

Regulations to implement the European Working Time Directive came into force in October 1998. The Regulations apply to all workers, including most agency and freelance workers. The regulations place limits on working hours and provide certain entitlements such as rest breaks and annual leave. The main regulations providing rights and obligations are explained and discussed in greater detail in Chapter 12.

Industrial relations

The term 'industrial relations' has always been used to describe the *formal* relationships that exist between employers, employees and their representatives. In this book, space limitations prevent explanations and discussion of the total range and complexity of the subjects that are regarded as part of industrial relations. The aim of this section, therefore, is to provide you with an understanding of particular aspects of the UK industrial relations system which I hope you will find useful.

Unitary and pluralistic perspectives

How industrial relations are conducted within a particular organisation is determined by the frame of reference through which its top managers perceive the formal relationship with individuals and/or their representatives. Alan Fox (1966) suggested that managers may adopt one of two basic views: the unitary and the pluralist perspectives.

The unitary perspective

Managers who take this view regard themselves as the only legitimate source of power and authority which they value and protect. They see their role as one of controlling the activities of the workforce and assume that all employees share the common goals of the organisation, are loyal to the 'management team' and totally committed to the purposes of the organisation.

Reward for effort comes only if the organisation functions efficiently and effectively enough to achieve its economic and growth objectives. Where conflict occurs, its cause is attributed to communication failures or the foolish temperaments of those involved. Trade unions are unwelcome and the managers fiercely fend off their approaches for recognition. Armstrong (1999) says that the philosophy of HRM, with its emphasis on commitment and mutuality, is based on the unitary perspective.

The pluralistic perspective

Here, managers may allow and actively foster freedom of expression, and the development of groups which establish their own norms and elect their own informal leaders. In this way, power and control arise in several areas of the organisation and loyalty is commanded by the leaders of the groups, which are often in competition with each other for resources. The managers achieve results by joining the groups, encouraging participation, motivating employees and co-ordinating their work efforts. This, it is said, represents good leadership, although sometimes it can be difficult to achieve the necessary balance, in which the interests of all stakeholders have to be taken into account. However, according to Rensis Likert, when employees become involved in solving work-related problems and making decisions, they become involved in what they are doing and committed to the achievement of successful outcomes (Likert 1961).

Activity 28

Think about how your organisation (or one with which you are familiar) is managed. How do you think you are/were regarded by the managers? What does the managerial style indicate to you? In the light of what is said above, do you regard it as a unitary or a pluralistic organisation?

HRM and pluralism

There are aspects of HRM, such as *individual* commitment and *mutuality of interest* in the success of the organisation, which seem to be in sympathy with the unitary concept, and therefore in conflict with a pluralistic philosophy. But can HRM incorporate any of the aspects of pluralism? According to Armstrong, one of the:

> **prescriptions which constitute the HRM model for employee relations is ... the organisation of complementary forms of communication, such as team briefing, alongside traditional collective bargaining – i.e. approaching employees directly as individuals or in groups rather than through their representatives.**
>
> **(Armstrong 1999)**

This is an approach, of course, which excludes trade unions.

Collective bargaining

Where trade unions or staff associations are recognised by organisations, collective bargaining is the means used to address conflicting issues between the organisation and its employees. Collective bargaining also takes place when there are disputes between managers and employees at national level, such as, for example, the fire service disputes of 2003 and 2004.

This section explains and discusses the roles of the various participants in collective bargaining at national and organisational levels. These include shop stewards and managers, union officials and employers' associations.

Types of collective bargaining

There are two types of collecting bargaining, which may be referred to as distributive and integrative bargaining (Walton and McKersie 1965):

- *Distributive bargaining* is described as 'the complex system of activities instrumental to the attainment of one party's goals when they are in basic conflict with those of the other party'.
- *Integrative bargaining* is described as 'the system of activities which are not in fundamental conflict with those of the other party and which therefore can be integrated to some degree'. The objectives referred to are about 'an area of common concern, a purpose'.

To someone who has little experience of collective bargaining, the above definitions must seem to be something of a mystery. Nevertheless, it is important for you to attain a sound understanding of both definitions, and it is hoped that the following case study will be helpful. The case study is about job evaluation, a subject which is explained and discussed in Chapter 11.

Case study 12: Distributive and integrative bargaining

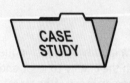

P and E Components (PEC) is a company distributing plumbing and electrical components to the trade. PEC is owned and managed by George Harris and Peter Gray. PEC has four operating geographic divisions in which there are 60 stores and four warehouses; it employs some 1500 people. Wages and salaries are individually negotiated at regional and local levels, depending on the seniority of the jobs. PEC recognises several trade unions which represent 75 per cent of the workforce, and there is a system of collective bargaining in place.

After reading a report by the HR manager, George and Peter decided they would like to introduce a system of job evaluation, which they thought would be more equitable than the current arrangements. Their first step was to approach the chief shop stewards to put the idea to them. The stewards decided to have a separate meeting, after which they went back to George and Peter to ask what kind of job evaluation scheme they had in mind.

Jointly, George, Peter and the stewards decided to have a larger meeting at which the HR manager would be present. After a long negotiation, the shop stewards agreed to put the idea to their members and to recommend that they voted in favour of a points rating scheme. In this scheme, the job factors are each evaluated and awarded a number of points. The number of points awarded, therefore, determines the salary of the job holder.

The trade union chiefs declared that after the scheme had been drawn up, they would wish to have further negotiations in order to try to agree the value of the points, and the managers agreed to this.

Discussion of the case study

The case study involves both integrative and distributive bargaining. Can you see which negotiations were 'integrative' and which were 'distributive'? The managers and shop stewards discussed the introduction of job evaluation and when they agreed about that, they moved on to discuss the kind of scheme that would be most appropriate to their company. That was integrative bargaining.

Integrative bargaining occurs when both sides recognise that they have common problems, the solution to which is to everyone's benefit. In this case they both wanted job evaluation but between them, they had to decide on a particular scheme. In other words they had to agree about the best way forward, or how they should go about doing things. What typifies this kind of integrative bargaining is that both sides adopt a joint problem-solving approach. They pool their knowledge and ideas in order to achieve something that meets the needs of both parties.

At the next session, however, when they were negotiating the value of the point, they were engaged in distributive bargaining. This occurs when the negotiators are in conflict over how something should be divided or distributed. The issues that divide them usually concern pay, time or power, which are all limited so that the main flavour of this kind of bargaining is a 'my loss is your gain' attitude. An obvious example is an employee's demand for a higher rate of pay. It is as if a cake is to be sliced in two and the question that arises is 'How big a slice do I get and how much do you keep?' Other examples may include demands for increased holiday entitlements or a reduction in working hours.

It is worth noting that this is discussed in 'either–or' terms, while in fact there are many 'mixed' sessions in which distributive and integrative take place simultaneously.

Products of collective bargaining

It was noted above that pay, working time and holiday entitlements are typical issues that are resolved through distributive bargaining. These are generally referred to as substantive issues: the outcomes alter employees' terms and conditions of employment. Agreements that are reached in this way, therefore are referred to as *substantive agreements*.

The agreements that are reached through integrative bargaining are referred to as *procedural agreements*, because the parties are engaged in 'how we shall go about doing things'. Typical internal issues are related to health and safety procedures and procedures that form part of the *internal justice system*, such as those for handling grievance and dealing with matters of discipline.

The internal justice system

All organisations have an internal justice system (IJS), which on the one hand, enables organisations to take action against individuals who misbehave, and on the other, enables the individual to seek a solution to perceived unfairness or ill-treatment. In this way, both sides of the employee relationship have access to a system through which redress may be sought. The formal processes of the IJS are managed through a *disciplinary procedure* and a *grievance procedure*.

The use of these procedures tends to be psychologically negative, since the disciplinary rules, for example, define unacceptable items of behaviour, ranging from minor indiscretions to comparatively serious offences which are referred to as 'gross misconduct'. Additionally, through the grievance procedure employees seek solutions to negative situations. Circumstances in which one party or the other is not satisfied by the outcomes of the process may lead to recourse to external institutions, such as employment tribunals or the courts.

The HR role in grievance and disciplinary matters

Understanding the purposes of these two procedures, knowing how they are structured, and having the ability to handle them are essential to the HR specialist. However, where an employee raises a grievance or it is alleged that he/she has breached a disciplinary rule, it is the line manager who invokes and carries out the procedure and in most cases, he/she does this with the advice and assistance of an HR practitioner.

Grievance procedures

The formal grievance procedure provides a channel through which employees can have their grievances heard by managers. Most grievances take the form of dissatisfactions and complaints. The procedure has a structure that comprises four stages, so that if an aggrieved employee does not obtain satisfaction at one stage, the process can move on to the next. In the event of repeated dissatisfaction, or if the issue is beyond the manager's control or authority, the grievance is heard at successively higher levels, ranging from the supervisor to a board member, such as the managing director or personnel director. Each stage takes the form of an interview between the manager and the employee, who may be accompanied by a trade union representative or colleague.

Note from 'Structure of the grievance procedure' below that the HR department does not get involved at the initial stage. Experience shows that most grievances are resolved at supervisory or line manager level. The procedure provides for a maximum amount of time to pass between the stages. Speed and fairness to all concerned are said to be the most essential ingredients of a good procedure.

If, at the close of the final stage, the matter still remains unresolved, a solution is sought through the organisation's disputes procedure, in which conciliation and arbitrative approaches are used. If the relevant trade union representatives feel strongly enough about the issue, they may take a vote for industrial action, although this is normally delayed until all possible avenues have been exhausted.

Structure of a grievance procedure

- *Preamble:* This is an informal stage in which the employee airs the grievance to his/her immediate manager/supervisor, and an attempt is made to resolve the issue.
- *Stage 1:* This takes place if the issue was not resolved at the preamble, and usually involves a more senior manager. The employee may be accompanied by a trade union representative or colleague. The employee states the grievance and an attempt is made to resolve it.
- *Stage 2:* This takes place if the issue was not resolved at the previous stage, and involves a more senior line manager and the HR manager. The grievance receives a full hearing and a final attempt is made to resolve it.
- *Stage 3:* If the grievance remains unresolved a meeting is held involving the employee, a senior director and, where appropriate, an area/regional union officer.

Few grievances reach Stage 3. Most are resolved at Stage 1 and many at Stage 2. In extreme circumstances, however, special panels may be set up, including the involvement of experienced external conciliators or arbitrators where appropriate, in attempts to resolve serious or complex grievances.

The initial grievance interview

Individuals may feel aggrieved for a variety of reasons. Grievances vary in their complexity and so, therefore, do the interviews. The initial interview has two purposes: first, for the employee to state the grievance, and second, for the manager to analyse what is being said, identify the cause and where possible, eliminate it.

Preparing for the interview

Employees are usually well prepared for such events and the manager should also prepare. Before the interview, the manager should obtain an understanding of the problem at the root of the grievance. In a small organisation, the employee is probably well known to the manager and, indeed, may be known to be an inveterate griper. In large organisations, however, where it is not possible to get to know everyone personally, it is a good idea to check such matters with associates, and take a look at the employee's record.

Making enquiries will provide the manager with several perceptions of the individual, and of the circumstances, so that when the employee's version of the grievance is expressed at the interview, the manager can put it into some kind of context, taking care not to jump to conclusions.

Conducting the interview

At the interview, the manager should listen attentively and allow the person to speak freely. There is no better way of getting the employee's perception of the situation. After the manager has heard the grievance and established mutual agreement with the employee over its nature, both parties can adopt a joint problem solving approach, in which the employee is encouraged to suggest solutions to the problem. Some suggestions may be impracticable, or outside the limitations of the organisation's policy, but the manager can offer the employee guidance about the possibilities. If agreement is reached over the solution to the problem, it is important for the manager to follow this up and ensure that any agreed action is taken.

Those who draft procedures try to write them in language that makes them watertight, so that the possibility of misinterpretation is reduced to a bare minimum. On the other hand, every case is different, and where a grievance has been shown to be justified, it is often possible for the manager to 'wriggle within the skin' of a procedure, in order to be fair to the employee and any others who may be involved.

Disciplinary rules

Standards of behaviour in organisations are regulated by systems of rules, codes of practice and procedures. The rules classify and define offences of which the organisation disapproves. While they vary from one kind of organisation to another, they may, for example, refer to:

- *General conduct*, such as violence, threatening/abusive behaviour and fooling around, such as horseplay.
- *Punctuality*, including arriving at and leaving the workplace at the agreed working times, being on time for meetings.
- *Absenteeism*, including regular attendance. This refers not only to arriving and being in the workplace, but to the employee's actual work station.
- *Health and safety*. This covers use of safety equipment on every occasion that the task demands and handling the equipment in a responsible manner so that no one is placed at risk.

- *Drug and alcohol abuse.* Being on the premises while under the influence of drugs and/or alcohol.
- *Stealing,* including the removal of any of the company's property from the place it normally occupies, unless written permission has been given.
- *Bringing the organisation into disrepute.* This includes behaviour within and outside the organisation which throws a negative light on the reputation of the employer.
- *Discriminatory behaviour.* This includes behaviour that indicates dislike or hatred of members of the opposite sex or people of a particular colour or ethnic background.

Offences may be classified and action taken according to their seriousness as follows:

- *minor offence,* such as arriving slightly late for work on several occasions, for which the employee may receive a reprimand or an oral warning
- *serious offence,* such as neglecting or misusing health and safety equipment, for which the employee may be given a written warning
- *gross misconduct,* such as violence or stealing, for which the penalty is usually instant dismissal without compensation.

The aim of the above section is to provide examples of disciplinary rules, show how they are classified and the typical actions that are taken when the disciplinary procedure is invoked.

Disciplinary procedures

Disciplinary procedures are usually compiled by the HR department, approved by the senior managers and agreed with the trade unions, where they are recognised. The organisation should have a separate procedure for dealing with matters of capability, which includes poor performance and cases of ill-health. The Advisory, Conciliation and Arbitration Service (ACAS), publish a code of practice entitled *Disciplinary and grievance procedures 2000.* This is a set of guidelines on the content and process of these procedures. ACAS also published an advisory booklet entitled *Discipline at work* which advises on the practical aspects of implementing the disciplinary procedure. Both documents have been written specifically for employers.

What the disciplinary procedure should do

The ACAS code outlines the structure and content of a disciplinary procedure as follows, saying that they should:

- be in writing
- specify to whom they apply
- be non-discriminatory
- provide for matters to be dealt with without undue delay
- provide for proceedings, witness statements and records to be kept confidential
- indicate the disciplinary actions which may be taken
- specify the levels of management which have the authority to take the various forms of disciplinary action
- provide for workers to be informed of the complaints against them and where possible, all relevant evidence before any hearing
- provide workers with an opportunity to state their case before decisions are reached
- provide workers with the right to be accompanied

- ensure that, except for gross misconduct, no worker is dismissed for a first breach of discipline
- ensure that disciplinary action is not taken until the case has been carefully investigated
- ensure that workers are given an explanation for any penalty imposed
- provide a right of appeal – normally to a more senior manager – and specify the procedure to be followed.

Handling the disciplinary procedure

The aims of a disciplinary procedure are to handle the process fairly and speedily. Because of its ultimate implications, a disciplinary procedure has to be seen to be fair to all who are involved. Fairness and justice should prevail and the approach, rules and practice surrounding the procedure should reflect this.

The Act of Parliament that provides for the individual rights of employees is the Employment Rights Act 1996 (ERA96). This Act states that employees have the right not to be unfairly dismissed, provided that they have at least one year's continuous service with the organisation, regardless of the numbers of hours worked.

Disciplinary procedures generally have been formulated with the law on unfair dismissal in mind. The structure that will be familiar to most practitioners provides for repeated offences and has three stages. The next section outlines a structure that is used in the large majority of organisations today.

Structure of a disciplinary procedure

- *Stage 1:* In this stage, an employee may be given a formal warning for committing a minor offence. The warning may be delivered orally or in writing; usually it is given orally. However it is given, it must advise the employee of the nature of the offence he/she has committed and of the possible consequences of repeating the offence.
- *Stage 2:* At this stage the employee is given a second formal warning for a repeated offence, or a formal warning for committing a more serious offence. Such warnings should always be given in writing, stating the time, date, place and nature of the offence. Again, the possible consequences of repeating the offence are pointed out, and in particular circumstances, the employee may be referred for counselling.
- *Stage 3:* Here, a third and final formal warning is given in writing. At this stage, the employee is in danger of receiving a severe penalty in the event of repeating the offence again, and this should be made very clear by the manager. The removal of privileges, suspension or even dismissal could result from a repeated offence after a final written warning.
- *Stage 4:* This takes the form of a hearing by a panel of senior managers, including the HR manager or director. After the hearing, decisions are made about the culpability of the employee and, where appropriate, the penalty to be applied. Most often at this stage the penalty is dismissal.

The personnel role

The role of the HR practitioner in disciplinary matters varies from one organisation to another, but usually it is to ensure that corporate policy, the procedure and the law are strictly adhered to. In cases where a dismissal looks possible, the matter should be referred to a senior manager to gain approval for the proposed action. Normally managers and supervisors have some authority in disciplinary matters, but in the absence of a senior manager, it is recommended that HR practitioners do not dismiss the person, even in cases of gross misconduct. The procedure should allow for an employee to be accompanied by a trade union representative or colleague when the formal warning is issued, and the manager too is advised to issue them in the presence of another manager or an appropriate HR specialist.

It is important that a thorough inquiry is carried out at every stage of the procedure, and all of the facts are collected and recorded, along with details of what happened when the procedure was implemented. If the dismissal of an employee results in an employment tribunal, one of the first questions from the bench is to check whether a thorough investigation had been carried out.

Invoking the disciplinary procedure

Managers and supervisors should not be too quick to invoke the procedure. Often, a manager under pressure, making a superficial assessment of the situation, does not get the whole story. For example, being late for work is an offence in most organisations, but if an employee who has a good record for punctuality suddenly starts arriving late, the manager should investigate the cause, rather than go straight for the rule book.

Good workers are hard to find, and if a manager can counsel an employee, or guide him/her towards the solution to say, a personal problem, a good worker can be turned into an even better, more loyal and motivated worker. The manager's first step, therefore, should be to ask for an explanation.

Case study 13: Late again, Price!

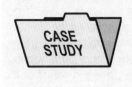

Joe Price was a section leader in the IT department. He had been with the organisation for six years, his performance was good and he was normally reliable and punctual. Jill Hartley, the IT manager, noticed that on several days in the past two weeks, Joe had been arriving late, sometimes by as much as 45 minutes, so she called him into her office to ask for an explanation.

It turned out that Joe's wife had left him. He now had his two children to look after, which included getting them ready in the mornings and taking them to school. His mother sometimes did this for him, but she was unable to do it every day, and those were the days on which he was late. After school, a reliable neighbour picked up the children and looked after them until Joe got home.

Jill's solution was to alter Joe's hours so that he started and finished work an hour later and that solved the problem. It was to be a temporary solution until Joe got himself sorted out. The idea of taking disciplinary action did not occur to Jill.

Except in cases where flagrant breaches of the rules occur, disciplinary processes should begin with a *preamble*, in which the manager and the employee get together to discuss the reasons why a rule has been broken. This gives the manager an opportunity to discover any problems, assess the employee's attitude towards his or her behaviour and to decide what action might be taken.

Absence management

This is one of the longest-running causes of serious concern to managers. Unapproved absence from work causes a multitude of problems to managers and involves the organisation in significant extra costs. According to Torrington and Hall (1998), the costing of absence needs to have a wider focus than just the pay of the absent individual. Other costs include:

- line manager costs in finding a temporary replacement or rescheduling work
- the actual cost of the temporary employee
- costs related to showing a temporary employee what to do
- costs associated with a slower work rate or more errors from a temporary employee
- costs of contracts being completed on time.

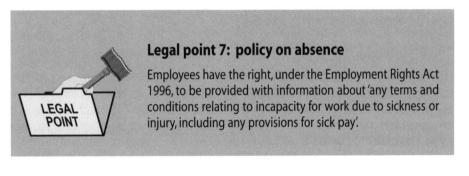

Legal point 7: policy on absence

Employees have the right, under the Employment Rights Act 1996, to be provided with information about 'any terms and conditions relating to incapacity for work due to sickness or injury, including any provisions for sick pay'.

Managing and controlling absence

Considerable attention has been paid to the problems related to absenteeism, and this has resulted in the use of management and control systems, some of which are linked to the disciplinary procedure. On the other hand, the objective in setting up an absence management system is to head off the need to use the disciplinary procedure. According to Foot and Hook (1999), the organisation achieves this 'by creating a culture in which everyone is aware of the importance of good attendance and of their value to the organisation'.

Reasons for absence

According to a CIPD survey report (2003a) there are many reasons that people take time off work. These can be categorised as:

- short-term sickness absence (uncertified, self-certified or covered by a doctor's certificate)
- long-term sickness absence
- unauthorised absence or persistent lateness
- other authorised absences, eg annual leave, maternity, paternity, adoption or parental leave; time off for public or trade union duties or to care for dependants; compassionate leave; educational leave.

One of the features of this list is that some of the reasons given are predictable, and therefore easier to manage since they can be planned ahead. On the other hand, unapproved absence is unpredictable and difficult to manage. Importantly, the former does not cause a reduction in productivity, whereas the latter does. Another cause of lost productivity is when an individual is on the premises but absent from his/her job without permission; this is a frequent occurrence that usually passes unnoticed.

Measuring absence

Managers know when there are absences from their daily contact with the staff, but only monitoring absence and measuring its frequency will reveal the true extent of the problem. If the problem is serious, then the task is to identify the causes and decide what to do about it. Persistent and widespread absence may be found in a particular department, in which case the department needs to be investigated to discover the cause. It might have been caused by unpopular changes in the work systems, the style with which the manager leads and communicates with the staff, or an increase in the workload.

On the other hand, absenteeism may be endemic across the whole organisation; it might be 'taken-for-granted' that the staff take unapproved time off, such as a 'duvet day'. In some cases, it is almost as if it is an entitlement.

The Bradford factor

There are several systems available for measuring absence. The Bradford factor is probably the most well known, and is used by many organisations. The system is designed to identify persistent short-term absences by measuring the number of spells of absence. It is calculated according to the formula: S x S x D, where S = the number of spells of absence by an individual in 52 weeks; and D = the total number of days of an individual's absence in 52 weeks.

> *Example: the Bradford factor*
> Ten one-day absences = 1000
> One ten-day absence = 10
> Five two-day absences = 250
> Two five-day absences = 40

It was noted above that when the causes have been identified, the next task is to decide what to do about it. The involvement of the line manager is key to the success of the steps that are taken to reduce absenteeism. First, he/she needs to keep a record of the frequency of the spells of absences and the number of days taken in each spell. As we shall see, the effectiveness of the action that he/she takes is determined by his/her leadership skills, since only as a last resort should the disciplinary procedure be invoked.

Return to work interviews

These have proved to be an effective intervention on the part of the line manager. They give the line manager the opportunity to talk to staff about the underlying causes of absence. The use of disciplinary procedures for unacceptable absence may be used if organisation wish to make it clear that unjustified absence will not be tolerated and that absence policies will be enforced (CIPD 2003a). Remember that the disciplinary procedure operates in stages, and therefore should act as a deterrent as each stage is triggered.

Self-test questions

1. How would you define the employment relationship?
2. What are the main differences between an employment contract and a commercial contract?
3. What is the difference between 'labour flexibility' and 'flexitime'?
4. What are the advantages of distance working to the employer?
5. How would you differentiate between your statutory rights and your contractual rights?
6. Why do you think it is said that the principles and practices of HRM have their roots in a unitary philosophy?
7. How would you distinguish *distributive bargaining* from *integrative bargaining*?
8. What are the main functions of the HR practitioner in handling grievance and dealing with matters of discipline?
9. What are the main objectives of disciplinary and grievance procedures?
10. What should line managers do before using the disciplinary procedure to control absence?

Employee reward

Chapter 12

Learning objectives

After studying this chapter you should:

- be able to describe the concept of employee reward

- understand how reward is managed, in terms of the organisation's reward policies, systems and procedures

- be able to explain what is meant by non-financial rewards

- be able to advise on suitable payment systems and make meaningful contributions to their development and implementation

- understand the law relating to pay and payment systems.

Introduction

This chapter introduces the concept of reward, including payment and non-cash rewards. As in the previous chapter, payment is seen as a component of the 'exchange' element of a contract (consideration); here it is also seen as a motivator and as an indication of how employees are valued by the organisation in terms of their contribution to the achievement of objectives.

The concepts of *incentive* and *equity* systems of payment are explained, including job evaluation, payment by results, performance-related pay and non-cash rewards. Reward also has strong implications for equal treatment, and the discussion here explains this in legal and business terms.

The chapter includes explanations of the management philosophies, strategies and policies that lead to the choice and development of reward systems, and an examination of the factors that determine pay levels. The discussion also includes new and traditional systems of payment.

Perceptions of reward

The terms *reward*, and *reward management* are relative newcomers to the managerial vocabulary. Before the 1980s, references were made to 'money', 'pay', and 'systems of payment', and today, the word 'reward' is often used to refer to payment.

Definitions

It is not possible to define reward in a single statement because perceptions of it vary from one person to another and from one situation to another. A manager, for example, might define reward as 'the payment that an employee receives in accordance with the value of his or her work contribution to the organisation'. An employee, on the other hand, may say that it is 'the return that he or she receives on the investment of his or her time, knowledge, skills, loyalty and commitment'. Non-financial factors such as the benefits and facilities that the organisation offers to its employees are also regarded as reward, as are recognition, praise and career development.

In fact, reward literally means something that is given or received in return for a service or for merit, and it is often financial. Where we refer to reward, in the United States the word *compensation* is used, but that sounds more like the outcome of a lawsuit than payment for a valued performance. Truly, 'pay' or 'payment' in the forms of wages and salaries are what spring to mind first when one thinks of reward in the organisational context, but since 'reward' entails more than just money, that is the word we will use here as a portmanteau description. When dealing with the detail, however, we shall call things what they are, such as *wages, salaries* and *payment*.

HRM and reward

According to Pointon and Ryan (2004), 'reward management' has often been viewed as the 'poor relation' of HRM, concerned with 'systems, figures and procedures'. On the other hand, organisations that have adopted the principles and practices of HRM say that their reward philosophies are consistent with and act in support of other HRM principles; for example, that they reward a good performance because that adds value to the organisation. The organisation sees its employees as its most important resource, and therefore it invests in that resource through the development of knowledge and skills in order to enhance employees' performance and thus get a return on its investment (see Chapter 2).

The new pay

Since 1990, when E.E. Lawler coined the phrase *new pay*, there has been a great deal of activity in industry concerning the fitness of the older and more traditional pay systems to serve the needs of modern organisations.

The managers of such organisations rightly believe that the success of the organisation is ultimately determined by the performance of its employees. It follows, therefore, that it needs to recruit and retain people who are appropriately skilled, flexible in their

Key concept 13: the 'new pay'

The underlying philosophy that follows the principles of HRM brought a fresh strategic approach to reward management. In this approach, reward is firmly linked to actual performance. According to Heery (1996), new pay, which reflects a unitary approach, is often contrasted with 'old pay', which reflects a pluralistic approach in that it (old pay) uses job-evaluated grade structures, payment by time, and seniority-based financial rewards and benefits.

outlook, prepared to become involved in and committed to the purposes of the organisation, and are at one with it in the belief that the achievement of objectives is a good thing, not only for the organisation, but for the employees too. From this, it follows that the reward systems must support the overall business strategy, indeed that they should flow from it, and that pay should be commensurate with such employees' contributions.

Schuster and Zingheim (1992), who further developed Lawler's concept of the new pay, stated that:

The new pay view provides that organizations effectively use all elements of pay – direct pay (cash compensation) and indirect pay (benefits) – to help them form a partnership between the organization and its employees. By means of this partnership, employees can understand the goals of the organization, know where they fit into those goals, become appropriately involved in decisions affecting them, and receive rewards to the extent they have assisted the organization to do so. New pay helps link the financial success of both the organization and its employees.

Non-financial rewards

The total range of what might be classified as 'reward' is considerable and may reach beyond the workplace. Few firms provide the complete range, and others prefer to provide only the statutory rights, such as, for example, a healthy and safe work environment and the provision of maternity and paternity rights. There is, however, a range of benefits and facilities that are designed to demonstrate to employees that the organisation values them and is therefore prepared to enhance the quality of their life at work. These might include:

- an attractive pension scheme (although in recent years the performance of company pension schemes has persuaded employees to make their own financial arrangements for a reasonable income in retirement)
- access to medical care
- help with long-term sickness
- assistance with family matters, such as bereavement, crèche facilities, help with schooling and transport for families who are moved around geographically
- counselling services
- access to occupational support scheme (OSS) and employee assistance programmes (EAP) (see Chapter 12)
- staff restaurant and social and recreational facilities
- preparation for redundancy and retirement
- advisory services for contemporary welfare issues, such as HIV/AIDS and sexual health generally; problems with drugs and alcohol and the formulation of policies on smoking in and around the workplace.

Rewards with financial value

People might receive special rewards, perhaps for performance, such as the successful outcome of a particular project, or for making a useful suggestion. One of the most important aspects of such rewards, however, is the influence of the element of individual differences. Porter and Lawler (1968), for example, point out that it is just that type of performance that produces job satisfaction, and that where an expected reward stands in different individuals' value systems determines how much they value the expected outcome (reward). The levels of values that people place upon rewards therefore differ from one individual to the next.

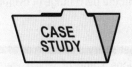

Case study 14: The wrong vintage

Roger Wynne was the IT manager of Green, Gross and Baker (GGB), a large firm of solicitors with its head office in Bristol and branches throughout the West Country. GGB employed 500 solicitors and some 1600 managerial and administrative staff.

In his spare time Roger was a keen collector and renovator of vintage cars, and he was very skilled at restoring them to their former glory. He often used his cars to travel to work, and the staff used to stop to admire them in the company car park; they regarded him as a 'perfectionist'. While he respected the technology that went into modern production-line cars, he did not like their design or the materials that were used in the interior.

The senior partners of GGB offered Roger the task of setting up a fully equipped computerised information service for the managers and specialist solicitors, and they told him that there would be a 'significant reward' for a good job, but they did not tell him the exact nature or value of the reward.

It was clear to Roger that the new system was important to GGB and he relished the challenge. It was a long and painstaking job but when it was finally up and running, it was obvious that Roger had upheld his reputation as a perfectionist.

A special presentation event was organised and took place in the spacious entrance hall of the head office. Imagine how Roger must have felt when the senior partners led him to the centre of the hall and proudly unveiled his reward, which was a modern 1800 cc 16-valve saloon car!

Factors that influence reward

Reward systems are founded upon the organisation's strategies and policies for compensating employees for their performance, and the investment of their time, knowledge, skills and competence. The rewards employees receive are based on their perceived value to the organisation, what their skills are worth on the employment market, the nature of the industry, and the financial health of the organisation.

The availability of labour rises and falls with the economy, and the intensity of competition for the right staff fluctuates accordingly. The new millennium brought with it a 'talent war', fuelled by the skill demands of ever-advancing technology and the fierceness of global competition. Obviously, the size and nature of the rewards that are being offered for those who possess the required skills will determine the organisation's ability to compete effectively for staff. The strategy adopted by the organisation addresses its need to obtain, retain and motivate committed, competent, experienced and loyal employees.

Determining reward strategy

The organisation has to be *financially able* to provide the levels of reward that enable it to compete with other organisations for staff. When formulating reward strategy, therefore, decisions have to be made about how much of the financial resource can be allocated for reward. Such decisions are influenced by the current and expected future profitability of the organisation, the negotiating positions of the relevant parties and the percentage of overall costs that are represented by pay.

The organisation's freedom to formulate reward strategy and set salary and wage rates is constrained by internal and external influences and obligations, some of which were discussed in Chapter 11. The main pressures may be summarised as follows:

- the organisation's ability to sustain pay levels
- comparisons with what other organisations pay
- national and industry-wide trends
- trade unions/employees' demands
- current and expected productivity levels
- legislation on pay
- UK government and European policies on pay
- changes in technology, the economy and the labour market
- cost of living increases
- the availability of particular skills
- levels of knowledge and competences required
- the evaluation of employee performance
- the relative values of the jobs as produced by job evaluation.

Reward systems

It is necessary for you to develop an understanding of both traditional and modern reward systems, since at particular times in your career, you may be expected to work effectively with both. Also, the point should be made here that although organisations with a modern outlook on reward have introduced 'new pay' systems, some still use traditional systems, and many organisations use both in order to reward different categories of employee appropriately.

The decline in manufacturing in the UK and the complementary increase in 'service' and sedentary types of work has reduced the demand for some of the traditional pay systems. Now, however, there is a demand for new and innovative pay systems, especially in the light of the need to attract, retain and motivate highly skilled staff.

Wages and salaries

Before we go any further it is important for you to understand the difference between *wages* and *salaries*. Wages are paid weekly to employees who are paid on an hourly or weekly rate, while employees who are on an annual salary are paid less frequently, usually monthly. It will become clear to you that the older and more traditional pay systems were largely designed to motivate and reward factory floor wage-earners in manufacturing companies.

Incentive and equity pay schemes

Systems of payment may be *incentive-based* or *equity-based*. Incentive-based schemes are designed to motivate a good performance in terms of the quantity and quality of what is produced. Equity systems tend more to link reward with the importance and value of the job, as well as to the person actually doing it.

Incentive systems of payment

It was in the early twentieth century that F.W. Taylor introduced a system of payment that was designed to motivate employees by rewarding their performance fairly. He devised what we now call *work study,* and after calculating how much work a human being could achieve in a particular amount of time, he linked employees' pay to their performance. Pay mechanisms such as these came to be referred to as *payment by results,* or PBR schemes. In organisations where they are now used, such schemes are more sophisticated than those of Taylor, but the basic principle remains the same.

His main objective was to increase productivity, and it seemed logical to him to simply show the workers how they might increase their rewards: 'The more you produce, the more you will earn.' He claimed that managers were ignorant of what men [sic] could produce, and criticised their lack of effort to find out. He believed that people worked in order to obtain financial rewards, rather than because they were interested in what they were doing. Clearly, they needed a reason to work (in addition to keeping their jobs), and he devised a system of payment by results in order to provide an attractive incentive.

Payment by results schemes

Payment by results schemes are those in which pay is tied to actual performance. The idea of pay being tied to actual performance is illustrated simply by *piecework*. This is where employees, whose job it is to produce a certain number of items daily or weekly, are paid in accordance with an agreed rate per item for the number of items produced. When this kind of system was introduced, almost 100 years ago, it worked in a totally direct fashion (see Figure 12.1).

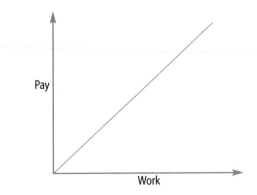

Figure 12.1 Example of a piecework scheme

This indicates that if the employee produced very few items, perhaps through being unwell, or being absent through sickness, he/she would receive very little, or even no pay. Where this system is still in use it has been modified to provide for a guaranteed basic wage, in which the worker receives at least the minimum wage. Beyond the guaranteed wage level, workers are given targets which, when exceeded, makes them eligible for a piece-rate bonus (see Figure 12.2).

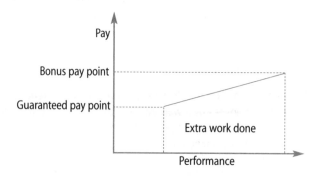

Figure 12.2 Guaranteed wage plus piece rate bonus

In Figure 12.2, note the angle of the curve beyond the 'guaranteed' point. Through the bargaining process, managers and workers negotiate what they call the steepness or flatness of the scheme. In a 'steep' scheme, as in Figure 12.1, fewer items may be produced in order to obtain a high bonus, whereas in a 'flat' scheme (Figure 12.2), a greater number of items would have to be produced to achieve the same bonus.

Criticisms of piecework include the idea that it places the productivity effort in the hands of the workers, instead of the managers, and that the 'money-motivated' rush for quantity adversely affects the quality of the product. Also, workers tend, informally, to standardise productivity beyond the guaranteed point, and trouble may arise when the need for productivity reduces. Trouble may occur since in the medium to long term, employees become accustomed to receiving regular weekly piece-rate bonuses, and unconsciously, they incorporate the extra cash into their perception of their 'income'. When they are asked to reduce productivity, therefore, the inevitable slimmer pay packet comes as a shock.

Obviously, workers who are paid in this way have an advantage over the support workers, such as clerks and administrators, who have less control over what is in their pay packets. This sometimes creates dissatisfaction among the support workers, and many companies have successfully minimised the discontent by introducing organisation-wide bonus schemes, in which all workers benefit from the profitability produced by their efforts, whether they are classed as 'direct' or 'support' employees.

Bonus scheme

This is a company-wide scheme in the which all employees are rewarded with an annual or biannual bonus on the basis of the organisation's productivity as a whole. The reward is usually a percentage of each person's annual pay. It is important to note that with this kind of scheme the productivity measure that is selected is one that genuinely reflects that the employees exceeded a previously agreed productivity standard over the relevant period. In this way, the amount of bonus paid is directly related to employee performance. The rationale for this kind of scheme is that employees will co-operate with each other and with the managers in order to achieve as high a bonus as possible.

Measured daywork

It was noted above that PBR schemes have been criticised because they place the control of productivity in the hands of the employees. One approach to solving this problem was to introduce measured daywork schemes, which became popular in the 1950s and 1960s when there was a large number of mass production factories in the UK. Armstrong (1999) describes this as a system that fixes employees' pay 'on the understanding that they will maintain a specified level of performance, but pay does not fluctuate in the short term with their performance' (as it would with a piecework scheme). Measured daywork provides an incentive for the employee to perform at a required level. This puts the employee under an obligation to meet that level since the incentive is guaranteed in advance.

Team reward scheme

Reputedly, this is a simple concept but it can be extremely difficult to administer. The idea is that an incentive-based pay system that rewards teams by reinforcing desired behaviour should lead to effective teamwork. One of the problems encountered is that managers tend to treat team members as individuals, rather than relating to them in terms of what the team can achieve (CIPD 2005). Furthermore, if all of the team members are to share the rewards equally, the assumption must be that all team members put in an exactly equal contribution to the effort that earned the reward!

Armstrong (1999), on the other hand, says that group and team incentive schemes 'provide for the payment of a bonus either equally or proportionately to individuals within a group or team'. It is also argued by Armstrong (1999) that pay systems that encourage the individual do not foster teamwork. Dealing with the individual, however, does seem to be more in keeping with an HRM approach, which is to deal directly with individuals, rather than their representatives or groups.

Pause for thought

Whenever a group or team is formed a leader appears. The leader may be one that is appointed by the organisation (a *formal leader*), or one that has emerged by mutual consent to represent the team (an *informal leader*). Leaders report to the people who put them where they are. A group, therefore, may have a two leaders. The question that arises is: which leader decides on the amount of work effort that is *actually put in*, and thereby controls the value of the bonus?

Equity-based schemes

Whereas incentive systems are tied to individual or a group's actual performance, in that they are rewarded for their productivity, equity systems relate to the value of the job itself, in that they reward the job holder at a level that reflects what it is worth to the organisation to have that particular job done. This involves the organisation in assessing the relative values of jobs, and setting up a pay structure that reflects those values so that everyone is rewarded equally for carrying out jobs that have been judged to be of equal value to the organisation. The most well-known and most used equity-based system of payment is *job evaluation*.

Job evaluation schemes

With these schemes, jobs are compared with each other and then graded according to their values. While the grades do not constitute a payment system, they do provide the basis for one. Job evaluation structures are developed/suggested by job evaluators and approved by a job evaluation committee or panel.

There are several approaches to job evaluation, some of which are 'non-analytical' and some 'analytical'. This is not to suggest that one approach is better than another, but choosing the most effective method for one particular organisation is an important decision, since they vary in their suitability. Sometimes, the greatest effectiveness is achieved by using different approaches in different parts of the organisation. Here, we shall discuss three approaches:

- job ranking
- job grading or job classification
- points rating.

Job ranking

This is a non-analytical process which simply compares whole jobs with each other without breaking them down into their component parts. Evaluators identify the positions of jobs and rank them hierarchically in order of their size. Jobs that are perceived to be of equal value are placed into groups. A criticism of job ranking is that it is a subjective process in that there are no reputed standards for assessing the sizes of the jobs, although it can be argued that employees will regard it as fair when they see where their jobs are ranked in relation to other jobs. In a sense, however, job evaluation in general may be seen as a subjective process, since as we shall see, even analytical systems are ultimately based on the consensus of a panel of evaluators.

EXAMPLE

Example 13: Job ranking

In this example, four jobs have been selected:

- admin assistant
- accountant
- office supervisor
- middle manager.

We can see immediately that each of them has a different value. Other office jobs are then ranked alongside the admin assistant, slightly higher jobs alongside the accountant, and so on. It is a rather crude and basic form of job evaluation, and it is sometimes necessary to grade certain jobs individually, since not all jobs fit neatly, even into broad categories on the hierarchy. Some jobs, as they say, 'stick out' as isolated entities.

Job grading/classification

Job grading, or job classification, as it is often called, is another non-analytical approach. It is similar to job ranking except that the evaluators decide on the groupings or pay grades in advance, after which a general job description is produced for all of the jobs in each group. A typical individual job is then identified and used as a benchmark. Finally, each job is compared with the general job description and the benchmark job, then placed in an appropriate grade. This can be useful in times of change, since new or redesigned jobs can be assessed according to the criteria, and placed at the appropriate level. On the other hand, modern thinking about organisational design tends to favour lean and flattened structures with a reduced number of levels, which can produce difficulties when categorising jobs in a scheme such as this.

Another approach to job grading is to categorise the jobs according to the criteria without considering their potential hierarchical position. In this way, criteria are related more directly to the actual work itself, so that the levels of knowledge, skills and competence required to do the work are taken into account, along with responsibilities and the importance of the decisions the job holder takes.

The process reveals a similarity between the methods of job grading and those of job ranking, in that when the committee is making comparisons, it treats jobs as whole entities. The job evaluation committee makes its decisions by reaching a consensus, but it is also open to consider appeals from employees who feel that their jobs have been unfairly or inappropriately graded. In some organisations, appeals are considered by independent panels.

Points rating method

This is an analytical method, and probably the most commonly used. The principal feature of points rating is that instead of comparing the value of whole jobs, as in non-analytical approaches, it analyses and compares jobs on the basis of such factors as qualifications and competences required, degree of responsibility, customer contact, job complexity, physical requirements and working conditions. Each of these factors carries a number of points, and the amount apportioned to each job is determined by the degree to which the factors are present within it. A hierarchical structure is produced on the basis of the points rating of each job. Pay for a particular job is determined according to the number of points it carries.

Job analysis is an essential precursor to a points rating system. When the factors mentioned above have been identified, job descriptions and specifications need to be reviewed, revised, and where necessary completely rewritten. The ultimate scheme has to be seen to be fair, and since the differences between jobs are measured in accordance with the degree to which the selected factors are present, great care must be taken over the analysis.

Deciding how many points to allocate to each factor is a well-known problem in points rating. The factors vary in their importance to each job, and the most complex or most important are allocated the greatest number of points. This is called the *weighting* of factors. The factors are placed in order of importance and complexity, and weighted according to a maximum number of points, bearing in mind the degree of importance that each factor has in a particular job. Each job is then graded according to the level at which the factors are present.

Fixed scales

Some organisations, particularly those in the public sector, have fixed incremental pay scales. Within each job there is a scale through which the job holder may progress in an annual 'step-up' fashion. (see Figure 12.3).

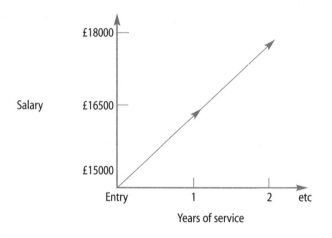

Figure 12.3 Example of a fixed incremental scale

In most organisations that use this system, the regular and unquestioned 'step up' has been replaced, so that now managerial discretion, usually based on performance ratings, may be used to reduce or increase the value of each increment.

Management consultants' schemes

Several management consultancy firms can provide 'tailor-made' job evaluation schemes (which are usually analytical), or the organisation can commission the consultancy to custom-build a scheme for it. As a 'do-it-yourself' exercise, the development of a job evaluation scheme can be costly and time-consuming, and it may ultimately be more cost-effective to engage a consultancy. Foot and Hook (1999) point out that an additional advantage of using a consultancy is that of 'giving access to extensive comparative data on job markets and rates of pay which designers of proprietary schemes collect'.

Performance-related pay

The bases for performance-related pay (P-rP) are fairness and equity. While the idea is to reward a good performance, it is hard to resist the notion that once it is established in an organisation, it also provides an incentive to perform well. *Merit* pay was a similar performance-based idea originated in the early twentieth century, which was an attempt to provide satisfactory rewards for the exercise of ability and current performance. According to Tyson and York (1996) 'Merit increases are ... given to show recognition and to imply the kinds of actions and attitudes which the company wishes to reward.' The same principle applies with P-rP, in which it is fair to reward various levels of performance differentially.

P-rP has been through varying levels of popularity and unpopularity over the years. In the 1970s, for example, when inflation was running in double figures, the percentage increases that were awarded seemed of little financial value. In the 1980s, however, inflation began to fall. A survey carried out by the Institute of Personnel and Development (now the CIPD) in 1998 found that although there had been a growth in the use of performance-based schemes, only 43 per cent of the responding organisations reported that they used performance pay for managerial and non-managerial staff.

There are arguments about P-rP as a motivator. We will not enter into the detail of these arguments here, but in broad terms surveys have indicated that while there is general support for the principle, most respondents did not believe that it had improved their motivation (Marsden and French 1998). Other research has suggested that P-rP is actually demotivating staff, rather than encouraging them (Bevan and Thompson 1991).

Influence of individual differences

Individually different perceptions of these schemes and of the purposes of reward in general have a strong influence on the results of such surveys. Some people, for example, adopt a particular profession because they feel naturally drawn to it, and while clearly they have to maintain a particular standard of living, it is the work itself that motivates them, rather than what they receive for carrying it out. On the other hand, Taylor's assumption (1911, 1947), that people work exclusively for money was based on his perception of entirely different types of worker. According to Goldthorpe (1968), we have seen that the same types of manual worker are motivated almost entirely by 'extrinsic' rewards. In other words, they see it as the means by which they are able to sustain a particular living standard.

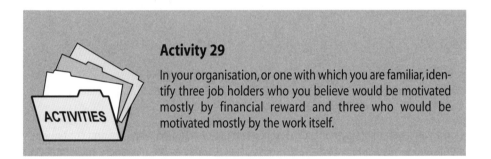

Activity 29

In your organisation, or one with which you are familiar, identify three job holders who you believe would be motivated mostly by financial reward and three who would be motivated mostly by the work itself.

ACTIVITIES

Guidelines to achieve acceptance

A set of guidelines for action designed to achieve a positive attitude towards a P-rP scheme might include:

- integrative bargaining for the optimal scheme
- the selection or creation of a scheme in which all employees may participate
- the onus of responsibility to identify the level of an employee's performance in relation to the minimum standard being placed firmly on the manager
- managers who operate the scheme being trained to do so, and given a thorough understanding of the spirit as well as the letter of its regulations
- steps being taken to ensure that all employees are provided with an explanation of the scheme and access to further explanatory information and advice
- employees being given the right of reassessment by request.

How performance-related pay works

The in-job performance of employees is appraised and there is a mechanism through which overall performance levels are identified. The gradings might be as follows:

Grade	Comment
1. Excellent	Has exceeded all standards and objectives.
2. Good	Has met standards and achieved objectives.
3. Average	Has met most standards and achieved objectives.
4. Poor or unsatisfactory	Has failed to meet standards or objectives.

There is an agreed reward, multiples of which are added to the general percentage increase across the organisation. The multiple applied is determined by which of the numbered grades the employee has been given. Table 12.1 is an example of how performance might be related to reward.

Table 12.1 Relating pay awards to performance

Performance level	Multiple of award given	Organisation-wide % of increase
1	X 2.5	
2	X 2.0	eg 5%
3	X 1.5	
4	0	

Source: Tyson and York (1996).

As with any system of payment, a P-rP scheme must be handled with care and continuously monitored for its fairness and effectiveness. The attitudes of the managers and employees towards a particular scheme are of critical importance, and if the basis on which the scheme is founded is perceived as flawed, or the approach to assessment is regarded as biased, the scheme will fall into disrepute.

Legislation

All organisations have to bear in mind the provisions of the legislation on pay, for example, the national minimum wage and the discrimination laws. When developing and administering a payment scheme, therefore, the organisation has to conform to the minimum standards, which include the provisions of:

- The Equal Pay Act 1970
- The Equal Pay (Amendment) Regulations 1983
- The Employment Rights Act 1996
- The National Minimum Wage Act 1998.

Equal Pay Act 1970

The aim of the Equal Pay Act (EPA) is to ensure that employees who are doing like work, which is work that is the same or broadly similar regardless of their sex, must receive the same rate of pay or be paid on the same salary scale. Organisations that pay such employees differentially are breaking the law. Similarly, men and women whose jobs may be different in character, but have been assessed similarly under a job evaluation scheme, must receive the same rate of pay.

Equal Pay (Amendment) Regulations 1983

These regulations supplemented the EPA with a clause that provides for equal pay for men and women when the jobs they do are of equal value, regardless of their type or how they have been classified under a job evaluation scheme. Equal value is measured according to the job's requirements in terms of competence, responsibility and level of decision-making.

Employment Rights Act 1996

This legislation consolidates employees' statutory rights in a single Act of Parliament. It affects employees' pay in that it proscribes unwarranted deductions from pay unless such deductions are made in particular circumstances. The Act therefore legitimises deductions if any of the following circumstances apply:

- when deductions are authorised by law, such as income tax, National Insurance contributions or court orders, such as for payment of maintenance to an ex-spouse
- when there is a statement in the employee's written contract which specifies that certain deductions may be made from wages and when the employee has already given written consent, for example when agreed deductions are made as a result of poor performance or rule breaking, such as unacceptable attendance times
- accidental overpayment of wages, or of expenses, even though this is likely to be the fault of the employer
- when the employee has been absent because he/she is taking industrial action
- in retail companies, to make good any cash deficiency in a till or a shortfall in the stock.

National Minimum Wage Act 1998

Workers are entitled to be paid at least the level of the statutory national minimum wage (NMW) for every hour they work for an employer. In October 2005 the NMW was increased, and the government has proposed further increases in October 2006. These changes are outlined in Table 12.2.

Table 12.2 Current and proposed national minimum wage rates

Category of employee	Current NMW since October 2005	Proposed NMW from October 2006
1 Adult workers aged 22 years or over	£5.05 an hour	£5.35 an hour
2 Workers aged 18–21 inclusive (development rate)	£4.25 an hour	£4.45 an hour
3 Workers aged 16 and 17	£3.00 an hour	Currently under review

The *development rate* (number 2 in Table 12.2) can also apply to workers aged 22 years and above during their first six months in a new job with a new employer and who are receiving accredited training.

Fair piece rates

In October 2004, a piece rate of 100 per cent of the NMW an hour was proposed by the government, and this was increased to 120 per cent in April 2005. At the same time (2005), homeworkers became eligible for the minimum wage.

Self-test questions

1. How would you define 'reward'? Would you prefer to use the US expression *compensation*, or would you use simply 'payment'? Why?
2. Why do you think E.E. Lawler proposed the *new pay*?
3. What are 'non-financial rewards'?
4. Why does an organisation offer particular benefits and facilities? What is in it for the organisation?
5. What are the constraints and obligations (or pressures) that influence the formulation of reward strategy?
6. What is meant by the term *fixed scales*?
7. Incentive schemes are so called because they are designed to have a positive influence on future performance, but what does a P-rP scheme reward?
8. What is the main purpose of the Employee Rights Act 1996?
9. Under what circumstances is it legitimate for an employer to make deductions from an employee's pay?
10. Under what circumstances may an organisation pay the development rate to an adult who is over the age of 21?

Health, safety and well-being

Introduction

Whenever the conversation turns to health and safety at work people usually talk about the organisation's obligations under the law. Undoubtedly, conformity to the provisions of the law are of paramount importance, but there is also a strong business case for providing a healthy and safe working environment. After all, if the organisation is good at attracting the right people, it is more likely to retain them if it looks after their health and safety and takes whatever steps are necessary to ensure their well-being while they are at work.

Although *health, safety* and *well-being* are inextricably linked, in this chapter they are discussed separately, and the relationships between them are explained within the context of the discussions. First, however, the relevant legislation is examined, and since the HR practitioner has a significant administrative and advisory role, there is guidance on how the provisions of the law may be implemented.

Health and safety law

Historically, the UK's long-term record for ensuring the health and safety of employees is poor. During the Industrial Revolution little was done to protect employees, visitors, local residents or passers-by from the hazards that arose from organisations' activities. Those most likely to be the victims of health and safety risks were the employees, and this is still the case. Several Factories and Shops Acts were passed in the early twentieth century but most employee protection was derived from the common law. Until 1949 there was no such thing as legal aid, and employees had to rely on the goodwill of their 'masters' to compensate them for injuries or health problems that were attributable to conditions in the workplace.

The Health and Safety at Work Act 1974

The Health and Safety at Work Act (HASAWA) places an obligation on everyone involved in the organisation to maintain standards in the health, safety and well-being of people throughout the workplace, whether they be fellow-employees, visitors, or members of the general public passing by or living close to the premises. The responsibility includes protecting and securing people's safety and preventing environmental pollution of any kind.

The 'Commission' and the 'Executive'

Under the provisions of the Act, the Secretary of State for the Department of Trade and Industry (DTI) established the *Health and Safety Commission* (HSC), with a *Health and Safety Executive* (HSE), which enforces the law, and offers advice. HSE inspectors have the right to enter premises without notice and examine records. They can issue *enforcement notices* and prosecute serious and persistent offenders. The point should be made, however, that HSE inspectors have these powers in case they need them, rather than to fill the courts with minor and accidental offenders. HSE inspectors advise organisations on health and safety at work, and persuade them to behave responsibly.

What organisations must do

There are particular steps an organisation must take in order to conform to the law. One way to explain this is to imagine that you have just set up a new organisation. There are 10 actions (steps) you must take to provide your organisation with a sound basis for health, safety and well-being, as listed below:

1. Write a *health and safety policy*. This means deciding how you are going to manage health and safety.
2. Set up a *risk assessment system*. Decide what could cause harm to people and how to take precautions.
3. Buy *employers liability insurance* and display the insurance certificate in your workplace. If you employ anyone, you must do this.
4. Provide free health and safety training for your workers so they know what hazards and risks they may face and how to deal with them.
5. Engage *competent advice* to help you to meet your health and safety duties. These can be your own workers, external consultants or a combination of these.
6. Provide toilets, washing facilities and drinking water for all of your employees, not forgetting those with disabilities. These are the basic health, safety and well-being needs.
7. Consult employees on health and safety matters. Most organisations have a *health and safety committee.*
8. Display the *health and safety law poster* or provide a leaflet containing similar information.
9. Report particular work-related accidents, diseases and dangerous events.
10. Register with the HSE or your local authority, depending on the kind of business you are in.

Health and safety policy

First, this is a statement of how the organisation intends to manage the health, safety and well-being of its employees, visitors and the general public. Second, it describes how health and safety will be organised and how the high standards that have been set will be achieved through the involvement of everyone, at all levels, throughout the organisation. Third, the statement includes details of how the policy will be implemented.

Pause for thought

Have you read your organisation's health and safety policy? Can you remember what it contains? Does it make you feel that the organisation is committed to providing a healthy and safe working environment?

Risk assessment

This is about the identification of current and potential hazards, analysing the possible attendant risks and making recommendations for the removal or reduction of the risks. The HSE (2005) says that health and safety is about preventing people from being harmed or becoming ill through work; a *hazard* is anything that can cause harm or make people ill.

Statutory regulations and code of practice

Risk assessment is regulated by the *Management of Health and Safety at Work Regulations 1992* and the *Code of Practice on Risk Assessment*, which offers guidance on implementation. The regulations say that the employer must 'carry out a risk assessment of the workplace and make all necessary changes to bring property, practices and procedures up to the required standard'.

Carrying out a risk assessment

If you employ five or more people, your risk assessments must be recorded. Clearly then, an employer who fails to carry out risk assessments is breaking the law, and the penalties can be severe. In the Code of Practice there is great emphasis on the identification of hazards, and the HSE, for example, points out various tasks and situations in which typically, high-risk hazards are found:

- receipt of raw materials, eg lifting, carrying
- stacking and storage, eg falling materials
- movement of people and materials, eg falls, collisions
- processing of raw materials, eg exposure to toxic substances
- maintenance of buildings, eg roof work, gutter cleaning
- maintenance of plant and machinery, eg lifting tackle, installation of equipment
- using electricity, eg using hand tools, extension leads
- operating machines, eg operating without sufficient clearance or at an unsafe speed; not using safety devices
- failure to wear protective equipment, eg hats, boots, clothing
- dealing with emergencies, eg spillages, fires, explosions
- health hazards arising from the use of equipment or methods of working, eg VDUs, repetitive strain injuries from badly designed work stations or working practices.

Five steps to risk assessment

The HSE explains the risk assessment process in five steps:

1. Look for hazards.
2. Decide who might be harmed and how.
3. Evaluate the risks arising from the hazards and decide whether existing precautions are adequate or if more should be done.
4. Record findings.
5. Review the assessment periodically and revise if necessary.

When carrying out the evaluation of risk, those involved should assess the level of risk in relation to each separate hazard. The severity of hazards may be classified on a short scale of, for example, 'slight risk', 'medium risk' and 'high risk'. Holt and Andrews (1993) proposed a severity rating scale as given in Table 13.1.

Table 13.1 Risk assessment: severity rating scale

1 Catastrophic	Imminent danger exists, hazard capable of causing death and illness on a wide scale
2 Critical	Hazard can result in serious illness, severe injury, property and equipment damage
3 Marginal	Hazard can cause illness, injury or equipment damage, but the results would not be expected to be serious
4 Negligible	Hazard will not result in serious injury or illness; remote possibility of damage beyond minor first aid case

Source: Holt and Andrews (1993).

The risk assessment process is not complete until action has been taken to eliminate any hazards found in the assessment and analytic process. Many organisations have staff members who are experts in the relevant fields, and the organisation's safety manager/officer will play a significant role in the whole process, and in ensuring that appropriate action is taken. Where it is needed, however, specific advice is also obtainable from the HSE.

The reviews may be regularly undertaken, say annually or biannually, but special reviews may be necessary when change takes place, such as the introduction of new technology or a reallocation of jobs.

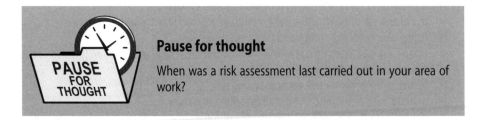

Pause for thought

When was a risk assessment last carried out in your area of work?

Accidents at work

References to accidents at work may invoke a variety of recollections ranging from those of our own individual experiences of witnessing or being personally involved in minor accidents or 'close shaves', to those major incidents that remain in our minds forever, such as large-scale factory fires, explosions in chemical plants, mining disasters and rail crashes. Even since the 1974 Act came into force, thousands of people have been killed or injured as a result of minor and major industrial accidents.

Discovering the causes of accidents, therefore, is an extremely important aspect of accident prevention. The causes identified through accident investigations may lead to appropriate preventive measures. Explanations for accidents are many and varied and attempts have been made to categorise them. These include: (i) environmental, (ii) behavioural, and (iii) physiological (Molander and Winterton 1994).

It is important to regard the three sources of explanation as interrelated. For example, individuals' responses to the environment and the factors within it are both behavioural and physiological. Also, particular items of behaviour, such as alcohol or drug abuse, cause perceptive and physiological disorders that produce a negative and often dangerous psychological state.

Environmental causes

The working environment is extremely important, especially in industries that clearly are very hazardous, such as working on railways, at sea on ships and oil rigs, chemical factories, and building and mining operations. In such industries, however, both organisational and employee awareness of risk is high, and significant progress has been made in training and the provision of safety equipment.

While this high level of safety consciousness has resulted in fewer accidents, such industries are still regarded as high risk, although industries which clearly are less hazardous by their nature have a higher incidence of minor accidents. With many people, environmental causes of accidents are thought of as 'factory floor' phenomena, but the point has to be made that an office environment, with illegal wires laid across the floor, faulty electrical fittings and insufficient working space, can be a dangerous place.

Office workers often attempt to make minor repairs and adjustments to their electrical equipment, lighting and so forth, without switching off the power supply and without the right equipment to reach the area in which they think there is a fault. Thus we find people standing on chairs to reach ceiling fittings, bending under desks to fiddle with connection boxes and so forth. Often, even the chairs they sit on are unsafe in one way or another.

Behavioural causes

Particular aspects of social learning are responsible for accidents at work. This refers to learning that has not been developed through formal education or training, but picked up from copying the behaviour of others, conformity to 'norms' and through trial and error. A new employee, for example, may notice that in order to achieve particular productivity levels – which carry extra pay – some workers breach health and safety regulations, by removing machine guards or engaging in other unsafe practices, which enable them to reach bonus figures.

Also, people experiencing stress undergo changes in behaviour. When they are worried about their marriage, home and family, job security and career prospects, they are thinking about those things when they should be concentrating on what they are doing. It has long been known that 'daydreaming' is a cause of accidents at work.

Physiological causes

In addition to those referred to above, there are several specific physiological causes of accidents. Poor eyesight, colour blindness, poor hearing, a limited sense of smell and other physiological problems can cause slow reactions to situations and might turn a prospective 'near miss' into an accident. Not everyone is fit and healthy, and managers and supervisors should be aware of their staff's state of health and fitness, in relation to the nature of the work that they assign to them.

Non-accidental health problems

Not all health and safety problems are accident-related. When we think of accidents we think of events that cause physical injuries or even death. Serious damage to health, however, can be caused in the workplace by inhaling noxious gases or ingesting certain substances, perhaps caused by a failure to use safety equipment, or alternatively caused by carelessness, incorrect storage or faults in production machinery and equipment. Office workers may experience visual problems when using computer terminals, and those who sit for long periods may not have the ideal chair. Repetitive strain injury (RSI) is the result of over-use of the same part of the body for too long a period.

Healthy workplace initiatives

Healthy workplace initiatives began in 1992, when the national initiative, *The health of the nation* was introduced in a white paper published by the Department of Health. The white paper recognised that the increasing concern of employers and their workforces over health issues provided opportunities to intensify health promotion in the workplace.

Task Force survey

A 'task force' was appointed to examine and expand this activity. The task force carried out a nationwide survey and the results were set out in a report, *Health promotion in the workplace*, published by the Health Education Authority (HEA). The survey was designed to gather information about the nature and frequency of 'health at work' activities, in terms of track record, the present situation and future plans. In total, 1344 organisations were examined.

Many aspects of workplace activity were covered by those questions, including:

- smoking and tobacco products
- healthy eating
- exercise/fitness/activity
- health screening
- blood pressure control
- back care
- heart health and heart disease
- cervical screening
- repetitive strain injury
- hearing

- alcohol and sensible drinking
- weight control
- stress management and relaxation
- cholesterol testing
- drugs/substance abuse
- HIV/AIDS
- breast screening
- lifestyle assessment
- eyesight testing
- women's health.

Not all organisations reported problems in every single area, so each of the 'healthy workplace' activities that were set up dealt with its own respective areas of concern. The initiative taken in the National Health Service, for example *Health at work in the NHS,* was based on five main areas of concern: (i) occupational stress, (ii) sexual health (HIV/AIDS etc), (iii) smoking, (iv) drug and alcohol abuse and (v) healthy lifestyle (eating habits, physical activity and so on).

Health and safety audits

Organisations should carry out health and safety audits, involving as many as possible of those directly concerned with health and safety issues. This may include health and safety officers and advisers, HR specialists, managers and trade union representatives. The purpose of such an audit is defined by Saunders (1992):

A safety audit will examine the whole organisation in order to test whether it is meeting its safety aims and objectives. It will examine hierarchies, safety planning processes, decision-making, delegation, policy-making and implementation as well as all areas of safety programme planning.

The audit should include practical and quantitative issues, such as the adequacy and implementation of the organisation's health and safety policies and procedures, and safety practices such as the efficiency and effectiveness of risk assessments and accident investigations. Additionally it should cover attitudinal and qualitative issues such as commitment to all aspects of health and safety at work and the level of seriousness adopted by involved groups, such as the health and safety committee.

As with all audits, the purpose of a health and safety audit is to identify problems and areas for improvement, and ensure that appropriate action is taken in order to resolve problems and improve the relevant areas.

Activity 30

Next time you are walking through the workplace or university campus, keep an eye open for posters and other notices about health and safety. Count how many there are and note what they say.

Employee well-being

The word *well-being*, rather than *welfare*, is used in this chapter because it covers the services that one associates with welfare, but it is also refers to individuals' physical and mental health, which implies that employees should be working in a physically safe and stress-free environment. Well-being is also concerned with employees' problems, such as their working hours, work overload, financial, home and marriage situations, susceptibility to stress and their general health and lifestyle.

Workplace stress

The main emphases in this section are on the causes of stress, the nature and identification of the symptoms, and the steps that can be taken by the organisation and the individual concerned.

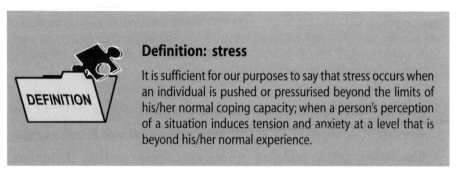

Definition: stress

It is sufficient for our purposes to say that stress occurs when an individual is pushed or pressurised beyond the limits of his/her normal coping capacity; when a person's perception of a situation induces tension and anxiety at a level that is beyond his/her normal experience.

Sources and causes of stress

Sources of stress are those areas of life in which stressors (see Glossary) are active. Research shows that there are six main areas of stress:

- the workplace
- marriage
- home and family
- personal finances
- living accommodation
- personal time and leisure.

However, more than 50 per cent of all stress is attributable to the workplace.

Stress as a commuter

The effects of stress that originate in one of the areas listed above travel around with people as they commute from one area to the next. For example, people take their workplace stress home with them where its effects are communicated to the family. If there are additional pressures at home, perhaps over finances, the accommodation itself, or 'neighbours from hell', then they will be added to the load like a rolling snowball and carried to the other areas, including the workplace. In a severe case the load becomes too much to bear and ill-health follows.

Stress and productivity

Stress adversely affects productivity. It has been estimated that around 100 million working days are lost annually through stress-related factors, such as sickness absence and reduced work performance. It is worth bearing in mind that these losses are 30 times greater than those associated with industrial relations problems, and an anomaly emerges when one compares the national and corporate investments that have gone into industrial peace with those dedicated to addressing stress problems.

The human function curve

This provides an explanation of what can happen when an individual is expected to cope with end-to-end emergencies, a continuously high workload or an excessive amount of time spent in the workplace. It is often said that 'a little stress is good for you' and that work performance increases as the pressure rises. 'It gets the adrenalin running', they say, 'and you experience an energy boost'. The truth, however, is that such stress *actually reduces* one's ability to cope with the job, which in turn, creates further stress (see Figure 13.1).

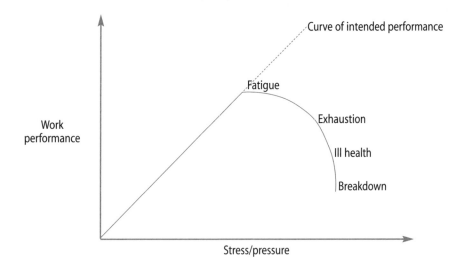

Figure 13.1 The human function curve

In Figure 13.1, the point at which *fatigue* appears on the curve will vary from one individual to the next, but the general principle is the same for everyone. *The curve of intended perform-ance* provides an indication of the employee's unfulfilled intentions. In cases of severe stress, the employee is not always aware that his/her work performance is being affected in the way that is indicated in Figure 13.1.

Dynamics of work stress

It was once thought that work-related stress was experienced mainly by company executives who claimed that time was their primary concern: always dashing about, attending breakfast meetings in the London boardroom and lunch meetings in Geneva. According to Smith *et al* (1978) and McLean (1979), however, stress-induced illnesses are not confined to either high or low-status workers.

Regardless of how one job may compare with another in terms of stress, it is helpful to recog-nise that every job has potential stress agents (stressors). Additionally, it is helpful to note that an event or situation that one person may regard as stressful might be seen by another as an interesting challenge or even a route to success at something. Furthermore, stress affects different people in relatively different ways. Some people find it easy to cope with pressure, while others have great difficulty.

Organisational causes

Researchers have identified five major categories of work stress (Cooper *et al* 1988). Common to all jobs, these factors vary in the degree to which they are found to be causally linked to stress in each job and to the illnesses that may result from the experience of stress (see Figure 13.2).

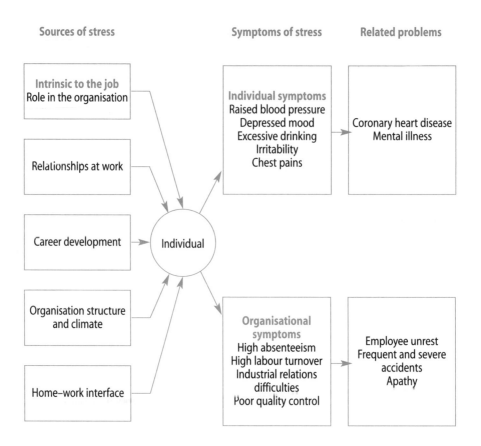

Figure 13.2 Dynamics of work stress

Source: Arnold *et al* (1991).

The role of the organisation

What can the organisation do to alleviate these problems? It was noted above that there are strong business reasons for the organisation to recognise the effects of stress and take action to alleviate it. In any case the organisation does have a social responsibility for the quality of life at work. Clearly, 'a little stress is good for you' is something that is not experienced by most people. Furthermore, it is pretty clear that employees who work in a benign culture that provides a stress-free environment are enabled to concentrate exclusively on their work.

Stress has been classified as *transient*, *post traumatic*, and *chronic*, all of which are related to the timing of the events that caused them:

- *Transient stress*: occurs at the same time as the cause and is a short-term experience. For example, it may be experienced by emergency services workers when they are dealing with events such as public disorder, accidents, fires and a variety of other types of incident.
- *Post-traumatic stress disorders (PTSD)*: occur after a shock caused by a critical life

event, such as involvement in a serious traffic accident, sustaining severe personal injury or being mugged.

■ *Chronic stress*: occurs as a result of continuous pressures being experienced by the individual for a period of time that is too long for the person to endure.

Managing stress

In this section, for the purposes of explanation, a distinction is drawn between *stress management* and *coping* with stress. Stress management consists of the arrangements that organisations, and others, make to minimise workplace stress, whereas coping with stress refers to the steps that an individual might take in order to moderate or eliminate his/her own personal stress.

Many organisations try to moderate the effects of stress by setting up an *occupational support service* (OSS), which is a section within the organisation through which employees may seek assistance when they experience the effects of stress. The scope of the service that may be offered by an OSS is determined by the number of employees and the kind of work in which the firm is engaged. A small to medium-sized organisation, for example, may arrange to access the skills of a nurse, an occupational psychologist and/or a stress counsellor, who can be called on as and when required. On the other hand a large organisation might employ such experts and set up the OSS as a special department.

Employee assistance programmes

Larger organisations may decide to outsource the service by using an *employee assistance programme* (EAP), which is an external agency, commissioned by the organisation to manage employee well-being on its behalf. The external agency is staffed by experts such as psychologists and counsellors, and there is also access to other experts such as solicitors, accountants and doctors, whose services might be required, depending upon the cause of stress experienced by an employee. EAPs are seen as an alternative to occupational support schemes. There are arguments for and against each kind of employee service.

It is thought that employees have greater confidence an EAP, since they may be somewhat suspicious of the OSS worker, who might be seen as a manager's informant. As an external agency, the EAP has the added advantage of objectivity, and having no internal political axe to grind, may be totally candid when it tells managers where there is room for improvement in the way they handle staff.

It has been noticed that organisations that avail themselves of such external services are well placed to demonstrate that they have a caring attitude towards their employees, for example, if an ex-employee has taken legal action against them on the grounds of a stress-related cause of illness and loss of employment.

The 'caring' organisation

Some managers are reluctant to offer advice and assistance to employees on developing a healthy lifestyle. They regard lifestyle as a very personal issue and think that 'interference' by the organisation may be regarded as an unwarranted intrusion. Within the organisation, however, they have an opportunity set an example by promoting a 'healthy workplace' by taking the following initiatives:

- *Smoke-free work areas.* This often means no smoking at all in any part of the workplace.
- *Consulting the workforce* about the kinds of food that are served in the staff restaurant. This is best achieved by agreement and having a food policy.
- *Providing employees with information* about healthy living, including information on physical activity, healthy eating, generally looking after oneself. Employees with health problems and disabled employees may need to consult a physician before adopting the advice.
- *Providing facilities,* where possible, for employees to engage in physical activity, and encouraging them to participate in sports.
- *Providing annual health checks.* There are 'well man' and 'well woman' schemes in which all occupational physicians are versed.
- *Creating and managing* a work environment that is physically safe and generally conducive to good health.

The law on employee well-being

The organisation is responsible for the well-being of its employees while they are working on its behalf: the organisation is said to have a 'duty of care' for its employees. Today, it is becoming commonplace for employees, or ex-employees to take legal action against their ex-employers for breaching their duty of care.

Increasingly, the kind of UK legislation that is related to employee well-being is the result of European directives that have been enacted in the 25 member countries of the European Union, where the bases of the policies are (i) equal treatment for all, (ii) fairness at work and (ii) family friendliness. It is important to bear in mind that much of this legislation is directed at non-work areas, as well as the area of employment.

Working Time Regulations

The Working Time Regulations (WTR) and the Protection of Young People at Work Regulations came into force on 1 October 1998. The regulations, which originated in the *European Fairness at Work* white paper, are concerned with four major aspects of work: (i) limits on working time, (ii) entitlement to rest breaks, (iii) night working and (iv) annual holiday entitlements. Clearly, these four factors are related to family friendliness and the well-being of the individual.

Limits on working time
Under this regulation, the employee does not have to work more than an average of 48 hours a week over a period of 17 weeks. The idea is to protect employees from being obliged to work longer hours, although the regulations allow the employer to request that an employee opts out of the regulatory working time. If this happens the agreement must be formalised in writing, and if the employee subsequently changes his/her mind, he/she has to give the employer three months' notice of his/her intention to work only the regulatory hours.

Entitlement to rest breaks
The regulation states that employees must have a 24-hour break in every seven-day period and 11 consecutive hours of rest in any 24-hour period. These, of course, are minimum standards, although in the UK, which is said to have the longest working hours in Europe, there

are many employees who work a five-day week, giving them a 48-hour break in every seven days: twice the minimum standard!

The chief purposes of the WTR are first, to improve safety standards, which may be accidentally breached if an individual is over-tired; second, to reduce workplace stress by limiting the amount of time spent in the workplace; and third, to move away from the 'open all hours' culture so that the individual is free to organise a satisfactory work–life balance.

Annual leave

The WTR requires employers to provide their employees with four weeks' annual leave with effect from 1999. Employers, in relatively recent history, have always made this provision, although the actual entitlement was usually subject to negotiation with the trade unions or staff association. The legislation specifies minimum entitlements that would outlaw rogue employers. In fact, most employers offer their staff a deal that is superior to the minimum standards provided by the legislation.

Opting out

The WTR provides for employees to opt out of the regulatory requirements, and it is legitimate for an employer to approach employees to request this. It is important to note that the weekly 48-hour average includes normal working time and any overtime. An employee, therefore, who is already on a 48-hour week is prevented from working overtime unless he/she agrees to opt out of the requirement.

Handling the 'opt out'

The process involves the employer in writing a letter to the employee containing an explanation of the employee's situation and the law that governs it. The letter should be accompanied by a legally correct form of agreement, which the employee may or may not sign. If the employee wishes to work overtime, and therefore signs the agreement, the arrangement is not necessarily permanent. The employee may reverse the decision but must provide the employer with three months' notice of his/her intention to do so.

It could be inferred from what is said above that being able to opt out legally is a dangerous provision. In particular trades, employees work an inordinate number of hours for which they are paid the bare minimum wage. Obviously their working time is illegal, unless, of course, they are persuaded to opt out of the regulations. Clearly, the WTR were produced for honourable employers.

Role of the HSE

Compliance with the regulations is monitored by the HSE, and officials have been given powers to inspect organisations' records. Employees' complaints made under the provisions of the WTR will be heard by employment tribunals.

This is quite a long and complex set of regulations, certainly too long for this book, but you can examine them in greater detail by referring to the *Industrial Relations Law Bulletin* or to the IDS briefing paper: *The implementation of the European Working Time Directive in the UK*, which is accessible by visiting http://www.incomesdata.co.uk/brief/wtimedir.htm.

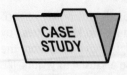

Case study 15: Protecting the wrong people

Phil Green had worked for seven years as a stock control computer operator in a large manufacturing company that supplied heavy machinery to industry. He was generally regarded as good at his job, reliable and always up to date. The shop floor was always busy so components were needed immediately on demand.

Phil was walking through the machine shop one day when he slipped on a patch of oil, lost his balance and fell to the floor, knocking his head on a machine on his way down. He was helped up and after a brief rest, felt fine, and so he went on his way and thought no more about it. He did not report the accident for fear of getting someone into trouble. In the past week, however, Phil has felt that his ability to concentrate was failing him, he has frequent headaches and thought that his eyesight was not all it should be.

Eight days later Jack Hartnell, the section manager, came roaring into Phil's office and started shouting about a shortage of components. After telling Phil that he had had complaints about the shortages, he said, 'Your job is to make sure the stuff's there when it's needed. I've had enough of this, you'd better buck your ideas up if you want to keep this job – and you'd better take this as a warning.'

Three days after this Jack Hartnell started disciplinary proceedings against Phil. There was a hearing which was chaired by Ian Cooper, the departmental manager, and attended by Jack Hartnell and Tim Johnson from the HR department.

Jack Hartnell's evidence emphasised the problems that were caused by Phil's poor performance. The shortage of components meant that the assemblers could not do their jobs, and productivity was falling badly as a result. He concluded by saying that Phil should be given a formal warning. Ian invited Phil to explain the sudden reduction in his performance, but Phil said that he was unable to do so. From Ian's demeanour it was clear that he was reluctant to proceed with a written warning. Eventually, Tim asked Ian to bring the meeting to a close, saying that they needed time to decide what action should be taken and would let Phil have their decision as soon as possible. Ian agreed and the meeting closed.

The following day, Ian and Tim invited Phil to Tim's office 'for a chat'.

Questions about the case
1. Did Phil do anything wrong? If so, what was it?
2. What should Jack Hartnell have done when he spoke to Phil in his office?
3. What was missing from Jack Hartnell's evidence?
4. Why do you think Ian and Tim wanted to see Phil?

Discussion about the case
Obviously Phil could have been suffering from the effects of the accident, which of course, he should have reported, not only for his own sake, but for others who might also have had

a fall. Action could have been taken to clean up the oil patch and then find out how the oil got there in the first place: one of the machines could have been leaking or it could have dripped from a fork-lift truck.

One of the first rules of management is that when something unexpected happens, the first response should always be to ask for an explanation and not jump to conclusions. Jack Hartnell failed in that respect. Clearly he was very annoyed, and it seemed that to him that productivity was more important than his staff. His general manner did not represent good leadership. Because of that he missed an opportunity to have a chat with Phil in order to get at the real problem.

Knowing that Phil had a good long-term reputation, Ian and Tim had recognised Jack Hartnell's shortcomings in handling the situation and wanted to talk to Phil to find out why his performance was suffering in this 'out-of-character' way.

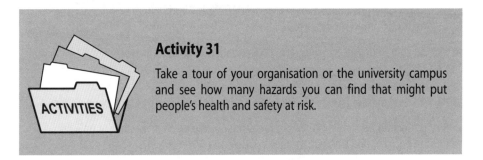

Activity 31

Take a tour of your organisation or the university campus and see how many hazards you can find that might put people's health and safety at risk.

Self-test questions

1. What should an organisation's health and safety policy contain?
2. What are the main purposes of carrying out risk assessments?
3. How are the three main categories of accidents at work classified?
4. What is the purpose of a health and safety audit?
5. Why should the organisation offer support and assistance to employees with non-work-related problems?
6. How would you define stress?
7. What types of worker are the most susceptible to stress?
8. What are the main differences between an occupational support service and an employee assistance programme?
9. What are the characteristics of a healthy workplace?
10. What are the advantages and disadvantages of the 'opt-out' provision in the Working Time Regulations?

Diversity and equality

Introduction

The aims of this chapter are first, to provide an understanding of diversity, including how it is managed in the organisation, its influence on the nature of social interaction and the general workplace culture. Second, the discussion includes how this aspect of organisational life is controlled by convention, and to a considerable degree by an ever-growing list of complex legislative measures. Third, the chapter provides an understanding of the concept of fairness at work.

The view taken in this chapter is that while it is critically important to conform to the law in matters of discrimination, it is only possible to legislate against behaviour that is discriminatory. Prejudice, for example, which is the main root cause of discrimination, is a personality characteristic and is impossible to detect unless the person's behaviour allows it out, which is when it becomes harmful to people's feelings, and indeed to their rights. Legislation is therefore only part of the solution to discrimination, and additional solutions are suggested later in the chapter.

Definitions

Diversity, prejudice and discrimination are expressions that are used in an everyday context, but they have also been defined here for specific usage and in order to assist your understanding of this chapter.

Definition: diversity

Diversity is present when, for whatever purpose, any number of individuals get together and interact. Generically the word *diversity* means variety. The term *organisational diversity* refers to the range of differences between the individuals and groups among employees.

Definition: prejudice

In *generic* terms, prejudice means the holding of an unreasoning opinion or like or dislike of something. Heery and Noon (2001, p279) say that in the context of *workplace discrimination*, prejudice means holding negative attitudes towards a particular group, and viewing all members of that group in a negative light, irrespective of their individual qualities and attributes.

Brown (1995) describes prejudice as:

The holding of derogatory social attitudes or cognitive beliefs, the expression of negative affect, or the display of hostile or discriminatory behaviour towards members of a group on account of their membership of that group.

Definition: discrimination

In very broad terms, we can say that discrimination occurs when, on grounds that are not relevant to a particular purpose, one person, or a group of people, is treated less favourably than others. Specific types of discrimination are defined separately by each of the relevant Acts of Parliament, and these are examined later in the chapter.

Organisational diversity

The general use of the word 'diversity' in relation to the make-up of an organisation's workforce is comparatively recent, but diversity itself is as old as humankind. The original concept is based upon individual differences, and since every individual is unique, organisations always have had diverse workforces. In modern terms, however, diversity also refers to differences between groups of different ethnic backgrounds, religious groups, sexual orientation, sex and marital status.

Individual differences

All individuals are different from each other; they are different psychologically, physically and behaviourally. The chance of finding two people who are exactly alike is the same as that of finding two people who have matching fingerprints. Individuals have their own personal values, beliefs, feelings and attitudes that have developed from their long-term perceptions and interpretations of the world around them. Wherever people go, from one country to another, from one organisation to another, their unique personality characteristics travel with them.

Differences between people become apparent when you watch them work. Everyone has his/her own unique way of learning, and of developing and using his/her knowledge, talents and skills. No two people work in exactly the same way. Even people who do the same job have their own peculiar way of doing it. All of this can be summarised in one word: *diversity*.

The influence of demographic changes

The demographic changes that have taken place in the UK population in recent years are reflected in organisations' workforces. Today's organisations employ people who hail from a range of national, religious, social, cultural and ethnic backgrounds. In addition, there are differences in age, gender and physical ability, including disability.

The demographic changes have broadened the diverse structure of the UK population, especially in terms of group types. In organisations, this has focused attention on the need to recognise diversity, learn how to manage it and how to eliminate discrimination. It is unlikely, however, that discrimination will ever be totally eliminated. The point was made above that discrimination is born of prejudice, which is a personality characteristic that causes particular individuals to discriminate against others simply on the grounds of their differences.

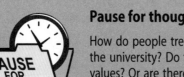

Pause for thought

How do people treat each other in your organisation or in the university? Do they all respect each other's beliefs and values? Or are there those whose prejudices show through now and again? Do you think it is important that people respect each other regardless of their background? Why?

What organisational diversity is about

According to Daniels and MacDonald (2005), diversity is:

about recognising this range of differences in people and valuing people as individuals, respecting their differences and their different needs. It is also about accommodating differences wherever possible so that an individual can play a full part in the working environment.

The CIPD says that diversity is about 'valuing everyone as individuals, as employees, customers and clients' (CIPD 2004). Foot and Hook (1999) say that diversity is about 'obtaining innovative ideas by promoting the involvement of employees from a wide variety of backgrounds, working in teams'.

Diversity: stacking up the evidence

The CIPD describe three types of diversity in terms of their potential effects:

- *Social category diversity* – which relates to differences in demographic characteristics such as age and race – has the potential to impact on group communication and cohesion.
- *Informational diversity* (also known as organisational diversity) – which refers to diversity of background, such as knowledge, education, experience, tenure and functional background – has the potential to cause higher task-related conflict, as well as to affect group co-ordination and cohesion.
- *Value diversity* (also known as psychological diversity) – which includes differences in personality and attitudes – can impinge on the organisation (CIPD 2004).

Combined, the three categories present a wide range of differences between people, and the effects that those differences can have on the technical functioning of a workforce and on the social interaction between and among its members.

Perspectives on diversity

Since 1970 there has been a stream of legislation, codes of practice and regulations on many forms of discrimination. Government-funded bodies, such as, *inter alia*, the Equal Opportunities Commission (EOC) and the Commission for Racial Equality (CRE) have been set up to advise on and administer the law. Despite all of this activity, discrimination in the workplace still occurs. In terms of providing equal opportunities in the workplace, the rights of individuals have become well known, and yet there still are gaps in some employers' understanding of the moral, ethical and legal aspects of managing diversity and the provision of equal opportunities.

Why be concerned with equality and diversity?

Mike Noon says that the question that needs to be addressed under this heading is, 'Why should managers care whether some people are disadvantaged and suffer unfair treatment?' He says that in answering this question, it is useful to distinguish between two different sets of arguments, which can be labelled 'the business case' and 'the social justice case' (Noon 2004, p233).

The business case
In discussing the link between HRM and equal opportunities, David Goss suggests two ways in which equal opportunities issues are located within the HRM debate. The first relates to:

concerns about *human capital*, in which opportunities to develop and progress are 'artificially' blocked for any particular group which results in the sub-optimal use of human resources; hence it is economically rational to ensure that all of those who have the ability also have the opportunity to exercise it on behalf of the organisation.

(Goss 1996)

Social justice

The second:

in contrast, emphasises the importance of *social justice*, in which equal opportunities is primarily a moral or ethical project that focuses on the processes giving rise to inequalities and seeks to address these in a qualitative sense, not by reducing social difference to a common economic currency, but by promoting its acceptance and understanding.

(Goss 1996)

It is worth noting that organisations that demonstrate an interest in promoting social equality tend to attract good employees. Ross and Schneider (1992) identified five main benefits that can result from this approach:

- The diverse workforce produces a wider range of ideas and can think from a broader range of perspectives than a workforce that is not diverse.
- Total quality management requires innovation and creativity. This is more easily achieved through a diverse workforce.
- If all people are treated equally, then people will be recruited and promoted on the basis of their skills and abilities. This will mean that it is more likely that the most capable people will achieve important positions in the organisation.
- If employees work in an organisation where they experience discrimination, or perceive that others are not treated equally, they are more likely to leave that organisation. Not only is this a drain of talent, it is also costly because of the significant expense of recruiting and training new employees.
- If employees are treated fairly, they will be more motivated and committed to the organisation. This is likely to lead to an increase in productivity, and a deeper commitment to the mission and goals of the organisation.

Equal opportunity as a legal obligation

The degree to which organisations are successful in the way they manage diversity is determined not only by the related policies and procedures but also by the collective attitudes of their managers: attitudes that lead to a particular approach. In broad terms, there are two types of approach. The first is to perceive equal opportunities as purely a legal obligation, something that has been imposed on the organisation from the outside, which implies that as long as the organisation conforms to the law and has acceptable policies and procedures in place, it will be regarded as a respectable employer in legal and ethical terms. The problem with this approach is that it reduces the concept of equal opportunity to little more than an administrative matter.

Recognising diversity

The second attitude bears in mind that the primary purposes of an organisation are to survive and develop so that it can continue to provide the best possible service for its public, or to provide the highest possible return to its shareholders. In order to achieve those ends, the organisation needs a knowledgeable and competent workforce. With this approach, its managers feel that the organisation cannot really afford to select employees on grounds that are not relevant to those primary purposes. To acquire such a workforce the organisation must select each individual purely because he/she is the best person for the job. This attitude is one that recognises the potential benefits that diversity can bring to the organisation.

> **Note**
>
> Later in your studies of this subject you will encounter arguments that have been extended beyond the discussion that is presented above. If access to them is required now, some of the titles in the bibliography at the end of the book provide more detailed and advanced arguments.

Prejudice

It is evident from the definitions given earlier that prejudicial attitudes are towards groups, because they are what they are, and towards individuals, because they are members of those groups.

The factors that arouse prejudice against groups are often based on appearance. According to Heery and Noon (2001), for example:

> **we typically think of prejudice as being against a particular group based on gender, race/ethnicity, religion, disability, age and sexual orientation. However, prejudice extends much further, and is frequently directed at other groups based on features such as accents, height, weight, hair colour, beards, body piercings, tattoos and clothes. It is extremely rare to find a person who is not prejudiced against any group – although most of us are reluctant to admit our prejudice.**

Stereotyping

It was noted above that prejudicial attitudes are against groups, and against individuals because they are members of particular groups.

Key concept 14: stereotyping

This is a tendency to label people with qualities and characteristics that the perceiver assumes are typical of particular groups, and therefore must also be typical of all individuals who belong to those groups.

Such biased perceptions occur when people rely on the stereotyped image and ignore factual information concerning individuals. For example, an elderly person will have outdated ideas; young drivers are reckless; men cannot cook and women are not good drivers. A glance at the facts, however, will tell you that none of these assumptions is true of all members of those groups. However, not all stereotyping results in creating negative images: the preconception can also be positive. For example, it might be believed all Welsh and Italian people are good singers.

Pause for thought

How do you think you would you react if you were presented with new information about an individual which contradicts your stereotyped image of him or her? Would the information cause you to alter your attitude towards that person? Or would you ignore the new information in order to maintain your original view?

Self-assessment

It would be rare to find a person who does not attribute particular characteristics to members of diverse groups. Problems of discrimination arise when we base our impressions of people on stereotype alone. According to McKenna (1994), what we should try to do is examine to what extent our impression of others is based on stereotypes alone, so that we can make adjustments accordingly.

Legislation on discrimination

Discrimination is a subjective term when used in normal daily life. When people make choices about what food or clothes to buy they *discriminate* in favour of some things and against others. Such decisions reflect people's tastes and opinions. In such contexts discrimination is perfectly legitimate. In some other contexts, however, discrimination has been made unlawful.

The law on discrimination is complex and extensive. For the purposes of this chapter, the emphasis is on employment law, although many of the legislative measures that are examined here, also apply to circumstances outside of employment situations. At present the legislation may be listed as follows:

- Equal Pay Act 1970. Purpose: pay and contracts must be the same for men and women doing like work.
- Sex Discrimination Act 1975. Purpose: makes it unlawful to treat less favourably on grounds of sex, sex-reassignment or marital status.
- Race Relations Act 1976. Purpose: makes it unlawful to treat less favourably on grounds of colour, race, ethnic origin or nationality.
- Trade Union and Labour Relations (Consolidation) Act 1992. Purpose: makes it unlawful to discriminate on the grounds of trade union membership.
- Disability Discrimination Act 1995. Purpose: makes it unlawful to discriminate against disabled people in their terms of employment, promotion opportunities, by dismissing them or by subjecting them to any other detriment.
- Part-Time Workers (Prevention of Less Favourable Treatment) Regulations 2000. Purpose: provides part-time workers, who are on the same type of contract as full-time workers, with equal treatment.
- Fixed-Term Employees (Prevention of Less Favourable Treatment) Regulations 2000. Purpose: provides fixed-term employees with the right to treatment that is equal to that of equivalent permanent employees.
- Employment Equality (Sexual Orientation) Regulations 2003. Purpose: protects people against discrimination on grounds of sexual orientation of any kind.
- Employment Equality (Religion or Belief) Regulations 2003. Purpose: makes it unlawful to discriminate on grounds of religion or belief.
- Employment Equality (Age) Regulations 2006. Purpose: prohibits unjustified age discrimination in employment and vocational training. (Subject to the approval of Parliament, these regulations will come into force on 1 October 2006.)

Discrimination

Workplace discrimination has been illegal since 1970, when the provisions of the Equal Pay Act became law. Since then, increases in the amount and complexity of legislation and case decisions have provided managers with the daunting task of keeping the organisation within the law and struggling to control discriminatory behaviour, not only in the implementation and interpretation of policy, but also on the part of employees. Discrimination may be viewed from two main perspectives: *individual discrimination* and *group discrimination*.

Individual discrimination

This occurs when, for example, in employment selection assessment and decision-making, selectors allow their prejudices to influence their decision-making. Also, when in employment, members of minority groups are often denied the opportunity to be trained and developed, and to exercise their competences and make career progress.

Group discrimination

Group discrimination occurs on national and organisation-wide bases. For example, on a national basis, statistical information shows that women working full-time are paid 18 per cent less than men, and those working part time are paid 40 per cent less then men (EOC 2001). About 30 per cent of managers are women, but they earn 24 per cent less than male managers. The higher up the management scale ones looks, the more the presence of women reduces. In the private sector, most of the women in top management positions founded their own companies.

Activity 32

Take a careful look at the management structure in your organisation or university, and note how many women and people from different ethnic backgrounds are on it, then work out the percentage. Repeat the exercise with the general body of the workforce, then compare the percentages to see if there is an imbalance.

In organisations, discrimination against groups becomes institutionalised if it is ignored or brushed aside; it becomes part of the culture. If it does become part of the culture, it may not be reported, since the employees may feel that their complaints, particularly of sex and race discrimination, will not be investigated thoroughly.

Pause for thought

When making a selection decision for say employment, promotion or to carry out a special project, selectors have to discriminate in favour of one candidate and against the others. However, the grounds on which such selection decisions are made are clearly prescribed by law. What approach do you think the selectors might adopt in order to ensure that such decisions are made without prejudice?

In the above activity, disproportionate results might be attributable to employment selection and internal promotion procedures. Written policy statements usually demonstrate good intentions in legal and ethical terms, but implementation through the related procedures does not always reflect those good intentions.

Categories of discrimination

Discriminatory decisions and behaviour may occur the grounds of sex, marital status, sexual orientation, race, religion, disability and age. We refer to these as 'prohibited grounds'. Such decisions and behaviour may be categorised as direct discrimination, indirect discrimination and victimisation.

Legal point 8: direct discrimination

This occurs when a person is treated less favourably than another worker on one of the prohibited grounds.

It is possible to place various interpretations on the term 'less favourably'. For example, a person who is treated differently from others might regard that treatment as less favourable than the treatment the others received. It might be, however, that the complainant's employment circumstances were different from those of the other employees; different treatment is not always less favourable treatment.

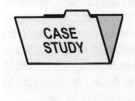

Case study 16: Direct sex discrimination

A woman pilot working for British Airways made a flexible working request to enable her to work part-time; her request was refused. Supported by her union, she won her employment tribunal claim for sex discrimination. British Airways appealed twice to the Employment Appeals Tribunal (EAT) but the appeal was rejected. (EAT/0306/05, 21 July 2005).

Legal point 9: indirect discrimination

Indirect discrimination occurs when a requirement or condition is applied universally, but places at a disadvantage members of groups that are non-representative on one or more of the prohibited grounds, eg sex, race or religion.

Case study 17: Indirect sex discrimination

In the case of *Price* v *The Civil Service Commission*, indirect sex discrimination was demonstrated when a maximum age limit of 28 years was imposed on entry to the 'executive officer' grade. It was argued that under this ruling women were considerably disadvantaged since they were often raising a family at that age, and that the imposed limit constituted indirect discrimination. This was not regarded as discrimination on grounds of age; the ruling given was that the imposed age limit constituted indirect discrimination (EOC Sex Discrimination Decisions no. 9).

Activity 33

Examine the definition of indirect discrimination (above), then study the case. The person who brought the legal action was a woman, so she was a member of the disadvantaged group.

Victimisation

This occurs when an employer treats an employee less favourably than other employees would be treated on the grounds that he/she has been, intends to be, or is suspected of, being involved in legal proceedings against the employer to seek redress for discrimination on one of the prohibited grounds.

Sex discrimination

The Equal Pay Act 1970 (EPA) prohibits unjustified differences in pay and contracts: that is, the terms and conditions of employment, which must be the same for men and women doing like work. The Sex Discrimination Act 1975 (SDA) makes it unlawful to treat individuals less favourably on the grounds of sex or marital status. The initial purpose of both the EPA and the SDA was to provide women with protection from discrimination. However, it is important to note that under these Acts, men and women have equal rights to protection, although the number of legal actions brought by women is far greater than that brought by men.

Genuine occupational qualifications

Employers may be exempt from observing the provisions of the SDA for jobs that have particular requirements which are known as *genuine occupational qualifications* or GOQs. The purpose of this is to maintain public decency and/or to meet certain expectations. For example it is lawful to look to employ a person of one specific sex in jobs such as actor, model, changing room attendant and toilet attendant.

Implications for employers

These two major pieces of legislation carry widespread implications for employers. The areas that are most affected are:

- *Recruitment and selection,* in which every stage and action, from drafting a job requisition through to making the selection decision, is subject to the law.
- *Employment contracts,* including the terms and conditions of employment.
- *Training and development,* in which both sexes must be given equal opportunities to undertake courses, not forgetting longer-term courses financially sponsored by the organisation and involving attendance at a local college or university.
- *Promotion,* in which again equal opportunities must be given.
- *Benefits, facilities and services* such as pension schemes, medical care, help with long-term sickness and counselling services, in which equal access must be available to both sexes in all circumstances.
- *Severance,* including terms and conditions for share options, selection for redundancy and redundancy payments, in which the criteria must apply equally to both sexes.

Gender reassignment

It has been estimated that there are about 5000 transexuals in the UK, and the likelihood of an individual HR professional encountering a discrimination case on these grounds is small. The purpose here is to cover the main points relating to discrimination on grounds of gender reassignment. More detail can be found by visiting the DfEE website.

The Sex Discrimination (Gender Reassignment) Regulations 1999 amended the SDA75. The regulations are a measure to prevent discrimination against transexual people on the grounds of sex in pay, vocational training and treatment in employment. The Regulations are a reflection of the European Court of Justice (ECJ) ruling that the dismissal of an employee on the grounds of his or her undergoing gender reassignment, which means undergoing a sex change, is contrary to the European Equal Treatment Directive.

Legal point 10: regulatory legislation

It is important to note that these regulations amend the SDA, and they become part of the Act itself. Thus, for the purposes of employment and vocational training, discrimination on grounds of gender reassignment constitutes discrimination on grounds of sex, which is a breach of the SDA. This means that any reference in the SDA to discrimination against men or women may be read as applying similarly to gender reassignment.

Discrimination: gender reassignment

Since the medical procedure that achieves gender reassignment is in two main stages, discrimination is unlawful at either or both of those stages, or after the reassignment procedure has been completed. The definition of gender reassignment discrimination, therefore, is that it is unlawful to discriminate against a person for the purpose of employment or vocational training on the ground that the person (i) intends to undergo gender reassignment; (ii) is undergoing gender reassignment; (iii) has at some time in the past undergone gender reassignment.

In such a case, 'unfavourable treatment' means treating a person less favourably on gender reassignment grounds than you treat, or would treat, a person for whom no gender reassignment grounds exist. This category of discrimination also applies to recruitment, unless a GOQ exists.

Sexual orientation

The relevant legislation for this is the Employment Equality (Sexual Orientation) Regulations 2003. The Regulations make discrimination by employers and trade unions on grounds of sexual orientation unlawful, and are intended to encourage tolerance and to protect the dignity of people in the workplace. Daniels and MacDonald (2005, p72) point out that numerous attempts had been made to assert that the Sex Discrimination Act 1975 should be interpreted so as to encompass discrimination on rounds of sexual orientation, but these arguments consistently failed both in the UK courts and at the ECJ. The word 'sex' in the Sex Discrimination Act 1975 clearly means gender and not 'sexual orientation' or 'sexual preference'.

The regulations cover direct and indirect discrimination, victimisation and harassment. The Regulations define sexual orientation as 'a sexual orientation towards':

- persons of the same sex, eg gay men or lesbian women
- persons of the opposite sex, eg heterosexual men and women
- persons of the same sex and the opposite sex, eg bisexual people.

The Regulations do not protect people whose sexual orientation leads them to become involved in such criminal activities as paedophilia and sado-masochism.

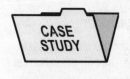

Case study 18: Sexual orientation

The first successful claim for this kind of discrimination was heard at Stratford Employment Tribunal in January 2005. The discriminatory acts against the claimant included senior colleagues nick-naming him 'Sebastian' after a camp character in BBC Television's *Little Britain* show, presenting him with a T-shirt with pink lettering before a conference of 60 colleagues, calling him a queer, queen and someone who liked poofy drinks (kir royale) and handbags. He was deeply offended and humiliated. His claims were for harassment, direct discrimination and constructive unfair dismissal. The tribunal awarded him £35,000 compensation.

Legal point 11

You may have noticed that the words 'or would have treated' appear in the definitions of the various types of discrimination. The legal point in relation to this is that if a person wishes to show that he/she has been discriminated against, he/she must also show that the treatment received was different from that offered to other employees in a similar situation. A lesbian woman, for example, would have to show that she was treated differently than a gay man would have been treated in a similar situation.

Racial discrimination

The legislation that prohibits racial discrimination in the UK is the Race Relations Act 1976 (RRA). Under this Act discrimination may occur on grounds of colour, race, nationality, ethnic origins and national origins. The Race Relations Act 1976 (Amendment Regulations) 2003 implemented the provisions of the European Race Directive (2000/43/EC) in UK law. The Regulations cover discrimination on grounds of ethnic, racial or national group, but not on grounds of nationality or colour.

The body appointed to enforce and advise on the law is the Commission for Racial Equality (CRE).

Genuine occupational qualifications

For certain types of work, discrimination is permitted for recruitment, selection, training or promotion on the grounds of GOQs. However, discriminatory treatment in the terms and conditions of employment is not permitted. The types of work are specified as:

1. *Entertainment*: if it is necessary to have a person of a particular racial group to achieve an authentic presentation.
2. *Artistic or photographic modelling*: if it is necessary to use a person from a particular racial group to provide authenticity for a work of art, visual image or sequence.
3. *Specialised restaurants*: if it is necessary to use a person from a particular racial group to sustain the special setting of an establishment where food or drink is served to the public.
4. *Community social workers*: if a person provides personal services to members of a particular racial group, and the services can best be provided by someone of the same racial group.

Disability

The initial legislative attempts to provide disabled people with protection from discrimination were the Disabled Persons (Employment) Acts of 1944 and 1958. The protection provided by these Acts was generally regarded as inadequate, and those representing disabled people actively campaigned for improvements. Their efforts eventually paid off when the Disability Discrimination Act 1995 (DDA95) was passed. The DDA95 came into force in 1996 and provides disabled people with the most comprehensive protection they have ever had, although some campaigners complain that it is still inadequate.

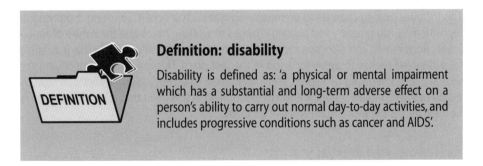

Definition: disability

Disability is defined as: 'a physical or mental impairment which has a substantial and long-term adverse effect on a person's ability to carry out normal day-to-day activities, and includes progressive conditions such as cancer and AIDS'.

People who have a disability, and those who have had a disability but no longer have one, are covered by the Act. For practical reasons it is important to understand the meanings of two of the expressions used in the definition.

1. 'Long-term' is defined as 12 months or more. The definition covers not only those who have been disabled for 12 months or more, but also those whose disability can be reasonably expected to last for at least 12 months.
2. 'Normal day-to-day activities' does not refer specifically to the day-to-day activities that are involved in the individual's job. It refers to the activities that most people carry out as normal parts of their lives. Thus, an individual who has an impairment that prevents him/her from carrying out particular tasks in his/her everyday life, for example at home, might not legally qualify as 'disabled' for the purposes of employment where the job does not include tasks that he/she is incapable of performing. The case overleaf, cited by Daniels and MacDonald (2005, p101), illustrates this point.

Case study 19: Quinlan v B&Q plc

As a result of open heart surgery, Quinlan was unable to lift heavy loads. In his job as a general assistant in a garden centre, he needed to life heavy loads, and he was dismissed because he was no longer able to carry out his duties. The EAT and the Employment Tribunal both concluded that he was not suffering from a disability because he was still able to carry smaller loads, even if he was not able to carry the loads required in his job.

Main provisions of the Act

There are two main provisions of the DDA95 which apply to employers:

1. It is unlawful to discriminate against potential or current employees for a reason that relates to an individual's disability, unless the discriminatory action can be justified. Employers therefore should not treat a disabled person less favourably than they treat or would treat others to whom the given reason does not or would not apply.
2. Employers must make reasonable adjustments to the workplace and to the employment arrangements in order to accommodate the individual needs of disabled individuals.

Reasonable adjustments

This includes making changes to premises – eg wheel-chair access, adjusting, modifying or repositioning equipment – and making changes to working hours and the nature of super-vision. Recruitment and selection procedures may be changed in order to make it possible for a disabled person to apply for a job in the first place. This may include modifying the design of documents, eg large print, and a willingness to accept job applications on tape, by e-mail or other suitable media. It is worth mentioning at this point that telecommuting may be ideal for people with certain types of disability.

Religion and belief

Discrimination in employment and vocational training on grounds of religion was made unlawful by the Employment Equality (Religion or Belief) Regulations 2003. 'Religion or belief' is defined as 'any religion, religious belief, or similar philosophical belief'. At the time of writing, there is no official body to enforce, advise on or support individuals bringing claims in this area of law. The new Commission for Equality and Human Rights will take on these responsibilities when it is formed.

Beliefs

Care needs to be taken over the interpretation of the word 'belief', since the beliefs that some people hold may not be religious. Many people believe in particular causes, and they confer virtue upon what those causes are designed to achieve. Some such beliefs are political, while others may be environmental. It would be interesting to see, for example, how an animal rights activist would fare at an employment tribunal with a claim of discrimination on grounds of his/her belief.

It is important to appreciate that diversity in religious belief is not a static concept. There are changes over time in the ways in which religions expect their adherents to behave. Within individual religions, different groups and individuals also have different standards of orthodoxy and devoutness, and may consider themselves to be bound by their religion to observe different forms or standards of behaviour.

Key concept 15: predominant forces

The UK is a secular country, and the most powerful influences over the way we live come from secular institutions, including industry. Christianity is the established religion in the UK, although different denominations predominate in different areas and among different sectors of the population. However there are many non-Christian religious minorities, some of them very sizeable, such as Muslims and Jews. The law requires organisations in the UK to respect the customs of adherents to all accepted religions, and not just to Christianity.

Implications for the organisation

The criteria for religious and belief discrimination are virtually the same as those for discrimination on grounds of race. While it is essential for employers, and particularly HR practitioners, to develop an understanding of the law in these respects, sound employment policies and practices are the real answer to ensuring the effectiveness of a diverse workforce. The degree of success in this respect is attributable to the culture of the organisation and how culture is managed (see Chapter 15).

Contrary to common assumption, the demographic changes referred to earlier in this chapter have only slightly increased the variety of religions and beliefs in the community. The more obvious effect is the raising of the profile of particular religions and beliefs, through a marked increase in their membership. This, of course, is reflected in workforces across the UK.

Employers must make sure that prejudice and stereotyping on the basis of people's ethnic origins and religious beliefs does not result in unfair decisions about jobs and training. Failure could lead not only to legal costs, lost productivity and damaged reputation when the law is broken, but also to lost opportunities to gain business advantage. Increasing evidence points to the importance of managing diversity to beat market competition in the delivery of value to a diverse customer base.

(CIPD 2005)

Further information on trends in recruitment is available from the CIPD, which publishes an annual recruitment survey. The current and earlier surveys are available at: http://www cipd.co.uk/onlineinfodocuments/surveys.htm.

Age discrimination

The consultation period for the Employment Equality (Age) Regulations ended in October 2005, and subject to parliamentary approval they will come into force in October 2006. In the draft, there are six main regulations, which are designed to:

- prohibit unjustified age discrimination in employment and vocational training
- require employers who set their retirement age below the default age of 65 to justify or change it
- introduce a new duty on employers to consider an employee's request to continue working beyond the normal retirement age
- require employers to inform employees in writing, and at least six months in advance, of their intended retirement date (which will allow people to plan for their retirement)
- remove the upper age limit for unfair dismissal and redundancy rights, giving older workers the same rights to claim unfair dismissal or receive a redundancy payment as younger workers unless there is a genuine retirement
- include provisions relating to service-related benefits and occupational pensions.

The Regulations will also remove the age limits for statutory payments such as those for sickness, maternity, adoption and paternity.

Harassment and bullying

Harassment and bullying at work may take many forms and are motivated by a variety of causes. Harassment and bullying are often one and same thing, and we shall use the word 'harassment' to cover both, except where a case is clearly one of just bullying. Harassment can have a serious effect on the health and well-being of individuals, who can become stressed and fretful, demotivated and unproductive. It also has a damaging effect on groups whose members become demoralised; they close ranks and become detached from their colleagues in other groups. This can have a deleterious effect on the organisation in terms of absenteeism, lost productivity, an increase in staff turnover, and ultimately failure to achieve objectives.

These points are reinforced in the *CIPD factsheet* (2005), which points out that:

> **harassment thrives in a workplace culture where it is not challenged, but is ignored or swept under the carpet. An organisation should not assume there are no problems because they have not received any complaints ... employees can be subject to fear, stress and anxiety, which can put great strains on personal and family life. The result is not just poor morale but higher labour turnover, reduced productivity, lower efficiency and divided teams.**

Facts do not cease to exist just because they are ignored or brushed aside, but it is possible for the top managers of the organisation not to be aware of what is going on at middle and junior levels. The following case study highlights what can happen if senior managers fail to keep themselves informed of what is happening in the organisation at other levels.

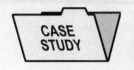

Case study 20: How not to manage

In a nationally known large plc, a supervisor was subjected to a continuous stream of harassment by his manager. The supervisor became seriously stressed and had a heart attack. After a period of sickness absence he returned to work; the harassment continued and he had another heart attack. Fortunately he survived the second attack, and was recovering at home when his manager sent him a memo saying that if he did not report for work within a week he would be disciplined. As a result of his reaction to this threat, he was taken back into hospital.

After he was discharged from hospital, he took the memo to his solicitor. Legal action was taken against the company, and that was the first indication of these events that the board of directors had received. Out-of-court settlements often result from this kind of action and this case was no exception. Eventually the company agreed to pay compensation in the sum of £250,000.

Discussion of the case

As you can see, the compensation was quite substantial, but that was not the total cost to the organisation. It had legal fees to pay, which were considerable, and further costs were involved in finding a replacement for the supervisor, who had been advised by his doctors that he should not return to work in the foreseeable future. The manager, who had admitted his behaviour towards the supervisor, resigned and a replacement had to be found for him.

Prospective litigants should be warned that when someone becomes ill and seeks compensation through legal channels, the individual must show that there is a definite causal link between what happened in the workplace and the illness. The task of establishing a causal link is eased considerably if the case is one of physical injury, but it can be more difficult if it is the kind of illness that someone might suffer as the result of harassment in the organisation.

The law on harassment

Harassment is not always linked to discrimination, but it can be based on one (or more) of the prohibited grounds for discrimination, and this possibility is specifically mentioned in the legislation. New definitions of harassment in respect of sex and gender reassignment were introduced in October 2005 when the Equal Treatment Amendment Directive was implemented into UK law. Individuals are therefore protected from harassment under all of the Acts of Parliament (including their related Statutory Regulations) that have been discussed above.

The main purpose of the Protection from Harassment Act 1997 is to protect individuals from stalkers. Under the Act, it is a criminal offence to pursue a course of conduct that amounts to harassment, or that causes a person to fear that violence will be used against him/her, on at least two occasions.

Legal point 12: the role of criminal law

Individuals are also protected against harassment by some laws which make forms of harassment a criminal offence: for example, the Criminal Justice and Public Order Act 1994 and the Protection from Harassment Act 1997. Under the Criminal Justice and Public Order Act, it can be a criminal offence for an individual to deliberately harass another person.

Legal point 13: beyond reasonable doubt versus balance of probabilities

For a prosecution to succeed in the criminal courts, the evidence must show *beyond any reasonable doubt* that the accused person (the defendant) committed the crime. The crime of harassment under the legislation discussed consists of first, of the deliberate intention to commit the illegal act, and second, its actual commission. For an action to succeed in the civil courts, the evidence must show that, on the *balance of probabilities*, the defendant is responsible for the damage done to the victim.

Here, the main concern is with workplace harassment, and this is normally something dealt with under civil law, where there is no need to prove intention. The CIPD notes that it is not the intention of the perpetrator that is the key in deciding whether harassment has occurred, but whether the behaviour is unacceptable by reasonable normal standards, and is disadvantageous or unwelcome to the person or people subjected to it or witnessing it (CIPD 2005).

Individuals are protected from harassment while they are applying for a job, during the period of employment, and after the working relationship has ended (for example in the provision of a verbal or written reference).

Definition: harassment

Harassment includes any unwanted behaviour that has the effect of violating dignity or creating an intimidating, hostile, degrading, humiliating or offensive environment. The Criminal Justice and Public Order Act 1994 defines harassment as 'intentionally to commit an act that causes another person harassment, alarm or distress either by using threatening, abusive or insulting language or behaviour, or disorderly behaviour or displaying any writing, sign or other visible representation which is threatening, abusive or insulting'.

There is also protection for people against harassment on the basis of their membership of a trade union, and in Northern Ireland on the basis of a political belief.

Fighting back

The responsibility for tackling workplace harassment belongs to everyone in the organisation. Usually, it is difficult for individuals to report harassment; sometimes it takes courage, for fear of intimidation and further victimisation. It helps if individuals genuinely feel that managers will support them in their quest for a solution. Sometimes, however, it is the victim's immediate boss against whom the complaint is to be made. If that is the case, then there is no alternative than to take the complaint beyond the manager to his/her boss, or to an HR practitioner.

The management role

A policy on dealing with harassment is the most effective approach to providing individuals with the confidence to present a complaint of harassment. They will feel more secure if there is a procedure in place which is specifically designed to hear the complaint, investigate it and take appropriate action.

Activity 34

Find out if your organisation or university has a policy on harassment and a procedure for dealing with it. If it does, ask if you may read the relevant documents. What do the documents contain? Do they cover training for managers and HR specialists in dealing with harassment? Does the organisation provide access to counselling in cases of severe distress caused by harassment or bullying?

Andrea Adams (1992) suggests that agenda-free meetings might be part of the solution:

> **In a business meeting, the agreed agenda is often essential for dealing with matters allied to the performance of the organisation. It can, of course, be used to stifle discussion, or at least to control its direction. If an organisation can tolerate examining what is really going on inside the working group, it will be necessary to move towards agenda-free meetings on a regular basis so that any problems can be brought to the surface and examined. Difficulties that have been disregarded or kept under wraps may surface on the back of other issues.**

Perpetrator beware!

It should be noted that when harassment is alleged, complaints handled inside the organisation might not bring an end to the matter. Those who harass their colleagues and subordinates could be committing a criminal offence, as was noted above. This is not an 'either–or' situation, since regardless of the action that is taken inside the organisation, the victim could also press criminal charges. The perpetrator could find him/herself personally liable and be ordered to pay compensation, in addition to any payment the organisation agrees to make, or is ordered to make by a court of law or an employment tribunal.

Sexual harassment

Sexual harassment is unwelcome physical, verbal or non-verbal conduct of a sexual nature. It includes:

- demeaning comments about a person's appearance
- indecent remarks
- questions about a person's sex life
- sexual demands by a member of the same sex or opposite sex
- name-calling using demeaning terminology which is gender-specific
- unwelcome physical contact and other conduct of a sexual nature that creates an intimidating, hostile or humiliating working environment.

It is important to note that it is possible for two people to develop a relationship at work that is warm and friendly, without being sexual. If the relationship does develop further and it is welcome on both sides, that is acceptable. However, it might lead to sexual harassment if only one of the parties to the relationship persists in trying to take the relationship further, while to the other, such advances are clearly unwelcome.

Damaging effects

In addition to the psychological harm that sexual harassment can do to individuals, it can be just as damaging to the organisation as other forms of harassment (see above). The Equal Opportunities Commission (EOC) has developed a five-step approach for the prevention of workplace sexual harassment. A précis of the five steps is:

1. *Develop a clear policy for preventing and tackling sexual harassment.* Make it clear to all employees that they are entitled to work in a climate of respect. Ensure that they all know what sexual harassment is and that it is unlawful. Indicate how seriously it is regarded and that it will not be tolerated. Explain how it is treated under the disciplinary code (normally it is defined as gross misconduct).
2. *Make sure everyone understands the policy.* Distribute copies of the policy (not forgetting new joiners), train employees in how to prevent sexual harassment, and provide staff with regular updates of changes to policy and related procedures.
3. *Treat sexual harassment as a health and safety issue.* Point out the mental and physical toll that it can take on a victim. Provide victims with support by offering access to a welfare officer, health professional or counsellor.
4. *Lead by example.* Make managers and supervisors responsible. Ensure they set a good example through their own behaviour so that a positive culture develops. Deal promptly with any complaints using the organisation's procedures.
5. *Monitor policy implementation.* Managers should review periodically whether the policy is successful and has produced a positive harassment-free working environment. Where complaints of sexual harassment have been made, managers should review the outcomes of the cases to check that procedures have been followed, that

any changes needed in the workplace have been made, and to act on any other learning points from the case.

The full version of the five-step approach can be accessed by visiting www.eoc.org.uk.

Assignment

Draft a policy on sex discrimination, including a procedure for those subject to sex discrimination to take action.

Self-test questions

1. How would you define the basic concept of unlawful discrimination, regardless of which of the prohibited grounds apply?
2. What do people mean when they talk or write about diversity in the organisation?
3. In terms of diversity, what effect have demographic changes made to society and to organisations?
4. How would you distinguish between the 'business case' and the 'social justice' case for recognising and respecting diversity?
5. What factors in an individual or group might arouse a person's prejudices?
6. How would you describe stereotyping?
7. It has been suggested that we should examine to what extent our impressions of others are based upon stereotyping. For what purpose might we do this?
8. What are the circumstances that distinguish 'direct' from 'indirect' discrimination?
9. Can you identify two situations in which it would be lawful to discriminate against an individual?
10. What steps can organisations take to prevent harassment?

Recommended reading

For those who wish to take a special and detailed interest in this subject the following text is recommended:

DANIELS, K. and MACDONALD, L. (2005) *Equality, diversity and discrimination.* London: CIPD.

Contemporary issues in HR

Aspects of culture

CHAPTER 15

Learning objectives

After studying this chapter you should:

- understand the concept of culture, its values and norms

- understand and take account of your organisation's culture in your role as an HR practitioner

- understand the importance of culture as a determinant of workplace behaviour

- be able to demonstrate an understanding of how history, corporate climate, managerial style and other factors contribute to the make-up of culture.

Introduction

The aim of this chapter is to provide an understanding of organisational culture: what it is, how it develops and its importance as the organisation's most powerful determinant of behaviour. In order for you to develop a complete understanding of what is meant by *organisational culture*, it will be helpful to provide first an account of how culture is perceived in the societal context. Reading about culture in extra-organisational contexts should help you to understand behaviour that occurs in a diverse workforce.

What is culture?

As far back as 1871, the anthropologist Edward Tylor defined culture as 'knowledge, belief, art, morals, law, custom and any other capabilities and habits acquired through membership of society'. In a narrower sense the term is used to describe the differences between one society and another. In this context, according to Giddens:

> **a culture is an all-pervasive system of beliefs and behaviours transmitted socially. Specifically, it consists of the sets of values and norms or rules held by a society, together with its material expressions.**
>
> **(Giddens 1989, p30)**

Values are internalised by young people as they learn what is good and what is desirable. They define for us what is important and worth striving for. Values represent the basic conviction that in a personal or social context, a specific mode of conduct is preferable to any other.

Definition: values

A *value* is an ideal to which an individual subscribes. People's values are learned during the socialisation process; individuals adopt them from the values of the society to which they belong.

In a Western society, for example, young people learn that achievement and wealth are important and indeed, the measure of an individual's achievement is usually indicated by the quality and quantity of his or her material possessions.

(Haralambos 1986)

Definition: norms

A norm is a tacit guideline that determines an individual's behaviour in particular situations. For example, as a member of a group or team, or of a student group, you learn that there are particular behaviours that conform to the group's expectations, and behaviours that do not. If you breach the code of behaviour, the group will demonstrate its disapproval, usually by applying formal or informal sanctions.

If a norm is breached in a serious way, the sanctions will be more severe. The sanctions are designed to elicit conformity, and are a significant feature of controlling overall behaviour and the maintenance of order in a society. Indeed, certain norms are incorporated into law, and conformity is enforced through punishment.

The power of values and norms

The relationship between values and norms becomes clear when a breach of norms defies the group's values; the establishment of behavioural norms reflects its values. This concept extends beyond the group, into larger groups, and out into the whole of society itself: for example the way people address each other, their table manners, and how they conduct themselves in public. People dress according to what is expected of them on special occasions, such as a formal ball, a funeral, an evening at the theatre or visiting a friend in hospital. All such situations demand certain attire and particular ways of behaving.

So, examined through its systems of norms and values, 'The culture of a society is the way of life of its members; the collection of ideas and habits which they learn, share and transmit from generation to generation' (Linton 1945). At birth, children are totally helpless and dependent on others to provide for their needs. In order to survive in the longer term, however, children must develop knowledge and skills, and must learn how those around them survive. In other words, children must learn the culture of the society into which they were born.

Culture therefore has to be learned, and for a society to operate effectively, its 'guidelines' must be shared by its members through their behaviour. Learning and sharing a culture is achieved largely without conscious control. It just happens as people develop and become socialised, and even though it directs their actions and thinking, and establishes their outlook on life, most members of a society take their culture for granted. People are hardly aware of their culture, even though their adoption of its values and conformity to its norms demonstrate a mutual understanding of what is and is not acceptable.

Definitions of culture

It is difficult to define overall culture since it is an elusive concept. Culture is a dichotomy in the sense that it constitutes first, visible and tangible factors, and second, abstract and intangible characteristics. For example, it was noted earlier that Giddens summarises culture as consisting of the sets of *values* and *norms* or rules held by a society, together with its material expressions. The term 'material expressions' refers to features of the environment that were put in place by people. This includes such tangible items as bridges, buildings, roads, tools, machinery and equipment. Values and norms, however, are among the abstract and intangible psychological characteristics of individuals and groups.

Herskovits (1948) defined culture as 'the man-made part of the human environment'. Triandis *et al* (1972) qualified this by pointing out that:

this includes both physical objects, such as roads, buildings and tools, which constitute *physical culture*, and subjective responses to what is 'man-made', such as myths, roles, values and attitudes, which constitute *subjective culture*.

Later, however, Triandis further qualified this saying that 'cultures are human creations but, unlike bridges, buildings, roads and other material objects of our making, cultures are subjective' (Triandis 1990, p36).

Undoubtedly there is a strong relationship between physical and subjective cultures. Subjective perceptions of how things are, how they should be and how they should look, for example, do vary from one society to another. For example, the architecture of buildings and the design of particular artefacts are determined by what, within a culture, is regarded subjectively as generally acceptable and right. This is reflected by the obvious differences in the appearance of buildings in different parts of the world. Even cooking utensils are specifically designed to meet idiosyncratic culinary needs, since what people eat and how their food is prepared vary from one culture to another.

It is in these and many other ways that cultures vary from one society to another, and since culture defines what is acceptable and what is not, frequent misunderstandings occur

Key concept 16: physical and subjective culture

It seems that the physical culture, which is created by people, may be separated from the subjective culture, which is apparent through the values and norms of societies. It is certainly true that academics who have produced non-organisational definitions of culture all include the physical culture. As we shall see later, however, those who define organisational culture tend to exclude the physical aspects

between members of different societies, as illustrated in the following example by Edward T. Hall (1973).

Example 14: Space invaders

Two men, one from North America and one from South America are chatting in a hall which is 40 feet long. They begin at one end of the hall and finish at the other end, the North American steadily retreating and the South American steadily advancing. Each is trying to establish the 'customary conversation distance' as defined by his culture. To the North American, his South American counterpart comes too close for comfort, whereas the South American feels uneasy conversing at the distance his partner demands. Sometimes it takes meetings such as this to reveal the pervasive nature of culturally determined behaviour.

Identifying cultures

Misunderstanding may occur if cultures are treated as discrete entities. Just as there is diversity within indigenous populations, there is also *intra-cultural diversity* created by individual and small-group differences. Within a culture, groups (sub-cultures) look across at each other and do not always approve of what they see and hear.

In-groups

According to Price (1997, p125), we look at people from other cultures, see that their ways are different and often dislike these ways. Triandis (1990, p34) supports this view, saying that we use our own culture as the standard and judge other cultures by the extent to which they meet our standard. This is referred to as *ethnocentrism*, and is similar to the *in-group* concept, the people with whom we identify.

Studies of ethnocentrism show that everyone tends to:

- define their own culture as 'natural' and 'correct' and other cultures as 'unnatural' and 'incorrect'

- perceive in-group customs as universally valid – what is good for us is good for everybody
- think that in-group norms, rules and values are obviously correct
- consider it natural to help and cooperate with members of one's in-group
- act in ways which favour the in-group
- feel proud of the in-group
- feel hostility towards out-groups.

(based on the work of Campbell and associates, cited in Triandis (1990, p35) and Price (1997, p125).

Pause for thought

If you were born and raised in, say, England, but felt in need of a change and wanted to abandon your roots to live elsewhere in the world, in what kind of society would you choose to live? A small tribal island in the Pacific Ocean? A Middle Eastern country? Central Africa? Could you survive in another culture? Would you try to continue living like an English person or would you try to adopt the culture into which you had moved? Do you think it would take courage to make such a move? Do you know anyone from an entirely different culture who has moved to the UK?

Where do we find culture?

When people speak and write about the 'English culture' or the 'Spanish culture', we somehow know what they mean. We take it that they are referring to particular idiosyncratic features that may only be found in England, and others that may only be found in Spain, but these might be thought of as *national differences*, as well as cultural differences. All countries have their own particular characteristics, and members of indigenous populations share dominant common values and conform to the accepted norms of their society.

While culture is not nationality, the two do interact. Within any country, there are groups whose members share additional values, or perceive one of the common values as more important than any of the others, as the following example shows.

Example 15: Animal rights

One of the values that most people in the UK share is their disapproval of cruelty to animals, which is a value that is not held in all countries. For example, groups of animal rights activists regard the cessation of animal experiments as highly important, to the extent that they seek out those whom they think are responsible and apply sanctions, sometimes including violence and other forms of intimidation. There are other, more moderate, animal rights groups who share the same singular value as the activists, but prefer to show their disapproval by staging peaceful demonstrations.

These groups place one of the national values at the top of their agenda. Examples of other national values that receive the attention of particular groups include concerns about health and the environment.

Differences within a culture

Sometimes it is useful to regard culture as the personality of the group. In the case of individuals, it is their personality characteristics such as attitudes, values and beliefs that direct their behaviour, and it is not difficult to read this across into the group culture. The relationship between the group and a 'strong-minded' individual member can be quite complex. Sometimes such a member attains the leadership position, and therefore has an element of control over the group's behaviour, but if this does not happen, there might be costs to the individual in the form of reduced freedom of action. William Foote Whyte (1955, p331) wrote that:

The group is a jealous master. It encourages participation, indeed it demands it, but it demands one kind of participation – its own kind and the better integrated with it a member becomes the less free he is to express himself in other ways.

Pause for thought: the individual and the group

At this point it is important to note that people's group behaviour is different from their individual behaviour. As we have seen, groups have values and norms to which their members adhere, but such conformity can be misleading. People place a high value on being accepted as group members, and when the situation demands it, they may suspend their values and conform to the group norms in order to sustain their group membership. Conversely, the value in question might be so deeply felt that they might decide not to conform to the norm and to leave the group rather than surrender that particular value.

The boundaries of culture

Cross-cultural studies involve making comparisons between one culture and another. Naroll, who was involved in cross-cultural studies, devised the term *cultunit* to describe people who are domestic speakers of a common district dialect of a language, and who belong to either the same state or the same 'contact group' (Naroll 1970). Some cross-cultural psychologists study cultunits (which are small cultures); others study larger units, including states. From their studies, it is clear that the attitudes and values that determine behaviour in the individual, group and state change with time.

The boundaries of the cultunit, therefore, are time, place and language: *time* because cultures change across time as old values and beliefs replace new ones; *place* because we emphasise interpersonal contact within the location of the culture; and *language* because it defines cultures by directing thinking and enables us to distinguish one culture from another. Consider the following example.

Example 16: Time, place and language

St Cyril, the ninth-century Greek missionary, travelled north out of Greece to preach Christianity. On his travels he encountered several tribes, each of which had its own encampment. Each was a discrete cultunit having its own location, language, values and rituals. The inter-group language barrier prevented communication between the tribes, who as a result were fearful and suspicious of each other.

St Cyril was unable to communicate with them and returned to Greece to consult his brother, St Methodius, and together they developed a new language. St Cyril returned to the tribes, taught them the new language and was then able to spread the Christian word. This also enabled the tribes to interact and integrate by forming themselves into larger units. The language had its roots in Greek, but since the ninth century it has become known as the Cyrillic language. Originally the Cyrillic alphabet had 43 characters, but continuously changing versions have reduced this to about 30. Eventually the language became widespread among many tribes.

The modern Cyrillic language is spoken in about 10 countries, including Russia, Belarus, Ukraine, Bulgaria, Serbia and other countries that were once part of the Soviet Union.

While this is an ancient example that demonstrates the linguistic ingenuity of the two Greek brothers, it also points to the effect that change can have upon cultures. The language, for example, removed the barriers between the tribes, extended the boundaries and helped to dispense with the fears and suspicions that they held about each other. Clearly, the tribes had integrated and shared the same, larger location.

Summary of culture

Culture may be perceived as *physical*, in the form of bridges, roads, machinery, tools, etc; and as *subjective*, such as attitudes, beliefs, values and tacit norms. While culture is not religion, sex, race or nationality, they all do interact. History shows that the physical and the subjective elements of a culture change across time as scientific innovation and intellectual advancements replace old structural designs, attitudes, values and beliefs. Cultures relocate themselves and their languages become more complex; they are therefore continuously evolving.

Organisational culture

Having studied the foregoing section, you should now have a sound understanding of the elements of culture. In this section, we examine the degree to which those elements can be read across into the organisational situation. First however, the following definitions will clarify the concept of organisational culture.

Definition: organisational culture

'Organisational or corporate culture is the pattern of values, norms, beliefs, attitudes and assumptions that may not have been articulated but shape the ways in which people behave and get things done' (Armstrong 1999).

Organisational culture refers to a system of shared meaning held by members that distinguish the organisation from other organisations. This system of shared meaning is ... a set of key characteristics that the organisation values.

(Robbins 2001, p510)

The CIPD defines culture as:

a system of shared values and beliefs about what is important, what behaviours are appropriate and about feelings and relationships internally and externally. Values and cultures need to be unique to the organisation, widely shared and reflected in daily practice and relevant to the company purpose and strategy. But there is no single best culture.

(CIPD 2005)

Organisational culture is the collection of relatively uniform and enduring values, beliefs, customs, traditions and practices that are shared by an organisation's members, learned by new recruits, and transmitted from one generation of employees to the next (Huczynski and Buchanan 2001).

You may have noticed that the above definitions of organisational culture include only the subjective culture, even though organisations do contain a physical culture, such as buildings, equipment, machinery and tools. The physical culture is determined by the organisation's location and the nature of its technology. If, for example, you studied the culture in a Ford manufacturing plant, and then did the same in a Vauxhall plant, you would find strong similarities. This is because of the similarity of the design of the buildings, the machinery, the noises and the work systems; the technology determines the activities that employees have to perform in order to do their work. You would find, however, that while there are similarities in the subjective culture, they do not match exactly.

Industrial culture

Motor car manufacturing companies all have very similar technology, including their capital equipment and workshop layouts. An employee who has moved from one firm to another would recognise the physical culture and very quickly adapt to the subjective culture.

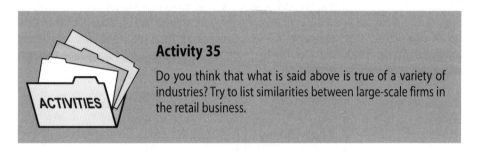

Activity 35

Do you think that what is said above is true of a variety of industries? Try to list similarities between large-scale firms in the retail business.

The influence of the physical culture is demonstrated in the following case, which is drawn from the industrial history of the UK.

Case study 21: The Luddites

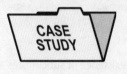

In the Lancashire cotton mills before the end of the eighteenth century, the cotton thread was spun by handi-craftsmen and women. In the 1770s Arkwright, Crompton and Hargreaves invented labour-saving spinning machines that were capable of producing material of a higher quality and at a greater speed that was previously possible. In 1811, the craft spinners saw the machines as a threat to their livelihood, and led by Ned Ludd, they vandalised the machines. The factory owners persisted with the machines, modified versions of which were used until the twentieth century.

One of the features of the machines that was disliked intensely by the workers was the very loud noise they made. Previously, there was a strong social culture in the workrooms, but with the machines, they could not hear each other speak. They added lip-reading to their repertoire of skills, but to use their words, 'this place will never be the same again'. The change to the physical culture had altered the subjective culture, showing that they are interrelated.

The position then is that while the physical culture does have a strong influence on the overall culture of the organisation, it is the subjective culture that principally interests managers and HR practitioners.

Robbins (2001, p53) supports this, saying that:

> **the physical properties of organisations tend to obscure the fact that organisations are really nothing other than an aggregate of individuals. Individuals, therefore, provide the foundation of the organisation; they bring it to life, and to understand why the organisation is what it is and why people behave in the way they do, you have to focus upon the individuals.**

Organisational subcultures

The interested parties, managers and academics, tend to talk and write about any single organisational culture as if it is a uniform phenomenon, while in fact organisations are made up of subcultures that represent different professions, locations, functions and levels (Hampden-Turner 1990). This reduces the number of attitudes and core values that are shared across the whole organisation.

Key concept 17: subcultures

It seems, therefore, that from this, one may deduce that the subculture on the workshop floor at say, location A, will be different from that of the marketing department at location B. Furthermore, organisations may have a boardroom subculture, a middle management subculture, a staff subculture and a shop-floor subculture.

The influence of subcultures

Furnham and Gunter (1993) describe the possible effects of the existence of subcultures at different levels and functions:

> **These sub-cultures can assume varying degrees of significance within the organisation, and can be beneficial if they adopt a common sense of purpose, but problems arise where they have different priorities and agendas. Then sub-cultures can clash with each other or with the overall corporate culture, impeding organisational functioning and performance.**

Why study organisational culture?

As a subject of concern for managers and of study for academics working in the field of organisational behaviour, organisational culture emerged in the 1980s. It was always there, hidden in the general atmosphere of the place, and since it was finally teased out and studied, it has achieved an importance that ranks it alongside other principal aspects of management and organisational studies. Understanding culture enables HR practitioners, managers and consultants to understand why people in organisations behave as they do, and enables them to alter the culture in order to make it more conducive to the achievement of sectional and overall objectives.

According to Moorhead and Griffin (1992), organisational culture probably exerts the greatest influence on individual behaviour when it is taken for granted. One of the major reasons that organisational culture is such a powerful influence on employees in an organisation is that it is not explicit. Instead, it is an implicit part of the employees' values and beliefs. It is for these reasons that managers and academics study organisational culture.

Individual differences within cultures

When you ask people about where they work, they tend to tell you something of the nature of the business, and perhaps its size and location. Then when you go to visit the organisation you see its buildings, the machinery and equipment. None of this tells you what it is like to work there; only the people can tell you that. If you were to ask them, however, you would get a different account from each of them, since they are a diverse group and each will have his/her own unique interpretation of the place and of its culture. As an outsider, it is only from this combination of perceptions that you begin to get an idea of the kind of culture in which they work.

Organisational values

The values and norms that make up the culture of the organisation are taken for granted by the employees ('the way things are around here') and there seems to be a degree of passive acceptance about this.

> **They – the organisational values and norms – are basic assumptions made by employees, do not necessarily appear in a document and are not transmitted in a training programme, although they can be expressed in written form.**
>
> **(McKenna 1994)**

If, however, you undertook to analyse the culture of an organisation in order to identify and describe it, you would find significant indications of its values in the:

- structure, which demonstrates the lateral layers of authority and decision-making and the vertical patterns of expertise
- documentation, particularly including HR policies such as the systems of performance and reward management
- managerial style, including the formal and informal modes of communication between managers and employees
- condition of the employee relationship including agreements reached, the absence and staff turnover rates
- nature of the business.

Identifying organisational culture

In the 1970s and 1980s several academics attempted, through analysis, to identify and classify organisational cultures with a view to altering their nature in order to make them more conducive to the achievement of objectives. As you will see, the names of the classifications indicate the predominant characteristic of each type of culture. There are strong similarities between some of these classifications; the following describes two which are somewhat different from each other.

Handy (1976) proposed four types of culture as follows:

- *Power culture* is one with a central power source that exercises control. There are few rules or procedures and the atmosphere is competitive, power-oriented and political.
- *Role culture* in which work is controlled by procedures and rules, and the role, or job description, is more important than the person who fills it. Power is associated with positions, not people.
- *Task culture* in which the aim is to bring together the right people and let them get on with it. Influence is based more on expert power than on position or personal power. The culture is adaptable and teamwork is important.
- *Person culture* in which the individual is the central point. The organisation exists only to serve and assist the individuals in it.

Schein (1985) also proposed four types of culture:

- *Power culture*, in which leadership resides in a few and rests on their ability, which tends to be entrepreneurial.
- *Role culture*, is one in which power is balanced between the leader and the bureaucratic structure. The environment is likely to be stable, and roles and rules are clearly defined.
- *Achievement culture*, in which personal motivation and commitment are stressed and action, excitement and impact are valued.
- *Support culture*, in which people contribute out of a sense of commitment and solidarity. Relationships are characterised by mutuality and trust.

Typologies such as these provide indications of what happens in organisations according to the ideologies of the top managers and the type of organisation. One could, for example, draw parallels between what is said about *power culture* and what other writers have said about the *unitary perspective* (eg Fox 1966); what is said about *role culture* and what writers have said about *bureaucracy* (eg Weber 1964); what is said about support culture and aspects of human resource management, such as commitment, solidarity, mutuality and trust.

This might be confusing to the student who is new to the study of culture, since the typologies say little about values and norms, which are two of the main components of culture. Particular attitudes and beliefs are implied by some of the qualifying descriptions; for example, 'strive to maintain absolute control over subordinates' and 'the role, or job description, is more important than the person who fills it'. If, on the other hand, we examine a perception that describes the dimensions of a single culture, we see it from a different perspective.

Trice and Beyer (1984) proposed an organisational culture consisting of four major dimensions: (i) company practices; (ii) company communications; (iii) physical cultural forms and (iv) common language.

- *Company practices* consist of events and ceremonies which help employees to identify with the organisation and its successes. These might include employees attending the ceremonial launching of a new product, and the opportunity to socialise informally at the annual ball or a sports event.

- *Company communications* consist, *inter alia*, of informal chats such as when long-serving employees tell newcomers about past events and relate the myths and legends that are associated with the organisation. There are also signs and symbols designed to convey positive messages about the organisation, such as the company slogan, its logo, messages contained in the mission statement and in the marketing information.
- *Physical cultural forms* include the design of the buildings and the nature of the capital equipment, which convey something distinctive about the organisation. It also includes the décor and the layout of the offices and workshops, including the posters, cartoons and even the screensavers that employees choose.
- *Common language* is probably the most significant indication of overall organisational culture and the nature of the subcultures within it. In any organisation there is a secondary language which is not understood by outsiders. It is based on technical vocabularies and the in-jargon of the place.

As you can see, the work of Trice and Beyer (1984) resembles more closely the accounts of culture that are given in the first half of this chapter. References to signs and symbols, myths and legends, and the sharing of a common language indicate that the components and boundaries of ethnic culture can be detected within, and read into, organisational culture.

Activity 36

Draw up a list of 15 words and terms that are taken for granted and used regularly by employees in your organisation (or an organisation with which you are familiar) but would not be understood if you used them at home or elsewhere.

ACTIVITIES

The importance of place

Earlier in this chapter it was noted that the boundaries of a cultunit are time, place and language. What follows is an explanation and discussion of the importance of *place* in relation to organisational cultures and subcultures. The discussion centres around the influence of the national differences between the geographical locations of organisations that have installations in several countries, and the subcultures that exist within UK national organisations that have installations in several areas of the country.

Ethnic vs organisational culture

There is always an element of ethnic culture in the organisational culture, and it is important to take this into account if we wish to prescribe a culture that matches the organisation's core values. Additionally, it is important to understand whether ethnic or organisational culture is the stronger in the organisation. Which culture would predominate in particular situations? Research supports the view that ethnic culture, rather than the organisation's culture, is more influential over employee behaviour (Adler 1997, p61–63). Muslim workers in the UK, for example, will be influenced more strongly by their ethnic culture than by that of the employing organisation.

Organisations that have installations in different parts of the world have to be able to predict, with a reasonable degree of accuracy, the behaviour of their overseas employees. It was noted earlier that culture is the greatest determinant of employee behaviour, but in situations in which the two cultures clash, the ethnic culture will predominate.

Cultural fit

One situation in which the task is that of predicting behaviour is the selection process. What one might call *cultural fit* is the degree to which a prospective employee's attitudes, beliefs, values and customary norms match those of the organisation. Is this something that should be assessed? According to Robbins (2001):

We should expect ... that the employee selection process will be used by multinationals to find and hire job applicants who are a good fit with their organisation's dominant culture, even if such applicants are somewhat atypical for members of their country.

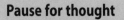

Pause for thought

From what is said in the above quote, do you think that multinational companies could risk rejecting the right person for the job by focusing on their culture rather than their suitability in terms of knowledge and skills? Could this develop into a discriminatory policy?

Culture shift

Human beings are the most adaptable creatures on Earth. They quickly acclimatise to unaccustomed conditions, and can move through a variety of different situations dealing with them as they go. People live their lives in stages, and they adopt roles as they move from one stage to the next; through infancy, teens, adulthood, and then middle age to old age. There are also stages in each day: the breakfast scene, the trip to work, the work situation, the trip home, the home scene.

Activity 37

Go through the above paragraph and think about how you behave in each of the stages and in each of the daily situations. Are you aware that your behaviour changes gradually during your life and frequently during each day?

One of the most important changes is the one that takes place as you enter the workplace. As you go through those doors, you put aside much of your ethnic culture and slip into the *place* where you spend *time* and where the *language* is different. By doing this, you and your workplace colleagues become part of a different culture. Without having to make a conscious effort, you adopt the workplace values and observe the norms. Furthermore, if you are a team member, you adapt again.

Pause for thought

How many different ethnic backgrounds are there in your team or classroom? Is there mutual understanding about what you have to do? How well do you work together?

The point that is being made here is that people from a variety of ethnic cultures join together to form a new culture in order to achieve particular objectives by working harmoniously together. This is not a description of an idealistic situation; it happens for real in all kinds of organisations every day. Indeed, there are times when team members have to close ranks in order to defend their position.

Integration of diverse elements

The organisation, therefore, is an ideal venue for integration. It is more disciplined than the external environment and is a space in which the organisation's own values and beliefs can be learned by all, regardless of their backgrounds.

Changing the culture

The foundations of the culture of any organisation are in its history. The traditions that have built up over time, including its methods of operating, tend to remain evident for as long as the organisation continues to succeed. What is done and how it is done are reinforced by success, and an 'if it ain't broke don't fix it' attitude emerges. The fact has to be faced, however, that things do change. Competition becomes more fierce, market demands change as technological innovation continues to progress, people (customers) have become more discerning and price-conscious, and living standards are raised continually – at least, that is the case in the more advanced countries. Sometimes, however, the more senior members of the organisation may be inclined to place a high value on tradition, as the following case study shows.

Case study 22: Mitsubishi Motors

In contrast to its main competitors, Honda and Daimler-Chrysler, Mitsubishi Motors experienced severe problems around the turn of the millennium. Unable to respond to the high demand for minivans and sport utility vehicles, it lost US$846 million in one year. The culprit was identified as the deeply rooted Mitsubishi culture, which was based on the traditions of the 1970s' market conditions. The company appointed a new president – Katsuhiko Kawasoe – to try to change the culture.

Other Japanese firms had broken from the country's long-held beliefs in the importance of tradition and history, but Mitsubishi had continued to move at its own pace. While other Japanese companies had abandoned such notions as the 'job-for-life' tradition, which was no longer realistic in a highly competitive world marketplace, Mitsubishi continued to do things in its own way. When the chairman of Mitsubishi Heavy was asked about laying off people, he replied, 'Employment is more important than profits! We are not concerned with return on equity … if foreign investors don't see merit in our stock, they can sell it' – which of course they did!

A consultant who works with Mitsubishi says the company is being held back by the lack of incentives, and nobody is holding management accountable. When something goes wrong, managers say, 'It would be un-Japanese to fire anyone or close plants.' At the time of writing, there is no visible improvement. New recruits are not lectured on the importance of competition or profits. Instead, company executives continue to talk about Mitsubishi's 'special place in history and duty to the country'.

Discussion of the case

It is not difficult to identify past organisations in the west whose demise was largely caused by their attempts to survive on their historical traditions. What should Mitsubishi do? The firm relies for its sales on the world markets but its deep-rooted culture is its main liability. In the 1980s, when global competition became a reality, and when speedy and sensitive responses to customer demands became the norm, deeply entrenched, old-fashioned cultures should have become redundant.

This was realised even as far back as 1966 by Burns and Stalker: 'Where customer demands are ever-changing, the organisation's speed of, and sensitivity to, response becomes the essence of success.' These writers were describing the kind of organisation that was most likely to succeed in a fast-moving and highly competitive market (what they referred to as *organic organisations*). It is worth bearing in mind that for their book to be published in 1966, they must have carried out the research for it in the early 1960s!

Making the change: can it be done?

Earlier in this chapter references are made to the work of several eminent writers on culture, and from these you will have seen that culture is made up of relatively stable characteristics. From reading the first part of the following discussion, you will see that changing an organisation's culture appears to be an extremely difficult task. We hope, however, the evidence from the second part of the discussion will indicate to you that cultures can be changed.

Part 1: Don't rock the boat

The long-held beliefs and deeply rooted values to which the employees of an organisation are strongly committed motivate them to maintain the culture. In mechanistic organisations (see

Chapter 1), there are forces that combine to reinforce the importance of adhering to the cultural norms. These include written policies, mission statements and philosophies that emanate from the top, the infrastructural design, the buildings, the hardware, the structure, the style of leadership, the general climate of the place, the policies on recruitment, selection, training and promotion, the rituals and historic myths about the organisation and its key people.

Historically, mechanistic organisations have always attracted employees who seek stable and structured positions. Senior managers are selected on the grounds that they are the most likely people to perpetuate 'the way things are'. We saw that when Mitsubishi put a new president in place, it seems that rather than change the culture, the culture changed him!

Part 2: Catalysts of culture change

If, in the organisation-wide sense, the culture matches the values and philosophies of those at the top, there is an overall cohesiveness which makes for a strong culture, which is the most difficult type of culture to change. In any organisational scenario, the culture change process presents a daunting prospect, but research and experience shows that it can be done.

In particular circumstances, organisations are vulnerable to culture change when a severe crisis arises, such as when a competitor suddenly and unpredictably launches a new major product on the market, or a critical financial downturn such as that suffered by MG-Rover in 2004. In such cases, organisations usually bring in a new chief executive; sadly for MG-Rover, it was too late to do that. On a more positive note, change becomes necessary when the predicted sales of a new product are exceeded dramatically and the organisation has to move quickly to fulfil the demand.

When a long-established and successful organisation sets up a new major division or a subsidiary company in order to fulfil a major contract, the new organisation is ripe for the development of a culture that is conducive to success. In such a case, the top managers may instil new values, demonstrate new rituals and generally make the employees aware of the kind of behaviour that is expected of them.

In those circumstances, however, sometimes the managers and specialists needed for the new organisation are drawn from the main company, and if the new set-up is put together as a matrix, it will need to draw upon the expert and administrative services of the main company. In other words, the new employees' contacts will be those who espouse the old culture.

The new organisation will be more likely to succeed in shifting along the *mechanistic–organic* dimension (see Chapter 1) if new managers develop a culture that is appropriate for the central task. It is important to note that if nothing is done about the development of a fresh culture, then one will evolve anyway.

Identifying the culture gap

In an organisation that has been established for several years, the managers may feel that the current culture is inappropriate for the achievement of corporate objectives. In such a case, the managers' first task is to envision the kind of culture that would be most appropriate for the foreseeable future. Second, they have to analyse and identify the true make-up of the current culture (see above), which will enable them to compare the two in order to identify the culture gap, at which stage they can develop a culture-change strategy; in other words, they have to fill the culture gap.

According to Armstrong (1999), culture change programmes can focus on particular aspects of the culture. The examples he cites include performance, commitment, quality, customer service, teamwork and organisational learning. All of these aspects have underpinning values which need to be defined. It would be necessary to prioritise by deciding which of them needs the most urgent attention.

The need for change

The need for change often arises from changes in the external environment, especially market demands and the activities of competitors. Sometimes changes are needed urgently, induced perhaps by a crisis, and they have to be implemented as quickly as possible, but there is a limit to what can be done in the short term. Experience shows that the most effective and enduring changes take place when they have been carefully planned and introduced in gradual, incremental stages. In order to develop a culture that is conducive to the achievement of objectives, the envisioned culture and the organisation's future plans should be considered concurrently, from the beginning of the change process.

Organisation development

Organisation development (OD) is the term used to describe a process through which, using the principles and practices of behavioural science, a change programme is applied in the organisation, often on an organisation-wide basis. OD is driven by the ultimate purpose of creating an effective organisation by altering the structure and changing employees' attitudes, beliefs and values. It is concerned not with *what* is done but with the *way* things are done, and with creating a new culture of cohesiveness, interdependence and mutual trust.

Definition

French and Bell (1990) defined OD as:

a planned systematic process in which applied behavioural science principles and practices are introduced into an ongoing organisation towards the goals of effecting organisational improvement, greater organisational competence, and greater organisational effectiveness.

The focus is on organisations and their improvement, or to put it another way, *total systems change*. The orientation is on action – achieving desired results as a result of planned activities.

Once the areas and aspects that require change have been identified, the next step is to introduce the ideas to the employees. Employees vary in their attitudes to significant change. In general terms, the longer-serving employees, who have a need for job security, may fear that they will lose their jobs, and therefore they tend to resist it more than the younger employees, who may see it as an interesting challenge. Chapter 1 covers this problem, and it will be helpful if you study the sections on 'Resistance to change' and 'Dealing with resistance'.

Change levers

These will have been identified from the analysis of the current culture, and decisions have to be made about putting them to optimum use. Some of the change levers described by Armstrong (1999) include:

- *performance*: performance-related or competence-related pay schemes, performance management processes, leadership training, skills development
- *commitment:* communication, participation and involvement programmes, developing a climate of cooperation and trust; clarifying the psychological contract
- *customer service*: customer-care programmes
- *teamwork*: team-building, team performance management, team rewards
- *organisational learning*: taking steps to enhance intellectual capital and the organisation's resource-based capability by developing a learning organisation
- *values*: gaining understanding, acceptance and commitment through involvement in defining values, performance management programmes and employee development interventions.

Managing the change process

While working on the change levers, the positive aspects of the old culture should be emphasised and re-affirmed, while the new values should be stated clearly and frequently. Employee behaviour that is conducive to the success of the change programme should be rewarded.

Consulting employees

While the total change process is introduced and driven by the managers, employee groups should be consulted about specific changes that affect their areas of work. Management-led group discussions will help to clarify the nature of and the reasons for the changes, and should be carried out in a way that confers a significant degree of ownership on the employees. This is achieved by seeking employees' opinions, particularly about how the change process should be handled. Their advice should be considered seriously and their experience will be valuable, since they are the people at the work interface. The bonus from this is that when ownership of the change is felt by employees, they are less likely to resist and more likely to ensure that it succeeds.

Embedding the culture

Finally, when an appropriate culture is in place, action should be taken to ensure that it remains there, at least until a further change becomes necessary. Schein (1985) listed five mechanisms for embedding and reinforcing the culture:

- what leaders pay attention to, measure and control
- leaders' reactions to critical incidents and crises
- deliberate role-modelling, teaching and coaching by leaders
- criteria for allocation of rewards and status
- criteria for recruitment, selection, promotion and commitment.

Self-test questions

1. How would you define organisational culture?
2. What is the relationship between values and norms?
3. Why is culture said to be a powerful determinant of behaviour?
4. How would you distinguish between the physical culture and the subjective culture? How do they influence each other?
5. What is ethnocentrism and why is it important in organisational culture?

6. What are the boundaries of culture?
7. In what circumstances do members of different ethnic cultures join forces to create a distinctive subculture?
8. What value is there in defining different types of organisational culture?
9. In what circumstances might it be appropriate to identify an individual's 'cultural fit'?
10. What is meant by the term 'culture shift'?
11. Write down four levels of organisational subculture
12. What are the positive and negative influences of organisational subcultures?
13. What are the possible consequences of allowing an out-of-date culture to persist at a time of significant external change?
14. Why would an organisation change its position on the 'mechanistic–organic dimension'?
15. What is the advantage of identifying the 'culture gap'?

Essay question

1. Explain and discuss the similarities and differences between subcultural aspects as determinants of group behaviour and personality factors as determinants of individual behaviour.

Work–life balance

CHAPTER 16

Learning objectives

After studying this chapter you should:

- be able to define work–life balance

- understand the variety of reasons why people work

- be able to advise your employer on what can be done to assist employees in achieving a satisfactory work–life balance

- as an HR practitioner, be able to assist and offer employees appropriate advice about work–life balance

- understand the law affecting work–life balance.

Introduction

This chapter is concerned with the role of work in relation to the other aspects of a person's life. These include attending to their responsibilities and obligations at home and in their family life, marriage, what people do to relax and the time they need to pursue personal interests. Additionally, it examines and discusses:

- the role that employers have in providing practical support to employees with their need to balance their commitments at work with those at home
- the business case for encouraging employees to achieve work–life balance, including the benefits to employers from doing so
- the legislation that is relevant to work–life balance.

The Work Foundation (website, 2005) says that work–life balance is about people having a

Definition: work–life balance

Work–life balance is a reflection of the importance that individuals attribute to each of the various aspects of their lives. It is a reflection of how much time and attention a person gives, and is able to give, to the responsibilities, obligations and activities, including leisure, that he/she carries out at work, home and elsewhere.

measure of control over when, where and how they work. It is achieved when an individual's right to a fulfilled life inside and outside of paid work is accepted and respected as the norm, to the mutual benefit of the individual, business and society.

The meaning of work

The word 'work' can mean many things. For example, people do work at home, such as house-work and DIY jobs. In another context, participating in sports may be regarded as work. In fact work is any physical or mental activity that expends energy. In the context of work–life balance, work refers to paid employment, which is usually a significant component of people's life structure. In the same context, the word 'life' refers to all of the non-work aspects of people's total lifestyle, while 'balance' refers to the reasonableness with which everything in their life fits together.

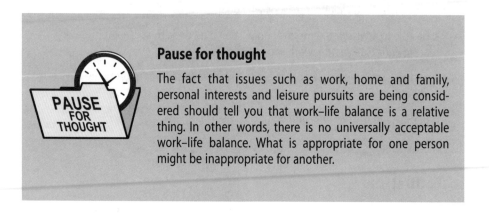

Pause for thought

The fact that issues such as work, home and family, personal interests and leisure pursuits are being consid-ered should tell you that work–life balance is a relative thing. In other words, there is no universally acceptable work–life balance. What is appropriate for one person might be inappropriate for another.

The role of work

Work is a central feature in the lives of most people. To some, it is simply a means to an end in that it supports a desired standard of living. To others, it is the main life interest, the all-consuming top priority, a so-called 'vocational calling'. However, the old 'either–or' saying that 'some people work to live and others live to work' is not totally accurate. People's attitudes to work vary widely, ranging from the perception of it as a chore they have to bear in order to provide for themselves and others, to being the main reason for their existence.

When people ask about your work they often say, 'What do you do for a living?' That well-worn phrase tells us about the traditional role that work has played since the beginning of the Industrial Revolution. For most people, work provides the central structure of their lives, while everything else is organised around it. It determines:

- where employees should be at particular times of the day and week
- the time of arrival at, and departure from, the workplace
- how much time they have to themselves
- their annual holiday entitlement
- their general standard of living (through finance).

In fact, work even tells them what time to get out of bed in the mornings!

Achieving work–life balance

Although we have said that there is no universally accepted work–life balance, there are common factors that people need to think about when attempting to achieve a work–life balance that is satisfactory to them. Clutterbuck (2003), for example, says that achieving a work–life balance can arguably be boiled down to:

- being aware of different demands on your time and energy
- having the ability to make choices in the allocation of time and energy
- knowing what values you wish to apply to choices
- making (conscious) choices.

Achieving a satisfactory work–life balance is not simply a question of summarising everything one does and putting it all into some kind of order. In fact it is quite a complex task that involves time management, deciding what the priorities are in terms of work, paying due consideration to the needs of important others – such as a spouse/partner and children (if any) – and of course making time and provision for personal interests, such as hobbies and leisure pursuits.

Time management

While this chapter is not about time management per se, how people allocate their time and energy to their obligations, responsibilities and pleasures does play a significant role in their achieving a satisfactory work–life balance. Everyone, regardless of who they are or what they do for a living, is allocated exactly the same amount of time, and the question is, 'What do you do with yours?'

Consider the following four facts:

1. There are 120 hours in a five-day week.
2. According to the Working Time Regulations (WTR) employers can demand no more than 48 hours a week, although employees can opt out of that limit.
3. The average 'home to work and back' travel time is two hours daily.
4. Many people (31 per cent of us) sleep for between seven and a half and eight hours in a period of 24 hours (Dingwall 1983).

What do these facts give us? If we add the time spent on the activities in 2, 3 and 4 and subtract the result from 120, we are left with 22 hours to ourselves in the working week, or 4.4 hours a day. Or are we? A large number of people do not fit exactly into the nine-to-five pattern.

Long hours culture

Many employees in the UK work longer hours than the WTR limit of 48 hours a week. This is a phenomenon that takes many forms:

- Some either opt out of the WTR limit or, without formally opting out, simply continue working voluntarily beyond the contracted time. This practice is often called *presenteeism*, which is done because some people think that staying on implies commitment.
- Others work more than the contractual time by taking work home.

■ Low-paid employees have to work overtime simply in order to earn a reasonable living.
■ Further considerations include the time spent talking and thinking about work.

Research into long hours

The information on working hours in this section comes from surveys carried out by the Office for National Statistics (ONS), the Department of Trade and Industry (DTI) and the CIPD. The ONS surveys show that (in the UK) just under a quarter of people in employment (6.3 million, or 22 per cent) work more than 45 hours a week. This is a high proportion by EU standards, though other developed countries such as Australia, Japan and the United States have more long-hours workers than the UK.

According to a survey carried out by the DTI and *Men's Health* magazine, UK employees work longer hours than those in most other parts of Europe. From the same survey, an item of data that should interest employers is that 71 per cent of men believe that their failure to strike a balance between life and job is affecting their performance at work.

A recent independent study of long hours working published by the DTI (2004) found that those working the longest hours in the UK are men aged 30–49 with children and employed in the private sector. Unlike other EU countries where people working long hours are most likely to be found working in hotels and restaurants, in the UK they are more commonly found in manufacturing. However, full-time managers in the UK, often stereotyped as 'workaholics', on average do not work longer hours than their EU counterparts.

In 2003, the CIPD commissioned a survey among a representative sample of UK workers, with a particular emphasis on those working more than 48 hours a week. The findings showed that the main reason for working long hours was workload. However, one in two workers said that working longer hours is 'totally (their) own choice – doesn't mind working long hours', which is up from two out of five respondents saying the same thing in a previous survey conducted in 1998. In the survey:

■ more than one in four respondents reported some sort of negative impact on health
■ more than two out of five respondents reported a negative impact on their relationships
■ most respondents reported negative effects on their job performance.

Organisations in which there is a so-called 'long hours culture' need to understand the negative effects of long hours on productivity and on the physical and mental health of employees. According to the DTI/*Men's Health* magazine survey referred to above, 63 per cent of the respondents said that they made mistakes, 74 per cent admitted to taking longer to complete a task and the same percentage said that they were performing less.

Organising work–life balance

It is unlikely that an individual will achieve a satisfactory work–life balance without the co-operation and assistance of others. The employer has a significant role to play in this. Gradually, employers are becoming more flexible and understanding of their employees' commitments, and there is also legislation that requires employers to assist in particular circumstances (see later). Ultimately, however, it is up to the individual to envisage a work–life balance that would be satisfactory.

Not a strict regime

When you start to consider your own situation in terms of how important each aspect of your life is to you and how they all fit into your life, you will find that work–life balance is a fluid concept. That is to say, the time and attention that you give to different aspects of your life varies from one day to another, from one week to another. For example, emergencies might happen to those closest to you, such as your spouse/partner and your children. If a child falls ill or is having problems at school, he/she will claim your attention at the expense of the other aspects. A satisfactory work–life balance, therefore, cannot be achieved simply by allocating set amounts of time in accordance with their importance.

The point here is that the aspects of our lives, including work, create conflict in that they compete with each other for our time and attention. Individuals have to be prepared to decide which aspects they wish to attend to at any particular time, and which go on their waiting list; and difficult as it may be, there will be times when they have to say 'no'.

Having the 'right' job

The likelihood that a person will achieve a satisfactory work–life balance depends to a considerable extent on his/her employer, and it is important to be able to distinguish between 'good' and 'bad' employers. Work–life balance involves more than juggling with time; it also includes people's health and happiness, which are best achieved by having a job they enjoy and in which they are treated fairly and with respect.

Choosing an employer

For many years, it was traditional for the job selection decision to be entirely in the hands of the employer. In the past, employers tended to give the job to a candidate, the implication being that it is a one-sided choice and that the candidate should somehow be grateful. Candidates too have played their parts in this; they enter the interview room eager to please and hoping to be selected, while in fact the decision should be mutual.

Before applying for a job, a person should find out as much as possible about the organisation. Does it have a good reputation for the way employees are treated? If the organisation is local, its reputation as an employers should be easy to discover. A prospective candidate should seek information about:

- its employment policies and procedures
- the training, development and career opportunities
- its policies and practices on equal opportunities
- the normal terms and conditions of employment
- what it is like to work there.

If the information gathered from such enquiries turns out to be positive and leads to a decision to apply for the job, the written response from the organisation to the application, which usually includes the job description and material about the organisation, will provide further information about its style and culture. If a prospective candidate who makes preliminary enquiries in this way, progresses to the selection stage, he/she will be in a good position to consider the organisation as a prospective employer.

Considering the offer

A candidate who is offered employment will have been through the selection procedure, perhaps involving a tour around the workplace and meeting managers and employees, and might have come to regard the organisation as a 'good' employer. However, he/she still should consider whether he/she feels comfortable in terms of fitting into the culture and how working there is likely to affect the other aspects of his/her life.

This is a vitally important decision, because if an individual finds that he/she is working for a 'bad' employer who fails to recognise that employees are individually different, and does not consider their non-work needs, then the ability of that individual to achieve a satisfactory work–life balance will be severely inhibited.

Unhealthy organisations

According to Susan Newell, 'bad' employers control 'unhealthy' organisations that have not adopted the policies, procedures and structures which give recognition to individual employee needs and remove sources of discrimination, nor do they have cultures which promote moral and social responsibility considerations. Instead, in such organisations, employees work in environments which do not promote physical and psychological well-being and work in jobs which induce stress (Newell 1995, p9). Stress is an important factor that seriously inhibits the achievement of a satisfactory work–life balance (see Chapter 13).

Work–life balance: action plan

If individuals are dissatisfied with their current work–life situation, there are a number of steps they could take in order to turn things around:

- Analyse and review the current situation.
- Identify the aspects that need to be changed, especially work and home, which are the two main aspects for most people, and are the areas from which they need the most support.
- Tell people about your intention to make change, including the nature of the changes and how they too would benefit from your proposed actions.
- Implementation should start with the workplace.

Who benefits?

Much of the discussion of work–life balance has focused on the 'family-friendly' aspect of childcare, and the problems faced by people with babies, toddlers and school-age children. But placing all of the emphasis on them is too narrow a focus, and can alienate some employees, as it is not only children who are dependent on others. In the UK, several million people already act as carers for elderly or disabled friends or members of their family (CIPD 2005). Clearly, all such dependants would benefit.

Benefits to the employer

One of the prime beneficiaries, however, is the employer, and there is a good business case for providing support to those who need to make the changes that are outlined above. The benefits to business include:

- higher productivity and competitiveness

- increased flexibility and customer service, for example, to cover for absence and holidays
- raised morale, motivation, commitment and engagement
- reduced absenteeism
- improved recruitment and retention of a diverse workforce
- wanting to become an employer of choice
- meeting legal requirements.

So what can employers do?

It was noted above that the employer has a significant role to play in work–life balance, and in fact the employer can make a contribution that will make an important difference. Here, we examine and discuss first, what employers can do to assist, and second, what the law says they must do.

Getting started

According to Business Link (2005), employers should regard the achievement of work–life balance not as a 'one-off' exercise, but as a long-term commitment to operating the business in a way that respects their employees' responsibilities outside of work. The policies that are designed to achieve this need to strike a balance between the needs of the business and those of the employees.

Clearly, employers will know what they wish to achieve in terms of their core business requirements, but if they regard the long-term well-being of the employees as important, then the employees, along with their representatives (trade unions), need to be consulted about what they too wish to achieve. The employer should:

- take the lead in demonstrating a commitment to work–life balance
- explain any changes to employees and keep them abreast of regulatory changes, eg the right for parents to request flexible working.

David Clutterbuck says that employers should give employees the tools to create their own work–life balance. For example, a number of employers, such as the Nationwide Building Society, have offered employees briefings or training in how to set about creating a better balance of work and non-work for their own lives. There are a number of issues that people might need help to tackle, including:

- what they actually want from each aspect of their lives – how important each aspect is to them now and how important they expect it to be in the future
- how they sort out conflicting demands on their time and physical and emotional energy
- how they achieve the self-discipline required to set boundaries and to say no when demands from others threaten to breach those boundaries
- how to recognise and manage the stress that comes from conflicting or excessive demands upon them.
  (Clutterbuck 2003)

Organisations that do not offer training/counselling on these issues have found that increasingly, employees are consulting the organisation's *occupational support system* or the *employee assistance programme* over matters of work–life conflict (see Chapter 13).

The role of HR

While it is the line manager who is in the best possible position to observe employees and identify those in need of assistance, it is primarily the role of HR to advise and assist in the development of a workplace culture that is supportive of employees striving to achieve a satisfactory work–life balance (WLB). Clutterbuck (2003, p4) maintains that:

> **only HR can make a convincing case for the business impact of investing time and money in promoting good work–life balance; only HR can craft and sell in to top management viable strategies for taking advantage of the competitive potential that a proactive approach to WLB brings; only HR can design and integrate the wide portfolio of policies needed; and only HR can develop and implement the processes for measuring progress against WLB goals.**

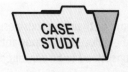

Case study 23: Happy Ltd

Happy Ltd is an award-winning training company with around 40 staff. The company has been following a positive work–life balance agenda for several years and was the first in London to achieve the Investors in People Work–life Balance Model. Managing director Cathy Busani explained how its family-friendly policies have delivered excellent staff morale, better customer service and low staff turnover.

Making a decision

Says Cathy, 'The idea for a defined policy on work–life balance began when a member of staff became pregnant. After working out a package that would allow her the flexibility she needed, we decided we wanted to offer the same opportunities to all of our staff. We already had a flexible working culture, but things needed to be formalised. So that we could be absolutely confident that everyone at Happy knew what was on offer, we ran a staff meeting to discuss all of the options available.'

Put ideas into practice

Cathy continues, 'We now use a variety of methods, many of which address the needs of families, but the flexibility we offer is available to all. Flexible hours, compressed hours, job sharing and dependency leave are all part of the mix. Parents can even bring children into the office during the school holidays if an urgent need arises. Achieving a better work–life balance is a cultural mindset, not just a set of policies. A key element is a can do attitude. We always consider unusual requests or new methods within the context of business needs. In practice, we've never had an instance where a workable solution couldn't be found. It is also important that managers provide a role model for healthy work–life balance. I work a four-day week and our CEO takes Wednesday mornings off to attend a reading class at his daughter's school.'

Involve people

'We explain our policies at induction and hold twice-yearly appraisals that include a question on work–life balance. Because we're flexible with staff and they feel involved, they're flexible with us. They often come up with solutions to staffing issues that we hadn't thought possible. Ultimately, customer service has improved.

'Our workforce is highly, motivated and staff turnover is about two-thirds of the national average for our sector. Our policies have also led to several national awards that have enhanced our reputation with both clients and employees. We're constantly approached by people who want to work here and we no longer pay for recruitment advertising. The only negative of pursuing family friendly-policies is that calculating salaries and annual leave is more complicated. However, the benefits far outweigh the disadvantages.'

What would I do differently?

'I'd do it sooner! Our family-friendly policies have worked so well and improved customer service so much, that I wish we'd introduced them even earlier in the business development.'

Happy Ltd is reproduced with the kind permission of Business Link, and is available at http://www.businesslink.gov.uk/bdotg/action/detail

Discussion of the case study

The case of Happy Ltd is a clear example of mutual understanding and trust between the organisation and its staff. The leader has practicable policies, and the can do attitude indicates a joint problem-solving approach that leads to the satisfaction of the needs of both the organisation and its employees.

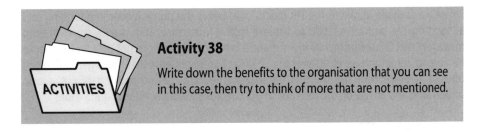

ACTIVITIES

Activity 38

Write down the benefits to the organisation that you can see in this case, then try to think of more that are not mentioned.

No one best way

It was noted earlier in this chapter that there is no universal prescription for a satisfactory work–life balance for individuals, and since all organisations are different from each other, the same applies to the achievement of a mutually satisfying pattern of working in terms of attendance. In the case study Cathy Busani mentions four attendance patterns that are in use concurrently.

The CIPD survey, *Flexible working and paternity leave*, found that part-time working was the most common option of flexible working offered by organisations. Table 16.1, taken from that survey, details the popularity of other options.

Table 16.1 The popularity of flexible working options by percentage of respondents indicating that their work involves at least that option

	Total %	Male %	Female %
Base: all full/part-time workers	(1,193)	(591)	(602)
Working part-time	53	38	71
Variable working hours (coming in/leaving late or early)	51	49	52
Job sharing	28	23	34
Working from home	20	21	20
Term-time-only working	19	14	26
Annualised hours	18	17	18
Nine-day fortnight	10	10	10
Other	3	2	5
Don't know	1	1	1
None	19	26	12

Source: CIPD (2005).

The law affecting work–life balance

Reference is made above to the HR practitioner being the prime mover in designing and integrating the policies needed to achieve work–life balance, and in convincing the top managers that it is a worthwhile investment. It is essential, therefore, not only for him/her to be able to communicate effectively the voluntary arrangements that the organisation can offer to its employees and the benefits that accrue from making such offers, but also to understand and advise on the relevant law, of which, incidentally, there is quite a lot.

Keeping track of the law

HR practitioners are faced not only with understanding the law but also with keeping abreast of the changes and the rate at which those changes are made. The law that has been explained and discussed in the previous chapters – much of which affects work–life balance – was up to date at the time of writing, but as an HR practitioner who is responsible for advising senior and line managers, you will need to keep a constant watch on the publication of new legislation and amendments to established laws. The chapters that include reference to the legislation that affects work–life balance are Chapters 6, 10, 13 and 14.

Family-friendliness

This is an area of employment law that features a large number of Acts and Amendments and which significantly affect work–life balance. Their purpose is to support a reasonable work–life balance for working parents. The provisions of the 'equal treatment' aspects of this legislation were first contained in the Equal Pay Act 1970, but since then there has been a train of measures including the Employment Rights Act 1996 and the Employment Act 2002, and the variety of amendments that are explained and discussed in Chapter 11.

Many employers were already offering flexibility to their employees before the legislation was formally enacted, but the purposes of the legislation are to set minimum standards and to ensure that all employers are treating their employees fairly and reasonably.

How does the legislation affect work–life balance?

For the most part, the legislation provides employees with a set of rights that apply in particular circumstances. The CIPD (2005) cite examples of these rights as:

- *Annual leave.* All employees are entitled to a minimum of 20 days' paid annual leave.
- *Working time.* The working time week is limited to 48 hours, averaged over 17 weeks for employees who have not 'opted out'. The Working Time Regulations also provide for minimum rest periods and make special provision for night work.
- *Parental leave.* There is a right to 13 weeks' unpaid parental leave for men and women, with at least a year's service, at any time up to the child's fifth birthday. This must be taken in blocks or multiples of one week, with 21 days' notice given to the employer.
- *Time off for dependant care.* The right to take unpaid time off to deal with family emergencies (eg concerning an elderly parent, partner, child or other person living as part of the family).
- *Maternity leave.* Women giving birth are entitled to 26 weeks' maternity leave. Employees with at least 26 weeks' service are entitled to an extra 26 weeks' additional maternity leave, making 52 weeks in total. It is unlawful to dismiss anyone of the grounds of pregnancy and childbirth, and contracts of employment continue during all periods of statutory maternity leave.
- *Paternity leave.* Fathers with at least 26 weeks' service are entitled to two weeks' paid paternity leave, which can be taken as a single block of one or two weeks within the 56 days following the child's birth.
- *Adoption leave.* Employees adopting a child and having at least 26 weeks' service are entitled to 26 weeks' ordinary adoption leave and 26 weeks' additional adoption leave. Only one parent may take adoption leave. If he/she qualifies, the other parent may take paternity leave.
- *Right to request flexible working.* Employees with children aged under 6 (under 18 if disabled) can request a change in their hours, time or place of work. The employer can refuse such a request on specific business grounds, but must follow a detailed procedure.
- *Part-time work.* Part-timers are entitled to the same hourly rate of pay and the same entitlements to annual leave and maternity/parental leave on a pro rata basis as

full-timers. Part-timers must also have the same entitlement to contractual sick pay and no less favourable treatment in access to training.

Requests and entitlements

When studying employee rights in these respects, it is important to distinguish between situations in which the employee has a 'right to request' and those in which there is a clear 'statutory right'. Every one of the rights listed above is related to attendance, and it has to be borne in mind that in order to survive, develop and attend to customer demands, organisations have business needs and priorities which, at times, may conflict with the needs of employees.

Consultation

The kind of conflict described above highlights the importance of adopting a joint problem-solving approach to both sets of needs. The Happy Ltd case study (above) portrays the ideal situation: that is to say, ideal for Happy Ltd. All organisations and all employees, however, have individually different needs, so there is little to be gained from looking over the fence. In any organisation, the strategy for work–life balance has to be specifically tailored to meet both business and individual needs. It involves more than simply conforming to the law; it means finding out directly from the employees about their personal needs and priorities, then considering how they can be met in ways that positively support business needs and priorities.

Voluntary measures

There are several benefits that an employer may offer above and beyond the legal standards that may help employees to achieve a satisfactory work–life balance. Some of these are beneficial to the organisation as well as the employee. They may include unpaid career breaks, paid sabbatical schemes and financing educational and training courses. Additionally, there are more informal benefits such as allowing the occasional paid or unpaid day off to attend to an important, but non-urgent matter at home or in the community. Furthermore, the minimum standards set down in legislation for maternity, paternity and other matters could be enhanced by offering higher pay and/or longer leave.

Such schemes not only give employees a great measure of control over how their working lives fit in with everything else they do, they also foster goodwill, loyalty, motivation and commitment.

Why bother?

Advancing technology has created the need for knowledgeable and highly skilled people who are deeply involved in the kind of work they do, and organisations are in competition for such staff. This so-called 'talent war' puts such employees in a position that enables them to be selective when it comes to choosing an employer. By implication, this means that organisations have to ensure they have sound retention plans. An attractive work–life balance policy, which has been constructed with the co-operation of, and contributions from, the staff will demonstrate the organisation's commitment to its employees' quality of life.

What HR can do

The HR contribution to the formulation of a feasible work–life balance policy is probably more significant than any other. The objective is to ensure that the organisation is one that encourages a healthy balance between work and non-work commitments among its employees. The task is eased if the top managers genuinely value their employees and are open to suggestions about a way forward. In the first instance, there are several steps that can be taken:

1. Organise a meeting with the employees and managers to tell them about your intentions and find out from them where they think improvements might be made.
2. Gather relevant information about the business needs and identify the how the implementation of a policy will contribute to the achievement of business objectives.
3. Formulate a work–life strategy that will benefit both the business and the employees. The essence of the strategy is that the organisation and its employees are working in a mutually beneficial partnership.
4. Consider the arrangements that will be needed to cover for absence, to preserve goodwill with customers and between the employer and employees.
5. Draft a feasible and cost-effective action plan to accompany the strategy.
6. Take the package to the top managers and explain to them how and why the right work–life balance policy will benefit the organisation and its employees.

The package should include:

- policies that match operation needs
- reward and performance measures based on staff effectiveness in terms of results
- clear guidelines about the proposal, particularly for the line managers
- details of a meeting with staff to explain the new policies
- arrangements to have a joint meeting with staff to hear their views, discuss any ideas they may have for further improvement
- arrangements to have regular meetings with staff to advise them on any changes and listen to their ideas
- a monitoring system to check progress and identify and correct faults.

Assignment briefs

1. In your organisation or one with which you are familiar, construct an investigative survey questionnaire designed to collect data about employees' perceptions of what the organisation could do to help them to achieve a satisfactory work–life balance.
2. Prepare a briefing session that introduces the concept of work–life balance to a group of senior managers, including the benefits to the organisation and the workforce.
3. Name and briefly describe two statutory employee rights that are designed to assist in the achievement of work–life balance.

Self-test questions

1. How would you define work–life balance?
2. In what circumstances might the Working Time Regulations be ineffective?
3. What are the negative effects of working long hours?
4. Why is work–life balance a 'fluid' concept?
5. How would you go about choosing a job that would enable you to achieve a satisfactory work–life balance?
6. Why should an employer be concerned about employees' lifestyles?

7. What benefits and facilities might an employer offer that exceed the minimum standards required by legislation?
8. How would you relate work–life balance to the retention of valuable staff?
9. How would you describe the role of HR in work–life balance?
10. The figures show that women more than men favour alternative patterns of flexible working. Why do you think this is?

References and further reading

ADAMS, A. (1992) *Bullying at work: how to confront and overcome it.* London: Virago.

ADAMS, J.S. (1961) Toward an understanding of inequity. In: R. Likert (ed), *New patterns of management.* Maidenhead: McGraw-Hill.

ADLER, N.J. (1997) *International dimensions of organizational behaviour.* 3rd ed. Cincinnati: Southwestern.

ALDERFER, C.P. (1972) *Existence, relatedness and growth: human needs in organisational settings.* New York: Free Press.

ANDERSON, A.H. (1994) *Effective personnel management: a skills and activity-based approach.* Oxford: Blackwell Business.

ANDERSON, N. and SHACKLETON, V. (1993) *Successful selection interviewing.* Oxford: Blackwell.

ANSOFF, H.I. (ed) (1987) *Corporate strategy.* London: Penguin.

ARENDT, H. (1958) *The human condition.* Chicago: University of Chicago Press.

ARMSTRONG, M. (1987) Human resource management: a case of the emperor's new clothes. *Personnel Management.* August. 30–35.

ARMSTRONG, M. (1999) *A handbook of HR management practice.* 7th ed. London: Kogan Page.

ARMSTRONG, M. (2001) *A handbook of human resource management practice.* 8th ed. London: Kogan Page.

ARMSTRONG, M. and BARON, D. (1998) *Performance management: the new realities.* London: Institute of Personnel Development (IPD) (now CIPD).

ARNOLD, J., ROBERTSON, I.T. and COOPER, C.L. (1991) *Work psychology.* London: Pitman.

ARVEY, R.D. and CAMPION, J.E. (1982) The employment interview: a summary and review of recent research. *Personnel Psychology.* 35, 281–322.

ATTWOOD, M. (1989) *HR management.* London: Macmillan.

BATES, R.A. and HOLTON, E.F. (1995) Computerised performance monitoring: a review of human resource issues. *Human Resource Management Review.* Winter. 267–288.

BEARDWELL, J., HOLDEN, L. and CLAYDON, T. (2004) *Human resource management: a contemporary approach.* 4th ed. Harlow: Pearson Education.

BEARDWELL, J. and WRIGHT, M. (2004) In: I. Beardwell, L. Holden, L. and T. Claydon (eds), *Human resource management: a contemporary approach*. Harlow: Pearson Education.

BEATTIE, D. (2002) President's message, *Annual Report 2002*. London: CIPD.

BEAUMONT, P. (1993) *Human resource management: key concepts and skills*. London: Sage.

BEVAN, S. (1997) Quit stalling. *People Management*. 20 November.

BEVAN, S. and THOMPSON, M. (1991) Performance management at the crossroads. *Personnel Management*. November. 36–39.

BLAU, P.M. and SCOTT, W.R. (1966) *Formal organisations*. London: Routledge.

BRAMHAM, J. (1994) *Human resource planning*. London: IPD (now CIPD).

BRAMHAM, J. (1988) *Practical manpower planning*. London: Institute of Personnel Management (IPM) (now CIPD).

BRECH, E.F.L. (1965) *The principles and practice of management*. 3rd ed. London: Longman.

BROWN, R. (1995) *Prejudice: its social psychology*. Oxford: Blackwell.

BUCKINGHAM, G. (2000) Same indifference. *People Management*. 17 February. 44–46.

BULLA, D.N. and SCOTT, P.M. (1994) Manpower requirements forecasting: a case example. In: D. Ward, T.P. Bechet and R Tripp (eds), *Human resource forecasting and modelling*. New York: Human Resource Planning Society.

BURNS, T. and STALKER, G.M. (1966) *The management of innovation*. London: Tavistock.

BUSINESS LINK (2005) *Meet the need for work–life balance: practical advice for business*. A guide developed with the Department of Trade and Industry. Available at www.business link.gov.uk/bdotg/action/detail [accessed 14 December 2005].

CAPON, C. (2000) *Understanding organisational context*. Harlow: Pearson Education.

CHAMPY, J. and NOHRIA. N. (eds) (1996) *Fast forward: the best ideas on managing business change*. Boston: Harvard Business School Press.

CHARTERED INSTITUTE OF PERSONNEL AND DEVELOPMENT (CIPD) (2002) *Recruitment on the Internet: quick facts*. London: CIPD. www.cipd.co.uk/factsheets.

CIPD (2003a) *Living to work? Survey report*. London: CIPD. Available at www.cipd.co.uk/surveys [accessed 16 December 2005].

CIPD (2003b) *Employee absence 2003: a survey of management policy and practice*. London: CIPD.

CIPD (2004) Diversity: stacking up the evidence. *CIPD Bulletin*.

CIPD (2005) *Getting the right work–life balance.* London: CIPD. Available at www.cipd.co.uk/subjects/wrkgtime/wrktmewrklfbal [accessed 16 December 2005].

CHILD, J. (1988) *Organisation: a guide to problems and practice.* 2nd ed. London: Paul Chapman.

CLAYDON, T. (2004) Human resource management and the labour market. In: I. Beardwell, L. Holden and T. Claydon (eds), *Human resource management: a contemporary approach.* 4th ed. Harlow. Pearson Education.

CLUTTERBUCK, D. (2003) *Managing work-life balance.* London: CIPD.

COLLIN, A. (2004) Learning and development. In: I. Beardwell, L. Holden and T. Claydon, *Human resource management: a contemporary approach.* 4th ed. Harlow: Pearson Education.

COOPER, C.L., COOPER, R.D. and EAKER, L.H. (1988) *Living with stress.* Harmondsworth: Penguin.

COOPER, D. and ROBERTSON, I.T. (1995) *The psychology of personnel selection* (ed C. Fletcher). London: Routledge.

COURTIS, J. (1994) *Recruitment advertising: right first time.* London: IPD (now CIPD).

CURRAN, J and STANWORTH, J. (1988) The small firm: a neglected area of management. In: A.G. Gowling, M.J.K. Stanworth, R.D. Bennett, J. Curran and P. Lyons, *Behavioural sciences for managers.* 2nd ed. London: Edward Arnold.

CURRIE, D. (1990) *Stress in the NHS.* Southampton: Southampton Institute.

CURRIE, D. (1997) *Personnel in practice.* Oxford: Blackwell.

DANIELS, K. and MACDONALD, L. (2005) *Equality, diversity and discrimination.* London: CIPD.

DEPARTMENT FOR TRADE AND INDUSTRY (DTI) (2004) *Working time: widening the debate. A preliminary consultation on long hours working in the UK and the application and operation of the working time opt out.* London: DTI. Available at www.dti.gov.uk/er/work_time_regs/consultation.pdf [accessed 12 November 2005].

DINGWALL, R. (1983) *The management of stress.* Budleigh Salterton: Granary Press

DOWLING, P.J. and SCHULER, R.S. (1990) *International dimensions of HRM.* Boston, Mass.: PWS-Kent.

DRUCKER, P. (1977) *People and performance: the best of Peter Drucker on management.* London: Heinemann.

DRUCKER, P. (1988) The coming of the new organisation. *Harvard Business Review.* January–February. 45–53.

EASTERBY-SMITH, M. and MACKNESS, J. (1992) Completing the cycle of evaluation. *Personnel Management.* May. 42–45.

EQUAL OPPORTUNITIES COMMISSION (EOC) (2001) *The gender pay gap.* Available at: www.eoc.org.uk [accessed 20 September 2005].

FAYOL, H. (1949) *General and industrial management.* London: Pitman.

FELDMAN, D.C. and ARNOLD, H.J. (1985) Personality types and career patterns: some empirical evidence on Holland's model. *Canadian Journal of Administrative Sciences.* June. 192–210.

FINKLE, R.B. (1975) Managerial assessment centres. In: M.D. Dunnette (ed), *Handbook of industrial and organisational psychology.* Chicago: Rand-McNally.

FOOT, M. and HOOK, C. (1999) *Introducing human resource management.* 2nd ed. Harlow: Pearson Education.

FOWLER, A. (1987) When chief executives discover human resource management. *Personnel Management.* January. 3.

FOWLER, A. (1992) How to plan an assessment centre. *PM Plus.* December. 21–23.

FOWLER, A. (1996) *Induction.* 3rd edn. London: IPD (now CIPD).

FOX, A. (1966) *Industrial sociology and industrial relations.* Royal Commission on Trade Unions and Employers Associations. Research paper No. 3. London: HMSO.

FRASER, J.M. (1966) *Employment interviewing.* 5th ed. Plymouth: Macdonald and Evans.

FRENCH, W.L. and BELL, C.H. (1990) *Organization development.* Englewood Cliffs, NJ: Prentice-Hall.

FURNHAM, A. and GUNTER, B. (1993) Corporate culture: diagnosis and change. In: C.L. Cooper and I.T. Robertson (eds), *International review of industrial and organisational psychology.* Chichester: Wiley.

GAGNE, R.M. (1977) *The conditions of learning.* New York: Rinehart and Winston.

GANNON, M. (1995) Personal development planning. In: M. Walters (ed), *The performance management handbook.* London: IPD (now CIPD).

GEARY, J.F. (1992) Pay, control and commitment: linking appraisal and reward. *Human Resource Management Journal.* Vol. 2, No. 4. 36–54.

GIDDENS, A. (1989) *Sociology.* Oxford: Polity Press.

GILBRETH, F. and GILBRETH, L. (1917) *Applied motion study.* New York: Sturgis and Walton.

GOLDING, N. (2004) Strategic human resource management. In: I. Beardwell, L. Holden and T. Claydon (eds), *Human resource management: a contemporary approach.* 4th ed. Harlow: Pearson Education.

GOLDTHORPE, J.H. (1968) *The affluent worker: industrial attitudes and behaviour.* Cambridge: Cambridge University Press.

GOSS, D. (1996) *Principles of human resource management*. London: Routledge.

HACKMAN, J.R. and OLDHAM, G.R. (1976). Motivation through the design of work: test of a theory. *Organisational Behaviour and Human Performance.* 16. 250–279.

HACKMAN, J.R. and OLDHAM, G..R. (1980) *Work redesign*. Reading, Mass.: Addison-Wesley.

HALL, E.T. (1973) *The silent language*. New York: Doubleday.

HAMPDEN-TURNER, C. (1990) *Corporate cultures: from vicious to virtuous circles.* London: Random Century.

HANDY, C.B. (1976) *Understanding organisations.* Harmondsworth: Penguin.

HANDY, C.B. (1989) *The age of unreason*. London: Business Books.

HANDY, L., DEVINE, M. and HEATH, L. (1996). *360-degree feedback: unguided missile or powerful weapon?* Berkhamstead: Ashridge Management Group.

HARALAMBOS, M. (1986) *Sociology: themes and perspectives*. London: Bell and Hyman.

HEALTH AND SAFETY EXECUTIVE (HSE) (2005) *Five steps to risk assessment: a step by step guide to a safer and healthier workplace* (an HSE leaflet designed to aid and advise employers and the self-employed to assess risks in the workplace). London: HSE.

HEERY, E. (1996) *Risk representation and the new pay*. Paper presented to the BUIRA/EBEN Conference. Ethical issues in contemporary human resource management. Imperial College, London, 3 April.

HEERY, E. and NOON, M. (2001) *A dictionary of human resource management*. Oxford: Oxford University Press.

HENDRY, C. (1995). *Human resource management: a strategic approach to employment*. Oxford: Butterworth-Heinemann.

HERRIOT, P. (1989) *Recruitment in the nineties*. London: IPM (now CIPD).

HERSKOVITS, M.J. (1948) *Man and his works.* New York: Knopf.

HERZBERG, F.W., MAUSNER, B. and SNYDERMAN, B. (1957) *The motivation to work*. New York: Wiley.

HILL, J. and TRIST, E. (1955) Changes in accidents and other absences with length of service. *Human Relations.* Vol. 8. May.

HOLDEN, L. (2004) Human resource development: the organisation and the national framework. In: I. Beardwell, L. Holden, and T. Claydon, *Human resource management: a contemporary approach*. 4th ed. Harlow: Pearson Education.

HOLLAND, J. L. (1985) *Making vocational choices*. 2nd ed. New York: Prentice-Hall.

HOLT, A. and ANDREWS, H. (1993) *Principles of health and safety at work.* London IOSH Publishing.

HUCZYNSKI, A. and BUCHANAN, D. (2001) *Organizational behaviour: an introductory text.* Harlow: Pearson Education.

HUSSEY, D. (1996) *Business driven human resource management.* Chichester: Wiley.

HUWS, U. (1996) *Teleworking: an overview of the research.* London: HMSO.

INCOMES DATA SERVICES (IDS) (1996) *Teleworking.* IDS study 616. London: IDS.

IDS (2000). *Improving staff retention.* IDS study 692, July. London: IDS.

Institute of Personnel and Development (IPD) (1998) *Performance pay survey: executive summary.* London: IPD (now CIPD).

IRS MANAGEMENT REVIEW (1996) *Performance management* 1 (1). London: Industrial Relations Service.

KATZ, D. and KAHN, R.L. (1978) *The social psychology of organisations.* 2nd ed. New York: Wiley.

KEEP, E. (1989). Corporate training strategies: the vital component. In: J. Storey (ed), *New perspectives on human resource management.* London: Routledge.

KOEHLER, W. (1959) *The mentality of apes.* New York: Vintage.

KOLB, D.A. (1985) *Experiential learning: experience as the source of learning and development.* London: Prentice-Hall.

KRULIS-RANDA, J. (1990) Strategic human resource management in Europe after 1992. *International Journal of Human Resource Management.* Vol. 1, No. 2. 131–139.

LAWLER, E.E. (1990) *Strategic pay.* San Francisco, Calif.: Jossey-Bass.

LEGGE, K. (1995) *Human resource management: rhetoric and realities.* London: Macmillan.

LIKERT, R.A. (ed) (1961) *New patterns of management.* Maidenhead: McGraw-Hill.

LINTON, R. (1945) Present world conditions in cultural perspective. In: R Linton (ed), *The science of man in world crisis.* New York: Columbia University Press.

MARSDEN, D. and FRENCH, S. (1998) *What a performance: performance-related pay in the public services.* London: Centre for Economic Performance.

MARTIN, M. and JACKSON, T. (2003) *Personnel practice.* 3rd ed. London: CIPD.

MASLOW, A.H. (1954) *Motivation and personality.* 1st ed. New York: Harper & Row.

MASLOW, A.H. (1972) A theory of growth motivation. In: *Motivation and personality.* New York: Harper & Row.

MAUND, L. (2001) *An introduction to human resource management: theory and practice.* Basingstoke: Palgrave.

MAYO, A. (1998) Knowledge management: memory bankers. *People Management.* 22 January. 34–38.

MAYO, E. (1933) *The human problems of an industrial civilization.* New York: Macmillan.

McGREGOR, D. (1960) *The human side of enterprise.* New York: McGraw-Hill.

McKENNA, E. (1994) *Business psychology and organisational behaviour.* Hove: Lawrence Erlbaum.

McLEAN, A. (1979) *Work stress.* Reading, Mass.: Addison-Wesley.

MOLANDER, C. and WINTERTON, J. (1994) *Managing human resources.* London: Routledge.

MOORHEAD, G. and GRIFFIN, R.W. (1992) *Organisational behaviour.* 3rd ed. Boston, Mass.: Houghton Mifflin.

MULLINS, L. J. (1993) *Management and organisational behaviour.* London: Pitman.

MULLINS, L. (1999) *Management and organisational behaviour.* London: Prentice Hall.

MUMFORD, A. (1993) *Management development: strategies for action.* London: IPM (now CIPD).

NAROLL, R. (1970) The culture-bearing unit in cross-cultural surveys. In: R. Naroll, and R. Cohen (eds), *Handbook of method in cultural anthropology.* New York: Columbia University Press.

NEWELL, S. (1995) *The healthy organisation.* London: Routledge.

NOON, M. (2004) Managing equality and diversity. In: I. Beardwell, L. Holden and T. Claydon (eds), *Human resource management: a contemporary approach.* 4th ed. Harlow: Pearson Education.

PAVLOV, I.P. (1927) *Conditioned reflexes.* Oxford: Oxford University Press.

PIERCY, N. (1989) Diagnosing and solving implementation problems in strategic planning. *Journal of General Management.* Vol. 15, No. 1. 19–38.

PILBEAM, S. and CORBRIDGE, M. (2002) *People resourcing: HRM in practice.* Harlow: FT/Prentice Hall.

PLUMBLEY, P.R. (1976) *Recruitment and selection.* London: IPM (now CIPD).

PLUMBLEY, P.R. (1985) *Recruitment and selection.* 4th ed. London: Institute of Personnel and Development (now the Chartered Institute of Personnel and Development).

POINTON, J. and RYAN, A.J. (2004) Reward and performance management. In: I. Beardwell, L. Holden and T. Claydon (eds), *Human resource management: a contemporary approach.* 4th ed. Harlow: Pearson Education.

PORTEOUS, M. (1997) *Occupational psychology.* Hemel Hempstead: Prentice Hall Europe.

PORTER, L.W. and LAWLER, E.E. (1968) *Managerial attitudes and performance*. Homewood, Ill.: Irwin-Dorsey.

PRICE, A.J. (1997). *Human resource management in a business context*. London: International Thomson Business Press.

QUINN MILLS, D. (1983) Planning with people in mind. *Harvard Business Review*. November–December, 97–105.

RANA, E. (2000a). *Annual report*. London: CIPD.

RANA, E. (2000b) Predictions: enter the people dimension. *People Management*. Vol. 6, No. 1, 6 January, 16–17.

RANDELL, G.R., PACKARD, P.M.A., SHAW, R.L. and SLATER, A.J.P. (1984) *Staff appraisal*. London: IPM (now CIPD).

RAUSCHENBERGER, J., SCHMITT, N. and HUNTER, J.E. (1980). A test of the need hierarchy concept by a Markov model of change in need strength. *Administrative Science Quarterly*. No. 25. 654–670.

REILLY, R.R. and CHAO, G.T. (1982) Validity and fairness of some alternative employee selection procedures. *Personnel Psychology*. No. 55. 12–37.

ROBBINS, S. P. (2001) *Organisational behaviour*. Upper Saddle River, NJ.: Prentice-Hall.

ROBERTS, I. (2001) Reward and performance management. In: I. Beardwell, L. Holden and T. Claydon (eds), *Human resource management: a contemporary approach*. 4th ed. Harlow: Pearson Education.

RODGER, A. (1952) *The seven point plan*. 3rd ed. London: National Institute of Industrial Psychology.

ROSS, R. and SCHNEIDER, R. (1992) *From equality to diversity: a business case for equal opportunities*. London: Pitman.

SALANCIK, G.R. and PFEFFER, J. (1977) An examination of need satisfaction models of job attitudes. *Administrative Science Quarterly.*, No. 22. 427–456.

SAUNDERS, R. (1992) *The safety audit*. London: Pitman.

SCHEIN, E.H. (1965) *Organisational psychology*. Englewood Cliffs, NJ.: Prentice-Hall.

SCHEIN, E.H. (1980) *Organisational psychology*, 3rd ed. Englewood Cliffs, NJ.: Prentice-Hall.

SCHEIN, E. (1985) *Organisational culture and leadership*. New York: Jossey Bass.

SCHUSTER, J.R. and ZINGHEIM, P.K. (1992) *The new pay*. New York: Lexington Books.

SENGE, P. (1990) *The fifth discipline: the art and practice of the learning organisation*. London: Century.

SISSON, K. (1995) Human resource management and the personnel function. In: J. Storey (ed), *Human resource management: a critical text.*. London: Routledge.

SISSON, K. (2001) Human resource management and the personnel function: a case of partial impact? In: J. Storey (ed), *Human resource management: a critical text.* 2nd ed. London: Thomson Learning.

SKINNER, B.F. (1953) *Science and human behaviour.* New York: Macmillan.

SMITH, M., COLLIGAN, M., SKJEI, E. and POLLY, S. (1978) *Occupational comparison of stress-related disease incidence.* Cincinnati, Ohio: National Institute for Occupational Safety and Health.

STOREY, J. (1992) *Development in the management of human resources: an analytical review.* London: Blackwell.

STOREY, J. (1995) *Human resource management: a critical text.* London: Routledge.

TAYLOR, F.W. (1911) *The principles of scientific management.* New York: Harper & Bros.

TAYLOR, F.W. (1947) *Scientific management.* New York: Harper & Row.

THORNDIKE, E.L. (1913) *The psychology of learning.* Columbia University: Teachers College Press.

TORRINGTON, D. and HALL, L. (1998) *Human resource management.* 4th ed. Hemel Hempstead: Prentice Hall Europe.

TORRINGTON, D., HALL, L. and TAYLOR, S. (2002) *Human resource management.* 5th ed. Harlow: Prentice Hall.

TRAINING COMMISSION. (1988) *Classifying the components of management competences.* Sheffield: Training Commission.

TRIANDIS, H.C. (1990) Theoretical concepts that are applicable to the analysis of ethnocentrism. In: R.W. Brislin (ed), *Applied cross-cultural psychology.* Chicago: Sage.

TRIANDIS, H.C., VASSILIOU, V., VASSILIOU, G., TANAKA, Y. and SHANMUGAM, A.V. (1972) *The analysis of subjective culture.* New York: Wiley.

TRICE, H.M. and BEYER, J.M. (1984) Studying organisational cultures through rites and rituals. *Academy of Management Review.* No. 9. 653–669.

TRIST, E.L., HIGGIN, G., POLLOCK, H.E. and MURRAY, H.A. (1963) *Organisational choice.* London: Tavistock.

TYLOR, E.B. (1874) *Primitive culture.* London: Murray.

TYSON, S. and YORK, A. (1996) *Human resource management.* Oxford: Butterworth-Heinemann.

VROOM, V.H. (1964) *Work and motivation*. New York: Wiley.

VROOM, V.H. (1970) *Management and motivation*. Harmondsworth: Penguin.

WAHBA, M.A. and BRIDWELL, L.G. (1976) A review of research on the need hierarchy. *Organisational Behaviour and Human Performance*. Available at www.emeraldinsight.com [accessed on 6 March 2006].

WALTON, R.E. and MCKERSIE, R.B. (1965) *Behavioural theory of labour negotiations*. New York: McGraw-Hill.

WARD, P. (1995) A 360 degree turn for the better. *People Management*. February. 20–22.

WATSON, J.B. and RAYNER, R. (1920) Conditioned emotional reactions. *Journal of Experimental Psychology*. Vol. 3. 1–14.

WEBER, M. (1964) *The theory of social and economic organisation*. London: Macmillan.

WHEELER, R. (1995) Developing IT strategies for human resources. *Human resource management yearbook*. London: APS.

WHITTINGTON, R. (1993) *What is strategy and does it matter?* London: Routledge.

WHYTE, W.F. (1955) *The organization man*. Harmondsworth: Penguin.

WILLIAMS, M. (2000) Transfixed assets. *People Management*. 3 August. 28–33.

WOODWARD, J. (1980) *Industrial organisation: theory and practice*. 2nd ed. Oxford: Oxford University Press.

WRIGHT, P., McMAHAN, G. and McWILLIAMS, A. (1994) Human resources and sustained competitive advantage: a resource-based perspective. *International Journal of Human Resource Management*. Vol. 5, No. 2. 301–326.

WRIGHT, P.L. and TAYLOR, D.S. (1984) *Improving leadership performance*. Harlow: Prentice Hall International.

Websites

CIPD: http://www.cipd.co.uk/onlineinfodocuments/surveys.htm

Department for Education and Employment (DfEE): www.pfc.org.uk/employ/dfeeguide.htm

Department for Education and Skills (DFES): www.dfes.gov.uk/skillsstrategy

Department of Trade and Industry (DTI): www.dti.gov.uk/work–lifebalance

Learning and Skills Council: www.lsc.gov.uk

Work Foundation: www.employersforwork–lifebalance.org.uk

Index

Students

Save 20% when buying direct from the CIPD using the Student Discount Scheme

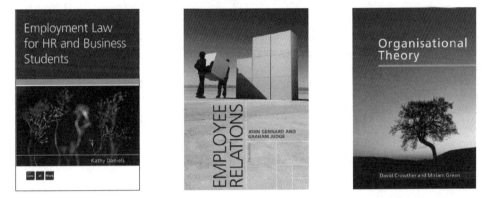

The Chartered Institute of Personnel and Development (CIPD) is the leading publisher of books and reports for personnel and training professionals, students, and for all those concerned with the effective management and development of people at work.

The CIPD offers ALL students a 20% discount on textbooks and selected practitioner titles.

To claim your discount, and to see a full list of titles available, call 0870 800 3366 quoting '*Student Discount Scheme 1964*' – alternatively, visit us online at **www.cipd.co.uk/bookstore**.

Order online at www.cipd.co.uk/bookstore or call us on 0870 800 3366

NB This offer is exclusive of any other offers from the CIPD and applies to CIPD Publishing textbooks only.

The Chartered Institute of Personnel and Development is the leading publisher of books and reports for personnel and training professionals, students and all those concerned with the effective management and development of people at work.

Also from CIPD Publishing . . .

Managing Performance:

Performance management in action

2nd Edition

Michael Armstrong and Angela Baron

Managing performance is a critical focus of HR activity. Well-designed strategies to recognise and improve performance and focus individual effort can have a dramatic effect on bottom-line results. The problem is to determine what the processes, tools and delivery mechanisms are that will improve performance in your organisation, as well as determine which ones are best avoided.

The authors have tracked performance management processes over the past seven years, and their comprehensive survey reveals what leading organisations are doing to manage their employees' performance and how they are delivering results.

With detailed illustrations from the real world, and clear practical advice, this text shows you how to improve the management of your employees' performance.

Managing Performance will help you:

- design performance management processes that reflect the context and nature of the organisation;
- create supportive delivery mechanisms for performance management; and
- evaluate and continuously develop performance management strategies to reflect the changing business environment.

Order your copy now online at www.cipd.co.uk/bookstore or call us on 0870 800 3366

Michael Armstrong is a Fellow of the Chartered Institute of Personnel and Development, and a Fellow of the Institute of Management Consultants. He has over 25 years experience in personnel management, including 12 as a personnel director. He has also been a management consultant for many years and is a former Chief Examiner, Employee Reward, for the CIPD. He has written a number of successful management books, including *The Job Evaluation Handbook* (1995) and *Strategic HRM* (2002), both co-written with Angela Baron; *Employee Reward* (third edition 2002); *Rewarding Teams* (2000); and *New Dimensions in Pay Management* (2001). All are published by the CIPD.

Angela Baron has been Advisor, Organisational and Resourcing at the Chartered Institute of Personnel and Development since 1990. Her other books, *The Job Evaluation Handbook* and *Strategic HRM* were both co-written with Michael Armstrong.

| Published 2004 | 1 84398 101 7 | Paperback | 192 pages |

The Chartered Institute of Personnel and Development is the leading publisher of books and reports for personnel and training professionals, students and all those concerned with the effective management and development of people at work.

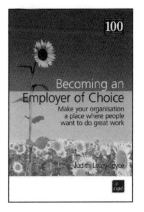